The Science of the Fastball

The Science of the Fastball

WILLIAM BLEWETT

McFarland & Company, Inc., Publishers
Jefferson, North Carolina, and London

LIBRARY OF CONGRESS CATALOG ONLINE DATA

Blewett, William, 1947–
The science of the fastball / William Blewett.
    p.   cm.
Includes bibliographical references and index.

ISBN 978-0-7864-7179-9
softcover : acid free paper ∞

1. Pitching (Baseball)
2. Pitchers (Baseball)   I. Title.
GV971.B54 2013   796.357'22—dc23   2012048862

BRITISH LIBRARY CATALOGUING DATA ARE AVAILABLE

© 2013 William Blewett. All rights reserved

No part of this book may be reproduced or transmitted in any form or by any means, electronic or mechanical, including photocopying or recording, or by any information storage and retrieval system, without permission in writing from the publisher.

On the cover: Houston Astros pitcher Nolan Ryan (National Baseball Hall of Fame Library, Cooperstown, New York)

Manufactured in the United States of America

*McFarland & Company, Inc., Publishers
Box 611, Jefferson, North Carolina 28640
www.mcfarlandpub.com*

To the many pitchers whose ascent in baseball
has been stalled by an insufficient gift of speed,
by a gift of speed that vanished too soon,
or by accepting as truth that one can never
be trained to pitch faster.

Acknowledgments

Dan Blewett provided the spark for this project, many of the experiences and observations that led to its analyses, expert critique, and counterpoints. As a pitcher he has demonstrated the benefits of strength training, proving Alva Bradley wrong by gaining 15 mph on his fastball velocity between high school and professional baseball.

Baseball-reference.com was a valuable source of pitching statistics in the research for this book. Its superb on-line database greatly facilitated this three-year writing project. Much of the literature search began with or included Wikipedia, the comprehensive and well-referenced on-line encyclopedia. The National Baseball Hall of Fame provided excellent support.

Several reviewers provided important comments, recommendations, and encouragement at various stages of writing the manuscript: Pete Bucha, Matt Rogers, Mark Mattson, Lucie L. Snodgrass, and my family of writers: Joann, J.D., Dan, and Annie Blewett.

Table of Contents

Acknowledgments vi
Preface 1

1. Three Fastball Prodigies — 5
2. The 107-mph Fastball? — 16
3. The Kinetic Chain of Pitching, Roughly Quantified — 25
4. The Four Elements of Pitching Power — 36
5. The Dalkowski Phenomenon: Under-Damped Biological Springs at Near-Resonance — 57
6. Triple Play: The Importance of Hand Speed — 73
7. The Fickle Flight of Koufax's Fast-Spinning Four-Seamer — 81
8. The Band and the Gap — 86
9. Diminishing Velocity: Five Effects That Link Eccentric Contractions to Power Loss — 93
10. Building Strength and Velocity with the "Magic" of Eccentric Contractions — 107
11. The Wild Card of Pitching Power — 130
12. Endurance, Durability, and Longevity: Amos Rusie vs. Pedro Martinez — 137
13. Differential Power Loss: Outliers, Slumps, and Downward Trends — 162
14. The Fourth Prodigy? — 177

Glossary of Technical Terms Related to Pitching Power 187
Chapter Notes 197
Bibliography 205
Index 211

Preface

This book is about pitching, but not about the art of pitching. It is about the science of the fastball. It is not a how-to book but a how-and-why book addressing some long-standing issues of pitching, such as: Why can some pitchers achieve phenomenal velocity while others cannot? How was a 17-year-old rookie named Bob Feller able to strike out major league batters in record numbers? Why is there more whiff-inducing hop on a fastball if it's thrown with a high spin rate and four-seam grip? Why do young pitchers with exceptional velocity often issue walks at an exceptional rate? Why do great pitchers occasionally pitch poorly? Why is exceptional hand speed important in striking out batters? Why is Nolan Ryan considered the fastest pitcher of all time? Why are pitchers so often afflicted with injuries to the elbow and shoulder? How does a pitcher achieve greater endurance on the mound? How can a pitcher most reliably increase his fastball velocity?

In addressing these and other questions, this book examines the science of generating, transmitting, and amplifying power from a pitcher's muscle fibers to a five-ounce baseball to achieve exceptional linear and rotational velocities. Illustrated by the experiences of some of baseball's greatest pitchers, it explains the science that applies in acquiring, improving, sustaining, and eventually losing phenomenal velocity.

Pitchers are baseball's practitioners of science. In their complex craft, they apply the science of aerodynamics to make the ball deviate from its initial trajectory, the science of biomechanics to control the flight of the ball and deceive the batter, and the science of muscle physiology to generate and transfer greater power to the ball. The pitcher's quest for better performance consequently involves a quest for better science, but in baseball, as in all sports, there exist both good and bad science. Bad science is readily accessible through word of mouth, but has never been proven valid. By contrast, good science has been validated, usually through controlled experiments. Yet good science is not easily accessible because of the great expense in acquiring it and the communication gap that exists between scientists and athletes.

A scientist typically views research as an end to itself and writes technical papers narrow in scope and filled with scientific jargon, language that is foreign to the pitcher and his coach. Scientists share their knowledge with other scientists almost exclusively, seldom with athletes and other non-scientists. The scientist is also highly specialized, focusing on miniature pieces in a grand puzzle of practical application. The athlete and his coach usually lack the knowledge that would allow them to translate scientific studies into better performance.

A related problem is that good science is not always accepted. The most rigorously developed experiments yield data that can be interpreted in different ways. People sometimes reject science that disagrees with what they have been taught or how they have been coached. Certain philosophies of training, like the harder-is-better approach, can become deeply imbedded in culture and difficult to change.

All athletes have an appetite for the science of their sport, but most tend to satisfy it with low-hanging fruit — folk science, newspaper science, internet science — which is sometimes bad science. A wide gap often exists between the low-hanging fruit and the out-of-reach science validated through carefully designed experiments. In pitching, this gap is especially wide because much of sports science emerges from medical research, where there is a high burden of proof. Bad science can be acquired through ill-conceived, uncontrolled experiments yielding illogical conclusions about causal relationships — as illustrated in the extreme by the pitcher whose one-hit gem comes on the day he switches from plain to barbeque-flavored sunflower seeds and thereafter employs the latter in his quest for pitching perfection. Because of this gap, the field of pitching abounds with theories that seem probable or even likely but that have not been subjected to scientific analysis. This book seeks to bridge that gap by using science to test anecdotal data about some important and persistent issues of pitching.

This book focuses on four areas of science relative to the fastball: biomechanics, the physics of power, aerodynamics, and the physiology and anatomy of muscles and connective tissue, all presented with a practical minimum of scientific jargon. The four words that appear most frequently in the book are: muscle, speed, power, and damage. In pitching, as in all sports, these four are closely related. Muscle fibers, the remarkable bio-molecular motors of the human body, provide the power for the roaring fastball. Damage, the physical result of stretching these fibers to structural failure, occurs routinely, both on the mound and in training. A pitcher develops greater power from these fibers, strangely enough, by optimizing the damage to them. Muscle damage beyond the optimum, however, produces a loss of power, a loss of speed. Greater strength yields greater speed. Strength training, properly applied, is the surest approach to greater speed. It is an avenue that has seen much higher traffic since the 1970s, but it is one on which the most prominent hazard is muscle damage. The most powerful type of muscle fiber is the most easily damaged. Hence, the pitcher must walk a fine line between optimal use and over-use of his biomolecular motors. No pitcher has ever achieved greatness without deviating from this line at some point.

The conclusion of this analysis is that the greatest power pitchers are those blessed by genetics with the most powerful type of muscle fiber in the arm and shoulder, exceptional biological springs in the arm and shoulder, the ability to coordinate complex movements near-perfectly at high speed, a naturally high level of testosterone that arrives in adolescence, and the knowledge of how to develop and preserve these gifts. The first four of these are natural gifts. Helping the pitcher acquire the fifth, knowledge, is the purpose of this book.

1

Three Fastball Prodigies

In the sport of baseball, the quest for perfection has long been the search for the ultimate pitcher, one who throws strikes with such velocity that no batter can put the ball in play. Unfortunately — or fortunately for the balance of the game — such a pitcher exists only in a boy's daydreams or in the movies, the latter being the case of Steve Nebraska. Though fictional, Mr. Nebraska symbolizes the ultimate pitcher, the most highly valued prize of the baseball scouting industry. In the 1994 Hollywood movie *The Scout,* Mr. Nebraska is discovered pitching in an obscure league in Mexico. He eventually reaches the World Series, where he pitches a perfect game. His is not merely a no-base-runners perfect game but a 27-strikeout, 81-pitch perfect game. He retires all 27 batters with three pitches each — a feat nine times better than any major league pitcher has ever accomplished. He consummates his performance with a fastball so powerful that it topples the catcher and the umpire in tandem.

Natural is the appropriate word for describing Mr. Nebraska and real-life pitching phenoms, just as it is for Olympic sprint champions Jesse Owens and Usain Bolt. They are naturals, prodigies of speed. As with speed afoot, prodigious fastball speed manifests itself in the teen years, often with little training required. Such manifestation is so rare, however, that an army of scouts is mobilized to a worldwide search that annually showers great wealth on male adolescents in hope that one of them will emerge as the real-life Steve Nebraska.

Perhaps the greatest fastball prodigy of all time, the closest scouts have come to finding a Steve Nebraska, was Bob Feller, a farm boy discovered in the corn country of Iowa in 1935. Feller was just 16 when he signed a major-league contract with the Cleveland Indians, receiving as his bonus the token sum of one dollar and a baseball autographed by the Indians' players. He was 17 when he threw his first pitch to a major-league batter. During the all-star break of 1936, two days after Independence

The Science of the Fastball

Day, the dimple-chinned kid from Van Meter donned Cleveland uniform no. 9 and pitched three innings of relief in an exhibition game against the St. Louis Cardinals. The second batter he faced in his professional debut was a feisty shortstop and future Hall of Fame manager named Leo Durocher. Feller fired the first pitch over Durocher's head, the second one behind him, and the third and fourth into the strike zone. Durocher's response after four Feller fastballs roared past him was to abandon the at-bat with a two-ball, two-strike count, saying, "I feel like a clay pigeon in a shooting gallery." The umpire coaxed Durocher to return from the dugout; standing well back from the plate, he took a feeble swing at the next pitch to become Feller's first major-league strikeout victim.[1]

Feller struck out eight batters in those three innings of relief. Six weeks later, he made his regular season debut and pitched a full nine-inning game against the St. Louis Browns. He struck out 15, an American League single-game record. Three weeks later, in his fifth major-league start, he struck out 17 against the Philadelphia Athletics to tie Dizzy Dean's major-league record. Soon thereafter, he was back on the Iowa farm, milking cows, doing farm chores, and riding a yellow school bus to and from Van Meter High School each day.

Feller didn't need to tell his 16 high-school classmates what he did on the summer vacation before his senior year. Newspapers, magazines, and radio conveyed that information. His picture appeared on the cover of *Time Magazine* the following spring, and NBC Radio covered his high school graduation live nationally from Van Meter, population 300. He had in that summer of '36 become America's boy wonder, its most famous teenager, aside from Shirley Temple, and perhaps the greatest source of boyhood sports fantasies in American history. He had in one brief season been transformed from farm boy to record-setting major-league pitcher by a phenomenal fastball.

If a Hollywood screenplay were to be written about Feller's remarkable summer, it would surely resort to dramatic enhancement by making his power for casting lightning bolts vanish as suddenly as it appeared. Such a scenario would seem appropriate to make his incredible season more believable. After all, major-league hitters are adaptive creatures who adjust quickly to new pitchers, and the liveliness of pitching arms is sometimes fleeting. He struck out 150 batters in 148 two-thirds innings in the 1937 season, but in 1938 his power did vanish, mysteriously, for three months before returning in the final game of the season. On that day, at age 19,

1. Three Fastball Prodigies

Bob Feller made his major league debut with the Cleveland Indians the summer before his senior year of high school (National Baseball Hall of Fame Library, Cooperstown, New York).

he fanned 18 Detroit Tigers to claim the major-league single-game strikeout record, a mark that would survive for 31 years. "I had a great curveball that day," he explained, "not at all uncommon for me as I had been throwing curves since I was 8 years old."[2] One of the Detroit batters in that record-setting game, Chet Laabs, accounted single-handedly for five strikeouts and 14 swinging strikes. Upon Feller's post-season return to his hometown, Van Meter turned out for an all-day celebration that included the governor and the local congressman.[3]

Feller became baseball's biggest drawing card. His photo appeared on Wheaties cereal boxes and his name was given to a candy bar. When he was scheduled to pitch, the Indians drew as many as 10,000 additional fans. He led the league in strikeouts from 1938 to 1941, before enlisting in the Navy two days after the attack on Pearl Harbor. He served throughout World War II, and then came back to have his best season in 1946 at age 27. He had returned from the war with a rejuvenated arm, and in his first full season back, he struck out 348 batters and won 26 games. In the same year, he threw for the Army ballisticians of Aberdeen Proving Ground the fastest pitch that had ever been timed with scientific instruments. Despite the four-year hiatus from baseball, he went on to accumulate 266 career victories before he retired in 1956.

It has long been assumed that Feller's strikeout ability, phenomenal for his youth, was simply a matter of his great fastball velocity. What gave him his ability to fan major-league batters, however, has remained as much a mystery as the source of his speed. No one has ever produced a good scientific explanation of either. Folk science explanations — of which baseball has an abundance — typically focus on physical characteristics, such as exceptional height, large hands, long arms, or peculiarities like Feller's high-kick windup.

Feller's physical characteristics provide no clue, however. He stood 5 feet, 10 inches tall as a high school junior — two inches less than his full height — and he was normally proportioned. So, in the reasoning of almost everyone, it had to be the farm work that produced his great velocity. He would later say that his fastball was indeed a product of the strength he developed tossing hay bales, milking cows, and generally working hard on the farm, which included doing chin-ups and pushups, and practicing on the baseball diamond he and his father built complete with bleachers, scoreboard, and his and her outhouses in 1931–32 (this was the original field of dreams, named Oak View because it was previously a grove of oak

1. Three Fastball Prodigies

trees). "Those hay bales were a great workout because I had to lift them sideways and toss them using the muscles of my wrists, hands, forearms, and back," said Feller in his *Little Black Book of Baseball Wisdom*. At first glance, this explanation of his phenomenal ability seems naïve. Countless young men have fortified their arms and shoulders in agriculture before and after Feller and have tested them on the baseball diamond. None of them has produced a fastball of his quality.

If there were an implication here that baseball scouts should haunt the farms of the heartland, there might also be one for them to focus on newspaper delivery boys. In his youth, Nolan Ryan flung copies of *The Houston Post* for four hours each early morning around his hometown of Alvin, Texas. Folk science might assert that newspaper-tossing in boyhood is the secret of developing a fastball recognized by the *Guinness Book of World Records*, except that the young right-hander tossed the newspapers with his left hand.

Feller and Ryan had much in common, including a modicum of wildness that yielded a substantial benefit through intimidation. In his 1992 autobiography, Ryan describes a three-batter sequence of wildness-induced intimidation in a 1965 high-school playoff game. He hit the first batter he faced in the helmet, splitting the helmet. He hit the next batter in the arm, breaking his arm. "The third kid went and begged his coach not to make him hit," explained Ryan. "That coach assaulted him verbally in front of everybody and shamed him into standing in there."[4] Ryan's book does not reveal the fate of the third batter.

Ryan, who once struck out 21 batters in a nine-inning high-school game, reached the major leagues in 1966 at age 19, a year after being drafted in the twelfth round. This, of course, was almost a decade before baseball scouts became radar gun operators, a capability that would have given them a more objective means of weighing Ryan's velocity against his lack of control. After a brief stint in the majors, his control problems got him sent back to the minors in the 1967 season, where he struck out batters at a rate of 1.5 per inning.

In his first full major league season, 1968 with the New York Mets, he struck out 133 batters in 134 innings as a reliever and spot starter. Two years later, he considered giving up baseball because he thought he lacked the ability to succeed as a pitcher. But by 1972, after being traded to the California Angels, he was on his way to becoming the all-time strikeout king of baseball. In three remarkable seasons, 1972, '73, and '74, he pitched

The Science of the Fastball

a total of 943 innings and struck out 1,079, winning 63 games in the three-year span. In the 1973 season, at age 26, he set the post–1900 record for the most strikeouts in a season, 383, and the fewest hits per nine innings, 5.26. He threw two of his seven career no-hitters that year.

In 1974, the same year he won 22 games and struck out 357, Ryan walked 202 batters, coming perilously close to Feller's major-league record of 208 in a single season (every sixth batter on average). In his 27-year career, Ryan set the major-league record for batters walked at 2,795 and for the most career wild pitches, 277. He also established one of the most exalted records in baseball — 5,714 career strikeouts, averaging over one strikeout per inning throughout his career. He had six 300-strikeout seasons, the sixth of which came at age 42. En route to his career strikeout record, on April 27, 1983, he erased the record of the legendary Walter Johnson when he recorded his 3,509th career strikeout. Johnson's mark had stood for 55 years. Ryan's may stand forever. Among his strikeout victims in achieving this record were 29 players who would enter baseball's Hall of Fame.

It is an unusual testament to the power of the fastball that public schools have been named in honor of these two strikeout record-setters — the Walter Johnson High School in Bethesda, Maryland, and the Nolan Ryan Junior High in Pearland, Texas, not far from the Nolan Ryan Expressway and 20 miles from Alvin. The two pitchers had other similarities as well — most notably a fastball that intimidated batters and upset their timing — but Johnson had two distinct differences. He had superb control from the beginning of his career, and he had a unique sidearm delivery.

Born on a farm near Humboldt, Kansas, Johnson spent his teenage years in the oil field town of Olinda, California, north of Los Angeles. He began playing baseball at 16 and immediately displayed an outstanding arm, first as a catcher and then as a pitcher with odd mechanics. In one game for Fullerton High School, he struck out 27 batters in 15 innings. After high school, he played for Weiser, Idaho, in the semi-professional Southern Idaho League, where he became known as the "Weiser Wonder." There, in the month of June 1907, he pitched 58 consecutive scoreless innings, threw a perfect game and no-hitter in back-to-back starts, and, in an eight-day period, struck out 44 in 27 innings while giving up only two hits and one walk.

The manager of the Washington Senators, Joe Cantillon, heard about Johnson and sent him a telegram offering a good salary and train fare to

1. Three Fastball Prodigies

Washington. When Johnson declined, Cantillon sent an emissary, a catcher from the team, to Weiser to convince him to sign. Again, he declined but sought the advice of his parents, hoping they would say no. When they offered no objection, he took the train 2,400 miles eastward to the nation's capital.

On August 2, 1907, the 19-year-old Johnson walked to the mound for his major-league debut against the Detroit Tigers and was greeted by a mocking, mooing sound from the Tigers' dugout. A Detroit player yelled, "Get your pitchfork ready, Joe [Cantillon]; your hayseed's on his way back to the barn."[5] One of those Detroit players was Ty Cobb, who later described Johnson as "a tall, shambling galoot with arms so long they hung far out of his sleeves, and with a sidearm delivery that looked unimpressive at first glance." His delivery made a strong impression, however, once Cobb entered the batter's box. "The first time I faced him," said Cobb. "I watched him take that easy windup — and then something went past me that made me flinch. I hardly saw the pitch, but I heard it. The thing just hissed with danger. Every one of us knew we'd met the most powerful arm ever turned loose in a ballpark."[6]

In a quiet setting, a pitcher receives an audible indication of his velocity. When he throws about 90 mph or faster, he hears a hiss the ball makes as he releases it. The sound of Johnson's fastball, however, was unlike that of any other pitcher of his era. The wake turbulence his fastball produced as it pierced the air created what some described as a roar. The roar of his fastball led to his nickname, "Big Train," given him by sportswriter Grantland Rice. Johnson's fastball reminded Rice of an express train roaring down the tracks.

Henry Thomas' biography of Johnson presents some subjective assessments of his phenomenol velocity. "I never saw a hurler with such terrific speed and perfect control," said Cantillon in 1924. Senators second baseman Jim Delahanty added: "No human being ever threw a ball so fast before." In 1910, legendary manager Connie Mack called Johnson's speed "the greatest I ever saw." "My players tell me that they had no trouble seeing the ball after it left his hand," reported Mack. "But that it seemed to jump at them before they could get their bats into motion."

Like Feller and Ryan, Johnson intimidated batters with his fastball, although he did so unintentionally. Many of those who faced Johnson would not dig in because of concern about being hit. That fear was produced not by wildness but by his sidearm delivery combined with great velocity. Johnson's strikeouts peaked at 313 in his fourth major-league season, 1910. In his 21-year career, he won 417 games, a number second only to Cy Young's 511. He had twelve 20-win seasons and twice topped 30 wins, recording 33 in 1912 and 36 in 1913. He threw 110 shutouts, more than any other pitcher in baseball history.

Johnson had much in common with the strikeout kings who succeeded him. All three naturally possessed phenomenal fastballs that lifted them into the major leagues as teenagers—Feller 29 years after Johnson and Ryan 30 years after Feller. A fastball of exceptional velocity has, of course, never been a ticket to the major leagues, but merely a ticket to try out. Among the fireballers who make it to the majors, almost all experience diminished strikeout rates as the result of facing highly skilled batters routinely. This was not so for Johnson, Feller, or Ryan, implying that there was something else, something other than raw speed that set them apart from thousands of other young men who have labored on the mound.

All three attributes of Johnson's fastball—control, movement, and velocity—were exceptional at the time of his major-league debut. Ryan and Feller excelled in two, velocity and movement. Although technology did not exist then to quantify the latter, the movement of their fastballs was probably just as important as velocity in producing their record-breaking strikeout numbers. Each of the three had very good off-speed pitches and the ability to use them to accentuate the fastball. Each apparently had exceptional muscle speed, strength, and elasticity in the kinetic chain of pitching, even though they had differences in mechanics. Each sustained his pitching superiority for at least 20 years by developing greater skill as velocity waned. Each pitched on a four-day cycle, although Ryan was part of a five-man rotation after his California Angels days.

Because Ryan's three outstanding seasons of 1972, '73, and '74 coincided with the advent of electronic speed measuring devices, Ryan led a major cultural shift, in which fastball velocity became the most prized attribute of a pitcher. Traditionally ranked below control and movement in fastball qualities, velocity became inflated in value by simple illogic that shows classic confusion between correlation and causation:

> *Nolan Ryan pitches with the greatest velocity ever measured and is the greatest strikeout pitcher ever. Ergo, strikeouts are a product of great velocity.*

The lead in the cultural shift fell to Ryan because he was a contemporary of the radar gun. Johnson and Feller came along even before radar itself

1. Three Fastball Prodigies

was developed for applications like national defense, weather forecasting, and traffic safety. Though Ryan maintained that velocity was not so important — stating in his autobiography, "It doesn't mean anything, because how fast you throw the ball isn't as important as where you throw it" — everyone else in and around baseball began to believe otherwise. Pitchers, coaches, managers, sportswriters, broadcasters, fans, scouts — the entire baseball community — began to take part in a grand pursuit of Ryan-like velocity using readings from a novel electronic device, the radar gun, to gauge pitching success. Pitching, one of the most complex skills in all of sports, became simplified, objectified, and reduced to a well-known common denominator — miles per hour, the same familiar units displayed on the dashboard of the family automobile. Velocity became the primary indicator of a pitcher's potential and status. Sportswriters, America's proponents of hyperbole, played a significant role of validating the folk science of pitching velocity. They spread the doctrine of speed, dismissing slower pitchers as soft-tossers and leading to the resurgence and institutionalization of maximal-effort pitching.

Maximal-effort pitching wasn't new. Ryan and radar merely revived it. Walter Johnson was a max-effort pitcher early in his major-league career. According to Ed Grillo, Johnson changed pitching style in his fourth season in the majors, 1910. "It used to be that he would go at top speed from the first inning to the last as long as his strength would hold out," Grillo wrote in the *Washington Star* on September 3, 1911. "Now he has adopted an entirely different policy. Johnson loafs in his games until he finds himself in a pinch, when he lets himself out to the fullest extent." Though all max-effort pitchers do not have the top-end velocity of Ryan, Feller, or Johnson, many have the capability to reach 100 mph or more by throwing with full exertion, and typically doing so with every fastball. Off-speed pitches are likewise thrown with maximum arm speed, as is necessary for deception.

Ryan himself was a max-effort pitcher in his four seasons with the New York Mets. "My idea of pitching was to throw as hard as you could," he told *Time Magazine* for the June 2, 1975, issue. That changed in his first year with the Angels. He found his cruising speed, improved his control, and complemented his roaring fastball with a silent partner — a deceptive off-speed pitch. For Ryan, that pitch was the curveball, which was said to be as good as any in the league. Ted Williams said Feller had "the best fastball and curve I've ever seen."[7] Johnson too had an outstanding curveball. In essence, some of the benefits of phenomenal velocity accrued because these three could retire batters with pitches thrown with less velocity. As Feller told a reporter on the 70th anniversary of his major-league debut, "Your out pitch is whatever you think the hitter isn't looking for."[8] He knew that even his magnificent fastball wasn't fast enough to blow past batters once they figured out the timing.

In the never-ending debate about the best pitchers of all time, Johnson, Feller, and Ryan are usually included. But they are most prominent when judged against the more narrow criteria of strikeout ability and speed. Were they the fastest of all time? How fast were they? These and other questions about the power of their pitching are addressed in the 13 chapters that follow. Namely:

- What natural attributes gave them such great power and velocity?
- Why haven't pitchers become faster over the years?
- What training is effective for increasing velocity?
- Was velocity the key to their strikeout records?
- How did their fastballs upset batters' timing?
- What is the role of arm-and-shoulder elasticity in generating high velocity?
- How does pitching damage the muscle fibers of the arm and shoulder?
- Why do great pitchers sometimes pitch poorly?

The caveat of this book is that these questions cannot be answered with the high level of confidence the world of science prefers. One cannot reverse the clock to acquire data from pitchers of the past, and data from pitchers present and future would take years to acquire. Even then, there are too many variables that affect pitching performance to support definitive conclusions. To be definitive, one should know, for example, the proportion of fast-glycolytic muscle fibers in Nolan Ryan's subscapularis muscle compared to that of other pitchers; the wrist-flexion angular velocity produced by Walter Johnson's right arm; the glycogen levels in Bob Feller's forearm flexor muscles in the summer of 1938; the spin rate of Sandy Koufax's fastball; the actual mound-to-plate deceleration of Feller's fastball on August 20, 1946; the modulus of elasticity of the anterior band of Steve Dalkowski's ulnar collateral ligament; the strength of his shoulder external-rotator muscles relative to pitchers of today, etc., etc. In the absence of such data, which is of course forever lost, the reader may view the analy-

1. Three Fastball Prodigies

sis in the following chapters as mere conjecture. The analysis, however, is based on the current state of knowledge in aerodynamics, biomechanics, the physics of power, and muscle anatomy and physiology. As such, it is not conjectural. Even with good science, however, it is difficult to establish absolute certainty. As Albert Einstein once said: "No amount of experimentation can ever prove me right; a single experiment can prove me wrong."

2

The 107-mph Fastball?

"We created a monster."— George Lederer, promoter of Nolan Ryan's 1974 speed measurement and contest

On August 20, 1946, Army scientists from Aberdeen Proving Ground, Maryland, loaded up a device used in military research and traveled 70 miles south to Griffith Stadium in Washington, D.C., the home of the Washington Senators. Their mission, unlike their usual military assignments in ballistics, was to address a decades-old question: "How fast is the world's fastest fastball?" There had been previous attempts to apply scientific instruments to this issue as early as 1912, and like this one, each had involved instruments designed for testing bullets or military projectiles in flight.

Pitching a baseball is ballistics of the manual type. It was appropriate, therefore, that Army ballisticians took on the task of measuring the velocity of Bob Feller's fastball, considered then to be the fastest in baseball. The scientific team was experienced in measuring velocities of weapons in support of World War II, which had ended less than a year earlier. The team came from a research laboratory that in the same year completed development of the first general-purpose electronic digital computer, the ENIAC, for calculating artillery tables. They brought to Griffith Stadium a Lumiline, a unique box-like timing device, and they would take velocity measurements before a night game because the baseball had to interrupt a pair of light beams in the Lumiline to start and stop a millisecond timer. It was thus more reliable in dim light than in the full light of day. The Lumiline was placed on home plate to measure the velocity of Feller's pitches at the instant they crossed the plate.

A crowd of 31,000 fans, about 20,000 more than a typical Tuesday night draw, turned out seeking an unusual baseball thrill near the end of the Senators' 76-win season. They came to see "Rapid Robert" throw a few strikes through the Lumiline's trapezoidal opening, a brief performance for which he negotiated a $700 fee. The final pitch was above the strike

2. The 107-mph Fastball?

zone, shattering the wooden frame atop the Lumiline's opening and terminating the proceedings with a bang.

Based on readings of the Lumiline timer, the highest velocity measured at home plate that evening was 98.6 mph. The Army team recorded temperature, humidity, atmospheric pressure, wind speed, and wind direction, then calculated the speed of the ball at the instant it left Feller's hand. To do this, they applied a standard formula of ballistics to estimate how much it decelerated between the mound and home plate. That calculation yielded a deceleration of 9 mph. They next determined the velocity out of Feller's hand — the sum of the plate speed and the estimated deceleration — to be 107.6 mph.

The problem with this approach was that the speed at release, the muzzle velocity in military terms, had to be calculated based on several variables, one of which — the coefficient of drag for the baseball — is particularly difficult to determine. From the instant a baseball leaves the pitcher's hand, nature applies the brakes to it in the form of drag. The ball transfers momentum to the air molecules in flight, and vicious wake turbulence forms behind the ball, converting its energy to noise and producing a hiss, hum, or roar in its flight to the plate. The noise of this wake turbulence is the source of Walter Johnson's nickname, and the tag commonly used for the fastball, the hummer.

The calculations used to estimate the deceleration were simple, but they were particularly sensitive to the value selected for the drag coefficient, a dimensionless value for aerodynamic efficiency. A higher drag coefficient means that an object, because of its shape, creates more turbulence as it moves through the air, producing more resistance and slowing more rapidly in flight. The drag coefficient for a streamlined Bonneville racecar, for example, is about 0.12, much lower than that of a typical box-shaped truck, which is about 0.60 or greater.

The ballistics team applied two equations with several variables, including drag coefficient[1]:

- The velocity correction equals air density relative to sea level times the projectile form-factor times the projectile diameter squared times the distance from the muzzle to the sensors times the drag coefficient divided by the projectile weight.
- The muzzle (release) velocity equals the instrument (home plate) velocity plus the velocity correction (deceleration).

17

The drag coefficient is not constant for a baseball. It changes with the ball's linear velocity, rotational velocity, surface roughness, air density, and the orientation of the seams relative to the spin axis (two-seam versus four-seam grip). The drag coefficient is near constant at 0.5 until the ball's velocity reaches about 50 mph. Then it decreases sharply as velocity increases into what is called the critical regime. There is considerable uncertainty about its value until it reaches about 100 mph, at which point the drag coefficient is about 0.3.[2] A four-seam grip produces a slightly lower drag coefficient than a two-seam grip, so even Feller's grip had an effect on the calculation used to estimate the deceleration.

The Army scientists applied a drag coefficient for a smooth sphere, which has a relatively constant value of about 0.5 until its drag crisis occurs at about 150 mph. In 1946, there were no wind-tunnel data specific to a spinning baseball and variations in its seam orientation, rate of spin, and velocity. It would be three years before aviation pioneer Igor Sikorsky had one of his engineers conduct experiments with a spinning baseball in a wind tunnel to develop the first such data.[3] Experiments showed that a ball with seams produces substantially less drag at the normal range of pitching speed than does a smooth ball. It may seem counter-intuitive that a rough ball has less drag than a smooth ball, but it is the same principle applied in the design of the dimpled golf ball to make it fly farther than a smooth golf ball. The airflow around a baseball goes through flow transitions as the velocity changes. At low velocity, two stable vortices form behind the ball, but as the velocity increases, the vortices become unstable and alternately break away. As velocity increases further, the flow becomes very turbulent with vortices of many sizes being shed in a turbulent wake. Each of these flow regimes produces a different amount of drag.

Results of different experiments agree that the drag coefficient of a baseball at 100 mph is approximately 0.3, a value that leads to a much lower estimate of the ball's deceleration between Feller's fingertips and the Lumiline atop home plate. On that summer evening in 1946, Feller's pitches *probably* decelerated about 5.4 mph rather than 9 mph. Using the 0.3 value, the estimated speed of Feller's fastball at release would thus be 104 mph. This is not to say conclusively that Feller failed to reach 107.6 mph out of the hand, but that there is great uncertainty in calculating — rather than directly measuring — the speed of a fastball at release.

At 100 mph, the drag on a baseball is about three ounces, according to calculations of a computer program developed by the National Aero-

2. The 107-mph Fastball?

nautics and Space Administration and available on the Internet, which applies the 0.3 drag coefficient.[4] In the conditions on August 20, 1946, Feller's pitch would probably have decelerated more than 5.4 mph had he used the two-seam grip on his fastball. Had he used a roughened-surface ball rather than a new ball, however, it would have slowed down less due to a lower drag coefficient. Had he thrown a new baseball in the early spring on, say, a 34-degree night, it would have been closer to 7 mph deceleration due to the higher air density.

Data from the optical Pitch Tracking System, PITCH f/x, installed in major-league stadiums beginning in 2007, indicate that a 100-mph fastball decelerates about 8 to 10 mph before reaching home plate. This two-camera system is a sort of remote Lumiline in that it measures the distance the ball's *image* travels in intervals of 1/60 of a second as it begins its flight to home plate. The PITCH f/x cameras, which must be calibrated regularly, gather a large volume of data on which many calculations are performed at high speed, not only to determine the speed of the pitch, but also to estimate its spin rate and plot its trajectory and ball position relative to the strike zone on the television screen with an accuracy of about 1 inch. The system always overestimates the deceleration because it applies a simplistic assumption that the baseball slows down at a constant rate. Deceleration is dependent on drag, however, and drag decreases as the ball loses speed. The NASA program calculates that the drag on the baseball released at 100 mph with a spin rate of 2,000 rpm on a 60-degree day at sea level is 3.7 ounces at the point of release and 3.3 ounces when it reaches the plate.

PITCH f/x measures the ball's velocity as it leaves the pitcher's hand, the point at which speed measurement is simplest and most consistent. That's the way it has been done since radar guns first appeared at ballparks in the 1970s. The least-desirable point at which to measure the baseball's speed is *between* the mound and home plate—a ballistician's no-man's land—which is where the measurement was made in 1974 to enter Nolan Ryan into the *Guinness Book of World Records*.

Ryan was the ace of the Angels at that time and was in a three-season stretch of record-breaking pitching. Despite his growing reputation as a strikeout phenom, attendance was low for Angels' games, with week-night crowds often dropping below 10,000. George Lederer, the Angels' Director of Public Relations and Promotions, came up with a marketing idea involving a high-tech instrument being developed at Rockwell International's research facility, just five miles from the Angels' stadium. Rockwell scientists were working on an infrared laser device for military use, which, like radar, applied the Doppler phase-shift effect to measure velocity remotely. The device had its limitations for baseball use, one of which was a very narrow beam. It was, consequently, an instrument of promotional convenience, rather than a device suitable for accurate, reliable, non-intrusive measurements of fastball velocity. This is attested to by the fact that after the two experiments with Ryan's fastball, a laser device was never again used to measure pitch velocity.

Lederer planned the promotion for September 7, 1974, a home game against the Chicago White Sox. He also announced a contest in which the fan closest to guessing Ryan's top speed would win a prize. The contest drew about 6,000 entries from California and 20 other states. Guesses ranged from 48 to 147.3 mph. "We created a monster," Lederer told *Los Angeles Times* columnist John Hall. "We never realized how much attention this would attract."[5]

In technical nomenclature, the speed-measuring device was a coherent infrared laser. Publicly, however, it was described as coherent infrared radar, dropping the term laser, because of concern that the public in 1974 would fear being subjected to some deadly beam being developed for space warfare. There were indeed safety concerns with the use of any laser device in a stadium filled with people. Particularly, there was no desire to risk blinding one of baseball's greatest stars, the man upon whom the promotion was based, and at the time the most highly paid pitcher, by pointing an experimental laser device at him from behind home plate. That's the way radar guns are employed, pointed at the pitcher from behind the plate, and that's the logical approach for measuring the speed of a fast-moving object, directly in line with its path of flight.

The concern for the safety of the future Hall of Famer forced Rockwell to place the laser device in the press box, aiming the beam downward to a point on the ground 9 or 10 feet in front of home plate. No one bothered to measure this point precisely or to calculate the correction to home plate to support a comparison to Bob Feller's record of 98.6 mph plate speed. Nor did they measure the angle between the ball's line of flight and the laser beam emanating from the press box, an angle that could have caused the speed to be underestimated. This was, after all, an event focused on promotion, not science.

The beam of a radar gun has a very wide cone, as much as 100 times

2. The 107-mph Fastball?

Nolan Ryan made his major league debut with the New York Mets at age 19 (Getty Images).

The Science of the Fastball

wider than that of the typical laser speed-measuring device. Using the laser, rather than radar, was like hunting ducks with a rifle rather than a shotgun. The Rockwell scientists recognized that some of Ryan's pitches would not be measured, and that was in fact the case, particularly with pitches wide of the strike zone. During the game, in which Ryan earned his 18th victory of the season, the highest velocity measured in each inning was posted on the scoreboard. His top speeds by inning were[6]:

87.6 mph, first inning	91.3 mph, sixth inning
93.4 mph, second inning	96.7 mph, seventh inning
94.1 mph, third inning	94.1 mph, eighth inning
98.8 mph, fourth inning	100.8 mph, ninth inning
96.4 mph, fifth inning	

Applying a rough correction to the 100.8 mph reading on a high fastball in the ninth inning yields a speed of 99.7 mph at home plate, assuming the ball intersected the laser beam 10 feet from the plate. No data were recorded on atmospheric pressure, wind speed, wind direction, temperature, or humidity, so the pitch speed can only be roughly estimated at 105 to 106 mph at release and 99 to 100 mph at the plate.

Eighteen days earlier, the Rockwell technicians measured the velocity of two of Ryan's pitches at 100.9 mph in an 11-inning game in which Ryan struck out 19 Detroit Tigers. This was a pilot test for the experimental method. Given the limited accuracy of the 10-foot correction to home plate, there is no significant difference in the readings on the two different days. Both are about 1 mph faster than Bob Feller's 98.6 mph at home plate.

Ryan's highest velocity measured on September 7 came in the ninth inning as he approached a total of 159 pitches, indicating either that his velocity was unaffected by fatigue, or that a substantial number of pitches from the early innings were missed by the laser beam, some of which might have been faster than those recorded. He was thus possibly denied a faster reading by the narrowness of the laser's beam.

From a scientific perspective, the best available military technology failed both Ryan and Feller in attempting to establish an accurate reference point, a standard against which all future fireballers could be measured. These two experiments, however, provided enough accuracy to indicate that Ryan and Feller were superior to pitchers of the radar-gun era.

On that night in Anaheim, non-intrusive speed measurement was

2. The 107-mph Fastball?

cautiously introduced to baseball. Since then, the radar gun has penetrated the tightly knit fabric of baseball, a sport that has resisted any technology that could alter the traditional balance of the game. In doing so, it has brought pitching velocity into sharper focus and has increased fan interest. But it has not been truly non-intrusive, which is an important factor if one wants to obtain accurate measurements of velocity. Even throwing into a strike-zone size target, as Feller did, can impose a small burden similar to having a 3–0 count with the bases loaded. Such was the case when Walter Johnson threw for speed measurement in 1912. Consequently, his measurement is considered inaccurate because of the methodology.

Being non-intrusive — as both radar and PITCH f/x are — ensures that measurements are most accurate because the readings can be taken during a game, an environment in which adrenalin and competitive pressure can affect velocity in a positive way. Radar guns are accurate when operating properly, but if the timing circuit of a gun becomes inaccurate, as is possible in any electronic clock, significant error, perhaps as much as 5 percent, can occur in the readings. "A lot of our electronics in America malfunction a lot," observed a Japanese baseball writer upon seeing a scoreboard radar reading he knew to be 4 to 5 mph high during a spring training game in 2012.[7]

Walter Johnson of course did not have the advantage of non-intrusive speed measuring device when he pitched to a bullet-testing device in Bridgeport, Connecticut, on October 16, 1912. Johnson traveled to the Remington Arms Company on that date to pitch at the company's test range. The speed-measuring instrument was incorporated in a 15-foot-long tunnel, with fine wires at the open end and a steel plate at the far end. The timing cycle began when the ball tripped the wires, and it ended when the ball struck the steel plate 15 feet down the tunnel, 75 feet from the pitcher.[8]

The opening of the device was about 60 feet away and was at shoulder height. As a sidearm pitcher, Johnson was said to have had difficulty getting his pitches through the two-foot-square opening. The device measured the average speed of the ball as it traveled through the 15 feet of tunnel. Thus, it measured the average speed about 67.5 feet from the pitcher (midpoint of the tunnel). Johnson's fastest of three pitches was 122 feet per second (83.2 mph) at 67.5 feet on his third try. The result: his calculated release velocity was about 90 to 91 mph.

There have been various other experiments, including Johnson's revisiting Bridgeport in 1917, but each time the methodology and lack of attention to detail in recording data and conditions made the results questionable.

The issue of who is the fastest pitcher continues into the 21st century with non-intrusive measurement capabilities of greater reliability but still requiring routine calibration. Joel Zumaya, a relief pitcher for the Detroit Tigers recorded a pitch speed of 104.8 mph on the radar gun on October 10, 2006, in Oakland's McAfee Coliseum. Aroldis Chapman, a 22-year-old Cuban who defected to the U.S. and received a six-year, $30 million contract with the Cincinnati Reds, threw 105.1 mph as recorded by the PITCH f/x system in Cincinnati on September 24, 2010. Sportswriters quickly declared Chapman to be the fastest pitcher of all time. His velocity, however, does not conclusively surpass that of Feller or Ryan.

Baseball, the sport with countless entries in its record books, does not have an official record for pitching velocity or a process for certifying one. Perhaps PITCH f/x now provides that capability. Or perhaps there should not be such a record. Velocity is, after all, a secondary measure of performance, a scouting statistic like the fastest time in running to first base. Baseball, more than any other sport, respects and honors the performances of those who played the game in the past. No one can go back in time to re-measure the fastball velocity of Johnson, Feller, or Ryan.

3

The Kinetic Chain of Pitching, Roughly Quantified

"You can observe a lot by watching."—Yogi Berra, as quoted in his 1988 book, *The Yogi Book*

    A corollary to Yogi Berra's truism is that you can observe a lot more by watching at 400 frames-per-second slow motion.
    Pitching a baseball involves a chain of explosive movements synchronized to produce an efficient transfer of energy from the pitcher's muscles to the ball. Pitching is often characterized as the work of the arm. It is more accurately described, however, as the collective work of many of the body's skeletal muscles, focusing their energy on accelerating the arm — both ends of it — towards home plate. Power is transferred from the muscles of the leg and torso to the shoulder and arm. It is amplified through elastic-strain energy storage and return to provide two bursts of energy to the arm — one from the contraction of the muscles in the shoulder and arm and one from the recoil of elastic-strain energy stored briefly in the shoulder and arm.
    At the end of this kinetic chain, the hand achieves the highest velocities of human movement. So rapid is the motion of the arm and hand that they appear as a blur in real time and at normal video-camera speed of $1/30$ of a second. The hand is a blur even at 200 to 250 frames per second, the speed range of slow-motion photography that has frequently been used in biomechanical studies of pitching. Like the wings of a hummingbird in flight, the arm and hand movements in pitching are so rapid that they are almost invisible, giving rise to misconceptions about the source of power. These misconceptions can be corrected by studying pitchers in slow motion.
    Scientific studies using slow-motion photography have involved hundreds of pitchers and have been conducted with the goal of reducing the

The Science of the Fastball

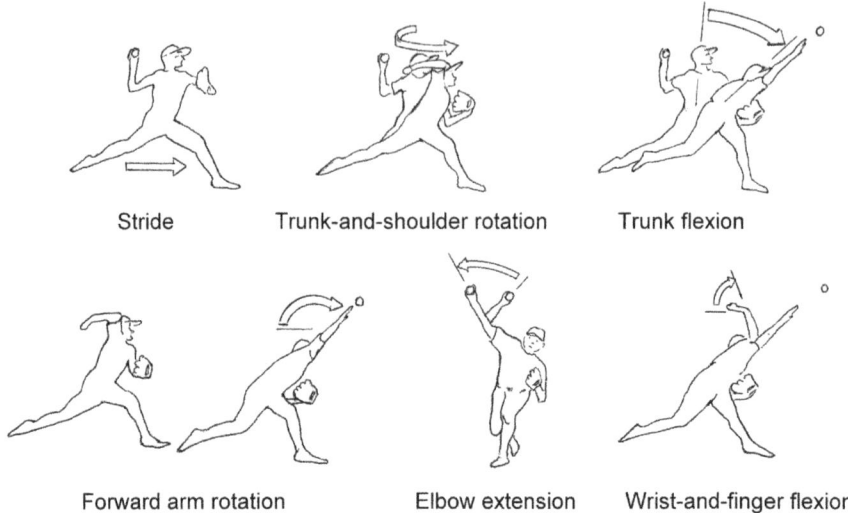

Figure 1: Three cocking movements and three launching movements of pitching.

rates of pitching injuries. The studies have seemingly made little progress in reducing injury rates, but they have yielded data relative to an issue that has existed since pitchers began throwing overhand in the 1880s: what differentiates exceptional pitchers like Johnson, Feller, or Ryan from their colleagues? The studies' limitations are that they acquire data in a laboratory setting, not on the playing field, and they typically include pitchers throwing at less than 90 mph. The large data set of the velocities, however, makes it possible to estimate, assuming a normal (bell curve) distribution, what Nolan Ryan's component velocities might have been in delivering his magnificent fastball.

There are six distinct movements in accelerating the fastball to its release velocity. *These are depicted in Figure 1.* The first of these, the stride, is linear, and the rest are rotational movements that occur between stride-foot contact and ball release and typically take a total of about 0.15 seconds to complete.

Arm-cocking movements:
- Stride
- Trunk-and-shoulder rotation
- Trunk flexion

3. The Kinetic Chain of Pitching, Roughly Quantified

Launching movements:
- Forward arm rotation
- Elbow extension
- Wrist-and-finger flexion

The first three of these movements accelerate the base of the arm, i.e., the shoulder joint, and serve mainly to store energy momentarily by cocking the arm. The latter three accelerate the opposite end of the arm rotationally relative to the shoulder joint. In these three, the arm and hand are accelerated rapidly by two sources of energy — contraction of arm and shoulder muscles and recoil, the release of energy stored in the biological springs of these muscles, tendons, and ligaments. The first three movements can thus be considered arm-cocking movements, and the second three to be launching movements. Two of these — the stride and elbow extension — differ from the other four in that they do not directly increase the ball velocity but transfer momentum. The stride makes the transition from linear to rotational, and the elbow extension makes the transition from rotational to linear.

How fast were each one of these movements in producing Nolan Ryan's 105- to 106-mph fastball? Pitching science would have benefited had the velocity of each movement been measured with slow-motion photography when Ryan's heater intersected the laser beam in 1974 or when Bob Feller pitched into the Lumiline in 1946. Technology will eventually make it possible to take such measurements on major leaguers as they pitch in a game. For the present, however, data on good-but-not-exceptional pitchers acquired by scientists such as Dr. Glenn Fleisig of the American Sports Medicine Institute in Birmingham, Alabama, have to suffice. In a study published in 1999, Fleisig and his colleagues measured the joint velocities of 29 college and professional pitchers who had an average fastball velocity of 86 mph.[1] In a second study, he analyzed 231 pitchers in four different age groups.[2] Using standard deviations in velocities for these groups allows an estimate of the component velocities of pitchers who attain much greater fastball velocities. Because these component velocities are rotational, they are measured in degrees per second. The more conventional units for rotational velocity are revolutions per minute (rpm). One rpm equals six degrees per second.

The Stride

The transfer of energy to the ball begins with the stride, which generates about 4 to 6 mph of linear velocity toward home plate. This stride velocity is not applied directly to ball velocity, however. It generates momentum (body mass times velocity) that is converted to rotational velocity as a forward flexing of the trunk. In the stride, the drive leg thrusts the pitcher's body forward, reaching maximum velocity *before* the stride foot firmly plants. If the forward knee braces firmly, the stride velocity drops to zero before the ball begins to accelerate toward the plate. If done properly, the momentum is not lost in this abrupt stop but is transferred into trunk flexion, a tilting of the trunk toward the plate, once the stride foot is planted five to six feet in front of the pitching rubber. Abdominal muscles and hip flexors contract to aid in this forward tilting. Without the momentum generated by the drive leg, the abdominal muscles and hip flexors would provide all the power of trunk flexion, which is the case when a catcher throws from his knees. The momentum produced by the stride also helps to counteract the retarding force the arm produces, giving the arm a stable platform when the arm explosively accelerates the ball to its release velocity. For every action there is a reaction, and here the action is the very rapid acceleration of the arm. This rearward force, which is imperceptible to the pitcher, can be observed by throwing a baseball while on roller skates. The more momentum the body has toward home plate, the firmer is the base with which to resist this rearward force. This is a positive effect of a pitcher having greater body weight and the leg strength to go with it.

Trunk-and-Shoulder Rotation

Once the stride foot is firmly planted, the trunk begins to rotate around a near-vertical axis to accelerate the throwing shoulder, the base of the arm, toward home plate. The trunk is not a rigid mass, and its rotation is actually a twisting motion in bottom-to-top sequence, pelvis first and shoulders last. The oblique and gluteus muscles provide the power, and in the twisting motion, energy is stored in the biological springs of these muscles to achieve greater velocity of rotation. The pitcher pulls his non-throwing arm close to his body to increase the speed of rotation, just as ice skaters draw their arms close to the body to twirl faster. The shoulder rotates about twice as far as the pelvis. Fleisig measured the maximum rotational velocity of the upper torso at about twice that of the pelvis, with the upper torso velocity measured at 1,230 degrees per second with

3. The Kinetic Chain of Pitching, Roughly Quantified

a standard deviation of 70 degrees per second. With the assumption of a normal distribution, adding two standard deviations to the average provides an estimate of the trunk-and-shoulder rotation velocity of the top two percent of pitchers. This value is 1,370 degrees per second.

Trunk Flexion

Trunk flexion, a tilting of the trunk toward home plate, has the lowest velocity of the rotational movements of pitching, because it involves moving a large mass with a relatively long moment arm; that is, relative to the other pitching movements, the center of mass is a greater distance from its point of rotation. It may be the most difficult movement to optimize because it involves coordinating a double transfer of energy. That is, energy from the stride is transferred to trunk flexion and is then transferred to the arm and shoulder to cock the arm. To ensure that maximum kinetic energy from the stride is transferred, the pitcher must establish rigid support with the forward knee, so that energy is not dissipated by flexing the knee after the foot is planted. To ensure that maximum energy is transferred from trunk flexion to the arm, the pitcher increases the speed of flexion with the assistance of the abdominal muscles and hip flexors. He can also improve the timing of trunk flexion by starting it from a substantial angle of extension, i.e., arching the back. This extension increases the arc through which the trunk flexes, yielding a higher angular velocity of flexion and bringing this maximum velocity closer to the point of full arm cocking (also referred to as maximum external rotation).

Hyperextension is best understood by watching Cy Young Award winner Tim Lincecum of the San Francisco Giants, who apparently develops more velocity from trunk flexion than most pitchers. Arching the back also stretches the muscles of the abdomen, storing energy elastically in these muscles to produce greater trunk-flexion velocity. Visible indicators of trunk-flexion velocity are the trunk angle at three points: the angle of extension, the angle when the arm is fully cocked, and the angle at release. The angle when the arm is fully cocked is the most important of these because it is the point at which the energy of the trunk becomes fully transferred to the biological springs of the arm and shoulder. Seven-time all-star closer Billy Wagner is a pitcher who derives exceptional power from trunk flexion, as seen in his high angle of trunk flexion at full arm-cocking.

Fleisig's data shows an average of 410 degrees per second trunk-flexion velocity for one group he studied, with a standard deviation of 70 degrees per second which indicates that the top two percent of pitchers would have a trunk-flexion velocity of about 550 degrees per second.

Forward Arm Rotation

The subscapularis muscle of the rotator cuff is the prime mover for forward rotation of the upper arm (humerus), which is also known as internal shoulder rotation. The humerus bone acts like an automobile's drive axle, rotating the forearm through an arc of about 120 degrees to the point of ball-release in just 0.02 to 0.03 seconds.[3] Most of the energy the ball has at release is transferred to it during this very rapid movement, often described as arm speed. It is not this quarter-pound muscle alone that produces the high velocity of arm rotation, however. Elastic-strain energy stored during the arm-cocking movements is released nearly simultaneously during forward arm rotation. Other muscles also play a smaller role in this high-speed movement — the latissimus dorsi, pectoralis major, and serratus anterior. Forward arm rotation is easily the fastest movement of pitching. Fleisig's research team found its average velocity among pitchers ranging from youth to professional to be about 7,720 degrees per second with a standard deviation of 1,040 degrees per second. With the assumption of a normal distribution, the speed of the top two percent of pitchers is estimated at 9,800 degrees per second. Data from another study by Fleisig indicate this velocity to be 9,390 and 9,420 degrees per second among college and professional pitchers. These data indicate that pitchers who exceed 100 mph probably have arm rotation velocities around 10,000 degrees per second.

Elbow Extension

Elbow extension, the straightening of the arm, occurs during forward arm rotation. Like the stride, the elbow extension makes a transition between rotational and linear velocity. Straightening the arm makes this transition occur, allowing the pitcher to control the direction of the ball's flight. The upper arm continues to rotate forward with the shoulder moving toward home plate, and the angle must increase to transition the ball to a linear path. Though the force applied in elbow extension does not contribute directly to ball velocity, this arm-straightening is important in determining velocity. The triceps muscle, aided by centrifugal force, extends the arm from an initial angle of about 90 degrees (at stride-foot contact) to one of about 157 degrees at release, on average. Before the elbow extends, while the angle is about 90 degrees, arm-rotation has its largest moment arm, which is equal to the length of the forearm and hand together. Once it extends to within about 23 degrees of full extension, the moment arm is reduced to about 39 percent of its maximum (the sine of 23 degrees). There is considerable variability in this angle, according to Fleisig's studies, with the standard deviation being five to seven degrees. Adding two standard deviations raises the moment arm for arm rotation at release to 54 percent of its maximum. The elbow extension velocity, the average rate of straightening measured by Fleisig, was 2,540 degrees per second with a standard deviation of 250 degrees per second, indicating that the top two percent of pitchers have an elbow extension velocity of 3,040 degrees per second. Extending rapidly is important because it allows the extension to occur later, keeping the moment arm large for a longer period so as to gain greater ball velocity from the high-speed arm rotation.

Wrist-and-Finger Flexion

The final and very important boost to ball velocity comes when the wrist and fingers snap toward the plate in well-timed flexion. Commonly referred to as hand speed, this rapid flexion produces a substantial acceleration in a period of about 0.01 seconds before the ball is released. There is also a retarding force from this rapid acceleration of the ball that slows the arm speed slightly. As is the case with trunk flexion, wrist flexion produces maximum velocity when the starting point is the hyper-extended position of the wrist, as will be discussed further in Chapter 6. Finger flexion provides an additional boost that is measured as part of wrist flexion. Wrist flexion velocity, which is quite variable among pitchers, has two visual indicators — maximum wrist angle of extension (the average is about 40 degrees) and wrist angle at release. For the fastball, the power for this final snap comes from the flexor muscles of the forearm — the flexor carpi radialis, flexor carpi ulnaris, flexor digitorum superficialis, and flexor digitorum profundus. An average wrist flexion velocity of about 2,950 degrees per second with a standard deviation of 790 degrees per second was measured in a study involving eight collegiate pitchers[4]. This indicates that the top two percent have a wrist flexion velocity of 4,520 degrees per second. A second study indicates 4,730 degrees per second.[5]

If perfectly synchronized, these six movements form a kinetic chain that transfers maximum energy to the ball from each of the many muscles involved. Perfect synchronization would require all the rotational movements (except elbow extension) to reach their maximum angular velocity at the same instant, as the ball is released. This is not possible, however, with the two movements involving the trunk. *Figure 2 shows* the timing of the rotational propulsive movements, with the left side of each bar being the start of acceleration and the right side being the point of maximum rotational velocity. Both trunk movements peak well before release, although trunk flexion is more variable and sometimes peaks after release. The pitcher's body accommodates this natural timing problem with elastic-energy storage and return in the biological springs of the arm and shoulder; that is, most of the kinetic energy from the trunk is stored momentarily in the arm and shoulder to bridge the 0.02-second timing gap. The energy storage is complete when the arm reaches the fully cocked position often referred to as maximum external rotation. The energy release begins a fraction of a second later with the recoil of these elastic components, coinciding with the explosive release of energy from the shoulder and arm muscles to rotate the arm forward at high speed. This effect is described in more detail in Chapter 5.

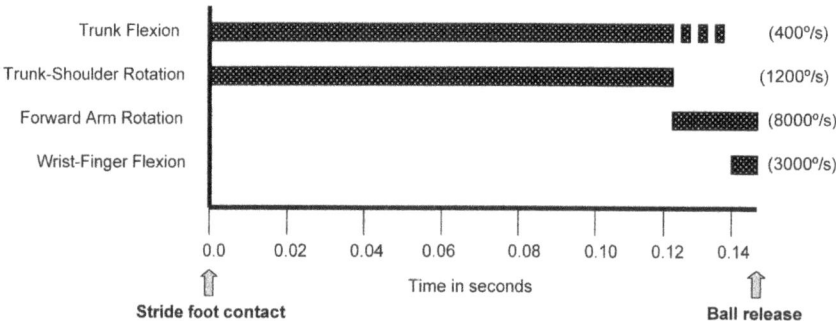

Figure 2: Relative timing of four pitching movements that accelerate the ball toward the plate. Note that each bar extends from zero velocity of the movement on the left to the maximum angular velocity on the right.

3. The Kinetic Chain of Pitching, Roughly Quantified

Walter Johnson about 1909, his third season of major league baseball (Library of Congress, LC-DIG-npcc-19194).

As indicated by the first two bars, trunk-and-shoulder rotation is about three times faster than trunk flexion but roughly coincides with the duration of the rotation because of the difference in the arc of movement, which is about three times greater for trunk-shoulder rotation. With the brief delay in storing and releasing the energy from trunk flexion and trunk-shoulder rotation, the pitcher delivers almost all the energy to the ball in the last 0.02 to 0.03 seconds of the pitch, during forward arm rotation and wrist-finger flexion. In this brief period, most of the energy stored in the cocking movements and all of the energy from the muscles of the shoulder and arm are transferred to the ball in rapid succession. A small portion of the total energy is supplied to the ball by the continued rotation of the shoulder and flexion of the trunk beyond the point at which the arm is fully cocked.

Each pitcher's coordination of the pitching movements is unique because of subtle individual differences in the strength, speed, and leverage of the various muscles in the kinetic chain. Bob Feller and Nolan Ryan pitched with the conventional timing diagrammed *in Figure 2*. Walter Johnson's sidearm delivery was unconventional. He began forward arm rotation and elbow extension earlier, during the rotation of the trunk and shoulder. Early elbow extension — commonly described as opening up early — usually generates less velocity because it lengthens the moment arm too soon, reducing the rate of acceleration in the trunk-and-shoulder rotation. Like the final movement of a discus throw, Johnson's delivery gave a greater role to the pectoralis major, the powerful chest muscle that typically has a large portion of fast-twitch muscle fibers. With conventional mechanics, this muscle makes a smaller contribution. Johnson made up for the retarding effect of the longer moment arm with exceptional hand speed. High wrist-and-finger-flexion velocity can account for perhaps 30 mph of ball speed, as will be discussed in Chapter 6. Although Johnson's fastball velocity was greater than that of typical sidearm pitchers, it was apparently not as great as Feller and Ryan produced with conventional mechanics, possibly because it did not employ the anterior band of the ulnar collateral ligament for power amplification. Johnson's pectoralis major likely had exceptional speed and strength, and he began his trunk rotation from a hyper-extended position to develop greater velocity. Though his arm appeared to the batter to be straight throughout the pitch, the elbow angle decreased to about 90 degrees as the arm and trunk began to accelerate out of sight of the batter. Though he extended his elbow earlier than pitchers with conventional mechanics, there was less stress on his elbow than most sidearm pitchers experience.

As Johnson's unique mechanics illustrate, the amount of energy transferred to the baseball in each movement varies from pitcher to pitcher, but the pitchers with the highest fastball velocity are those who transfer the

3. The Kinetic Chain of Pitching, Roughly Quantified

most energy to the ball during the launching phase, which allows them to complete forward arm rotation and wrist-and-finger flexion in the shortest time. To achieve great velocity, Johnson, Feller, and Ryan assuredly had fast, powerful muscles of the shoulder and arm, and they applied elastic-energy storage and return to great benefit. It is assumed that there was very little energy wasted in transition from one movement to the next and that they were able to maximize all the elements of pitching power described in the next chapter. It is noteworthy, and fortunate, that no coach ever altered Johnson's mechanics in an attempt to make them more conventional. He, like Feller and Ryan, developed his pitching mechanics naturally, early on. Though Johnson's mechanics were unusual, they were, to his ultimate benefit, highly efficient.

A demonstration of the six movements of pitching is available for visual analysis at every baseball game. The distinct movements are, however, indiscernible by the average fan because they unfold in two blinks of an eye. Without the aid of slow-motion video, the movements merge into a blur. The ability to evaluate the strengths and weaknesses of a pitcher's kinetic chain in real time is thus limited to those who have critically viewed thousands of pitches and consequently hold in their mind a dynamic image of perfect mechanics. Without the aid of slow-motion or sequential photography, a novice can examine only the beginning and ending positions and can evaluate movements only by carefully focusing attention on one movement at a time.

For those lacking the ability to visualize good and bad pitching mechanics, baseball games often provide a demonstration of very poor mechanics for comparison and contrast — in the ceremonial first pitch. This presentation of imperfect pitching occurs as a prelude to the game, when an old, young, or simply unskilled honoree throws in the direction of home plate a pitch that is a fastball in name only. This pitcher of the moment demonstrates very little strength, very little speed, and virtually no elastic-strain energy storage and return. But it is the poor coordination of the six movements that is perhaps most striking. It is coordination comparable to that of a 16-year-old learning to drive with a manual transmission. Later, for contrast, the closer stands at the same spot, and as his arm momentarily disappears in a blur of rapid motion, a fastball leaps from his hand with such energy that it emits a hum, maybe even a roar, and finally a pop as it hits the catcher's glove signaling: game over, demonstration complete.

4

The Four Elements of Pitching Power

"A kid pitcher has to have a fastball to succeed in the big leagues, for he can never learn how to pitch faster. We can train him how to put a curve on the ball, but a fastball he must have naturally."—
Alva Bradley, 1935[1]

A year before Bob Feller first donned his Cleveland Indians uniform, no. 9, the president of the Indians, Alva Bradley, made this contribution to the science of pitching. He presented what could be called Bradley's Observation on Natural Speed. Two-thirds of a century later, Bob Feller himself would renew and clarify Bradley's Observation: "You can learn control and how to pitch, but not how to throw several miles per hour faster."[2]

Bradley and Feller have been proven wrong. Fastball velocity is determined by the amount of energy the pitcher supplies to it in the brief period between stride-foot contact and ball-release. When the ball leaves the pitcher's hand, it has kinetic energy in the form of both linear velocity (in mph) and rotational velocity (spin, in rpm). Power is the *rate* of supplying energy to the ball, and it has two components, speed and force. Pitching power is muscle speed multiplied by muscle strength, a measure of force. Thus, pitching power is not a function of natural muscle speed alone, as one might infer from Bradley's observation. The reality is that strength training, once forbidden for pitchers, can increase a pitcher's power — and his fastball velocity — if done properly. A pitcher can indeed "learn" to pitch faster.

There are two other elements of pitching power, and these relate to how the energy from the muscles is transmitted to the ball. These also are determined by natural attributes, genetic gifts subject to little or no improvement. Only the element of strength can be substantially improved with training. Improvements in coordination and timing can yield greater velocity, but the ability to optimize timing — high-speed coordination and body control — is a natural attribute. The four elements of pitching power are:

- **Muscle strength.** The maximum strength of a muscle is determined by its size, specifically by its physiologic cross-section area. The cross-section area of a muscle is determined by the number, diameter, and angle of the muscle fibers.
- **Muscle Contraction Speed.** The quantities of fast-twitch and slow-twitch fibers in a muscle determine the speed at which the muscle can contract. The maximum speed of a muscle fiber is referred to as the twitch speed, the maximum speed with zero load on a single type of fiber. When a load, a resistance, is applied to the fiber, it contracts at a speed slower than its twitch speed. Consequently a stronger fiber, one having a larger diameter, will contract faster under load.
- **Elastic-strain energy storage and return.** The human body contains biological springs, elastic materials in tendons, ligaments, and muscles. By briefly storing and returning energy as they stretch and recoil, these springs act as power amplifiers. This effect is described in Chapter 5.
- **Transmission efficiency.** Efficient transmission of power from the muscles to the ball requires: (1) the capability for precise, high-speed timing and coordination of the muscles in the kinetic chain; and (2) stable joints, particularly the elbow and shoulder joints. The effect of joint stability on power transmission is discussed in Chapter 9.

Muscle Strength

In August 1996, a few days after the Olympic flame was extinguished in Atlanta, members of the Atlanta Braves coaching and scouting staffs gathered at their stadium to watch a 29-year-old man from the Czech Republic apply a pitching grip to a baseball for the first time.[3] There were high expectations for Jan Zelezny, upon whom the group's attention was focused, because he had won his second Olympic gold medal in the javelin throw four days earlier. He had flung the spear 289 feet to become the first man in 72 years to win consecutive gold medals in the Olympic javelin competition.

The Science of the Fastball

The gathering for Zelezny's first pitch was one of the more unusual events in the world-wide search for the preternatural pitching arm. This one, however, proved disappointing from the instant the first pitch left Zelezny's un-calloused fingertips. His fastball on that August day topped out at 85 mph on the radar gun, not exactly Bob Feller-like.

To say that a champion javelin thrower is always a good prospect for a major-league pitcher is like saying that Arnold Schwarzenegger, in his pre-gubernatorial body-building prime, would have been a good candidate for the Olympic sprint-relay team. He had great muscle size and strength but not necessarily great muscle speed. His equation for power was strength-dominant, not speed-dominant. His top speed afoot was limited by his natural muscle speed, and his bulging leg muscles would provide him speed superiority only under a heavy load. In his prime, Mr. Schwarzenegger could probably have towed an automobile at a faster speed than the best Olympic sprinter could have.

Zelezny possessed great throwing power, but his equation for power relied upon strength. At about 28 ounces, the javelin is 5½ times heavier than the baseball and typically thrown with a maximum velocity of about 70 mph. At this speed, a javelin has 2½ times as much kinetic energy as a 100-mph fastball. When it came to pitching a baseball, Zelezny was probably not exceptional in two of the four elements of power — muscle speed and transmission efficiency (timing specific to the baseball). Though he possessed great shoulder and arm strength, he might not have had exceptional arm speed, and with no experience in pitching, he had not developed the precise timing and coordination needed for an efficient propulsive chain with a 5-ounce baseball. He consequently threw the baseball at the velocity of an average collegiate pitcher.

Twelve years later, a pair of javelin throwers with speed-dominant power were discovered when baseball scouts cast a wider net in their talent search.[4] They staged a contest in India called The Million-Dollar Arm and selected finalists by having each of the 37,000 entrants throw toward a radar gun, with 85 mph being the criterion for advancement. The secondary purpose of the contest was to promote baseball in this country of 1.1 billion people, in which the sport of cricket is popular. The two finalists, right-hander Dinesh Patel and leftie Rinku Singh, had previously thrown the javelin competitively, although for distances about a third less than Zelezny. The two winners received training in California from highly regarded pitching coach Tom House and progressed well enough to sign

4. The Four Elements of Pitching Power

minor league contracts with the Pittsburgh Pirates in November 2008. Patel improved from 89 mph in the contest to 93 mph in the minor leagues; Singh progressed from 87 to 92 mph. As of 2011, both had pitched two seasons of Low-A ball, achieving creditable earned-run averages. Despite his low-90s fastball, Patel was cut in November 2010, while Singh survived to continue his quest. Singh, like many of the contestants, had a background in cricket, which uses a ball that is about 10 percent heavier than the baseball. Thrown by rule with a straight arm, the cricket ball has a maximum velocity from a cricket bowler of about 100 mph.

As the weight of the ball or object being thrown increases, the throwing motion changes to accommodate differences in power and leverage of the muscles of the kinetic chain. The body shifts the load to larger muscles, recruiting motor units of muscle fibers for the greater power and leverage needed to meet the greater demand for force. With the javelin, the arm straightens. With the 16-pound shot put, the arm motion changes to one of elbow extension. Likewise, throwing a 15-ounce football involves different mechanics,[5] and pitching with a 6-ounce baseball in a velocity-improvement program may alter the mechanics slightly and recruit muscle motor units different from those used in pitching a standard baseball.

Baseball's equivalent of the javelin throw was its long-throw competition. Throwing for distance was contested occasionally as a promotional event of professional baseball from the 1870s to the 1950s. Glen Gorbous, a 6-foot-2 Canadian who played third base for the Philadelphia Phillies, set what Guinness recognizes as the world record for the longest baseball throw on August 1, 1957. He took a six-step running start and threw 445 feet, 10 inches. Gorbous, who entered the major leagues in 1955 after being taken in the Rule Five Draft, retired in 1957 after an arm injury. The potential for arm injuries was apparently one reason the long-throw contests were discontinued.

With regard to conditions and record-keeping, long-throw contests were poorly controlled and imprecise. A pitcher named Don Grate threw 445–1 in 1956 to set the record Gorbous broke. Grate's throw, however, hit about 8 to 10 feet up the home-plate backstop 445 feet away.[6] The speed and direction of the wind had a strong effect on the distance of these throws. Sheldon Lejeune of the Evansville Baseball Club set the record in 1910, throwing 426–9½ downwind immediately after throwing 385–3 upwind. Rocky Colavito in San Diego in 1956 threw 415–7 hampered by a crosswind, then threw 435–10 with a slight tailwind.[7] Spin rate, air density, altitude, and vertical angle of the throw affect the distance as well. Spin rate affects the amount of lift the ball generates and can extend the duration of its flight, as discussed in Chapter 7. With no means of measuring the spin rate, or knowing the wind speed, wind direction and other conditions, there is no way to accurately determine the speed of release for Gorbous' 445-foot throw in Omaha, Nebraska. It could have been around 109 mph, according to a NASA computer model. The 47-year increase in long-throw distance, 4 percent from Lejeune in 1910 to Gorbous in 1957, is therefore likely due to uncontrolled variables or random error, rather than actual improvement in distance or velocity.

The world record for both the javelin throw and the shot put increased 35 percent in the 50-year period between 1934 and 1984. If the long-throw record had increased the same percentage in 50 years, baseball players in 2007 would have been throwing 600 feet. And if Bob Feller's velocity of about 105 mph could be considered the world record for pitchers in 1946, the 35 percent improvement seen in javelin and shot put would have had pitchers hitting 140 mph on the radar gun by the mid-1990s.

Why has there been no significant improvement in fastball velocity over the years? The answer may in part lie in a 19th-century theorem usually applied to impedance matching in the design of electrical sound systems. Jacobi's Theorem of Maximum Power Transfer states that load resistance must be equal to the internal resistance in order to achieve maximum transfer of power. In pitching, the load is the ball, and the internal resistance is the weight of the body, particularly the arm, hand, and trunk. In forward arm rotation, the movement in which most of the power is supplied to the ball, the internal resistance is the weight of the forearm and hand combined, about 67 ounces on average. With the ball (5 ounces) in the hand, the moment of inertia in arm rotation is increased by about 13 percent, so roughly 87 percent of the power is used to propel the arm and 13 percent to propel the ball. Consequently, only 13 percent of any increase in power of the shoulder muscles achieved with strength training results in greater ball velocity. For the 28-ounce javelin, thrown with a straight arm, the power transfer value is about 33 percent. Strength training is consequently more beneficial for throwing objects heavier than a baseball. Still, a pitcher who achieves significant strength gains can achieve a significant velocity gain.

For the muscles active in the arm-cocking phase of the pitch, the power transfer percentage is very low. Most of the energy a pitcher expends

4. The Four Elements of Pitching Power

in the stride, trunk rotation, and trunk flexion is wasted because of the very low power-transfer rate of these movements. The efficiency of power transfer increases with each subsequent movement of the pitch, because it involves moving lighter body parts. In the stride, energy is expended to move forward the whole body (e.g., 200 pounds). In the trunk flexion, energy is expended to tilt the trunk forward (about 120 pounds). In the arm rotation, energy is expended to rotate the forearm (3 pounds on average), hand (1.1 pounds on average) and ball (0.3 pounds). And in wrist-and-finger flexion, energy is expended to move just the hand and ball, only about 1.4 pounds.

The ceiling on a pitcher's velocity is determined by his power, which is governed by muscle speed, muscle strength, power transfer rate, and power amplification achieved with elastic-strain energy storage and return. All except muscle strength have naturally defined upper limits for any pitcher. Muscle speed, however, is more important in pitching than in javelin-throwing because the baseball is very light, presenting a smaller resistance; consequently, muscle speed is closer to the maximum contraction speed (speed with zero resistance) than it is in javelin-throwing. This leads to what may be the second reason there has been no improvement in fastball velocity over the years: pitchers have not yet fully exploited the potential of strength training. Since the culture of pitcher training began to change in the 1970s, the constraints of baseball's long, arduous playing season have kept pitchers from deriving as much benefit from strength training as a javelin thrower or shot-putter can during the longer off-season of track and field.

On which muscles should strength training be focused to achieve the most gain in velocity? On those having the least internal load — the muscles for wrist-finger flexion and forward arm rotation. These are the flexor muscles of the forearm and the subscapularis of the rotator cuff. Strengthening every prime mover of the kinetic chain benefits the pitcher, but strengthening the legs provides the least direct benefit in ball velocity. In the stride, the thrust leg propels about 200 pounds of body weight and 5 ounces of baseball, for a power transfer rate of less than 0.2 percent. It is noteworthy that a pitching machine requires much less power than a pitcher uses in delivering an equivalent fastball, because the machine's moving parts, mechanical arm or fast-spinning wheels, are designed to be very light, much closer to the weight of the ball than the parts of the pitcher's body that propel the ball.

Strength training can bring the pitcher to his maximum power potential — to his maximum velocity as limited by his genetically determined muscle speed and elasticity of the arm and shoulder. Strength training provides the greatest gains in velocity if the muscle strength in the pitcher's kinetic chain, particularly in the arm and shoulder, has not yet been fully developed. Though developing proper timing and coordination is important, the rate of velocity development is largely the rate of developing strength, and, to a lesser degree, optimal timing. Strength varies substantially among young pitchers. This is seen in the contrast between two pitchers who have often hit 100 mph on stadium radar guns as major leaguers. Justin Verlander of the Detroit Tigers, the 2011 American League Cy Young Award winner and MVP, was throwing 93 mph as a high-school junior. Billy Wagner, the seven-time All-Star closer, was topping out at 83 mph as a high-school senior.[8] Wagner experienced a growth spurt of six inches and 40 pounds in the year after high school and further increased the strength gains that came with the growth by lifting weights. He improved the net power he transferred to the ball by approximately 48 percent, while Verlander improved it by about 20 percent. The energy of the ball increases with the square of the velocity.

Wagner and Verlander are just two of the 48 major leaguers who reached 100 mph or faster on stadium radar guns or PITCH f/x between 1974 and 2011, according to *The Baseball Almanac*.[9] It has likely been the broader use of strength training that has increased the membership in this exclusive club. Strength training, however, has not produced ever-faster pitchers — not another Johnson, Feller, or Ryan — in part because of the limitation imposed by the other half of the power equation, muscle contraction speed.

Muscle Contraction Speed

Natural muscle contraction speed is the element of pitching power about which Alva Bradley was most accurate. In asserting that a kid pitcher can never learn to pitch faster, he was alluding to the reality that the quantity of fast-twitch muscle fibers in a pitcher's arm and shoulder is genetically determined. It is established soon after birth and cannot be increased with training.

The muscle fiber is a marvelous and extremely complex engine.

4. The Four Elements of Pitching Power

Explaining its intricate workings, how it repairs itself, and how it grows stronger in response to its demands has been as challenging as any endeavor of science. Even after many decades of research, many aspects of muscle structure and function are not fully understood. A muscle fiber consists of millions of microscopic motors called sarcomeres. These bio-molecular motors, each about the size of a dust particle floating in the air, are bound together end-to-end and side-by-side to form muscle fibers. The sarcomere, the smallest moving part of a muscle fiber, converts chemical energy to mechanical force and motion, contracting and relaxing with a sliding, ratchet-like action of filaments made of protein molecules.

Sarcomeres are attached end-to-end at joints called Z-disks to form thread-like fibrils. Several hundred to several thousand fibrils are bundled into one muscle fiber, so a one-inch-long muscle fiber contains millions of sarcomeres. The Z-disk, which anchors half the sliding filaments, is a weak point in the fiber, particularly in the fast-twitch fibers, making them susceptible to damage, as will be discussed in Chapter 9. Skeletal muscle has enormous plasticity, which means it adapts quickly in response to changes in activity such as strength training or endurance training, as well as changes in nutrition and the environment. This adaptation includes structural changes, not only to the muscle fiber, but also to its capillaries and motor neurons. The key component in plasticity is the satellite cell, a stem cell that lies dormant on the muscle fiber until activated by messenger molecules. When ordered into action, the satellite cells multiply, travel to the site of damage, and fuse to repair the fiber and return it to normal function. Much more complex and larger than other cells of the body, muscle fibers are not replaced as other types of cells are. They are repaired, regenerated, or remodeled.

There are three types of skeletal muscle fiber: fast-glycolytic, slow-oxidative, and fast-oxidative-glycolytic. The first type is designed for speed and power, the second for fuel-economy, and the third is a hybrid with intermediate levels of speed, power, and economy. As with automobile engines, space limitations mean that it is not practical to have both exceptional power and exceptional fuel economy from the same engine. There is insufficient space under the hood, or in the fiber. Fuel storage, fuel-oxygen processing devices (mitochondria), oxygen storage (myoglobin), supply lines (capillaries), wiring, power converters (sliding filaments), and enzyme storage each take up space. The fiber designed for speed and power allocates a lot of space for fibrils, sliding filaments, and fuel storage. It leaves little space for storing and processing oxygen. The economy fiber has a lot of the oxygen processing, oxygen storage, and capillaries and consequently there is less space available for fuel storage.

Two characteristics determine whether a muscle fiber is fast or slow: (1) the size and discharge frequency of the motor neurons that control the fibers grouped into motor units, and (2) the metabolic process that converts the stored energy to motion — aerobic (with oxygen) or anaerobic (without oxygen). Combinations of these determine the speed, strength, and economy of the three fiber types:

- **Fast-glycolytic fiber.** This is the high-performance fiber that makes a fastball roar. It provides explosive power for sprinting, jumping, and throwing. It is the fastest, strongest, and most elastic, but it is also the most easily fatigued, most easily damaged, and least durable of the three fiber types. It is activated by faster, larger-diameter motor neurons having a higher discharge frequency, and it applies the anaerobic process that converts energy most rapidly, about 100 times more rapidly than the aerobic process of the slower fibers. Requiring only 50 to 80 milliseconds for a twitch contraction, the fast-glycolytic fiber is about five times faster than the slow-oxidative fiber.[10] As the term glycolytic implies, it employs glycolysis for making adenosine triphosphate (ATP), the energy-transfer molecule that makes the filaments slide. Its main source of power is glycogen, a storage form of glucose (a simple sugar) produced by the liver and stored as microscopic granules in the muscle for rapid conversion to ATP. Though this anaerobic process is rapid, it is extremely inefficient in converting glycogen to ATP, releasing only 5 percent of the energy potential. With this poor efficiency, it produces a byproduct, lactic acid, which interferes with ATP production when it accumulates in the fiber. This byproduct and the rapid use of stored energy cause the fiber to fatigue rapidly; consequently, it is known as the fast-fatigable fiber. It stores more glycogen than the other fiber types, but it can still deplete glycogen rapidly because of its inefficiency. The fast-glycolytic is also the strongest fiber, having a larger diameter and more sliding filaments than the other fiber types. White in color, this fiber has little or no myoglobin, the protein that stores oxygen in muscle fibers for use when oxygen demand outpaces supply from the bloodstream. It also has a low capillary density and few mitochondria, the microscopic powerhouses that produce ATP with the aerobic process by oxidizing glucose or fatty acids supplied directly from the blood. Mitochondria take up less than two percent of the volume of the fast-glycolytic fiber.[11] This fiber has superior elasticity, because it has more of a large protein molecule called titin or connectin, which acts as a biological spring to maintain the structural integrity of the fiber by providing resistance to stretching. With a higher content of titin, this fiber provides better elastic-strain energy storage and return, as will be discussed in Chapter 5. Despite the titin, fast-glycolytic fibers are more susceptible to muscle damage in eccentric contractions, and they do not repair as quickly as slow-oxidative fibers because of the lower density of capillaries.

- **Slow-oxidative fiber.** This Type I slow-twitch fiber is the slowest, weakest, most energy-efficient, most durable, and most quickly repaired fiber. It is the fuel-economy fiber, and as such is referred to as the fatigue-resistant fiber. It is beneficial for tasks requiring endurance, such as long-distance running. With small motor neurons and the slower, aerobic energy conversion process, it has a twitch contraction time of 100 to 200 milliseconds, making it the least powerful and least desirable fiber in a pitcher's arm and shoulder. Red in color because of a high density of myoglobin, it has many mitochondria, which may take up as much as 20 percent of the muscle fiber volume. It is surrounded by many capillaries and is about half the diameter of the fast-glycolytic fiber, which scientists believe allows oxygen and fuels to diffuse more quickly from the surrounding capillaries into the fiber. Being smaller, it generates less force, less power. It also has a small capacity for glycogen storage, and when using glycogen, it synthesizes ATP from glycogen more slowly than the fast-glycolytic fiber.
- **Fast-oxidative-glycolytic fiber.** This hybrid fiber, which derives significant power from both the aerobic and anaerobic processes, might seem to be an ideal match for the arm and shoulder of a starting pitcher except that it is less powerful than the fast-glycolytic fiber. Also known as the fast-twitch red fiber, this is the intermediate model with speed, strength, and fatigue resistance between the slow-oxidative and the fast-glycolytic. It compromises power because of space constraints caused by the addition of mitochondria necessary for the oxidative metabolism. To make room for more mitochondria,

it gives up space for glycogen storage. At peak exertion, however, the mitochondria can produce only about one-third of the ATP needed, so glycogen remains the main energy source for explosive exertions like pitching. With its combination of power and fatigue-resistance, it is the ideal fiber for thoroughbred racehorses and middle-distance runners. It is activated by high-frequency nerves and neurons, which are faster than those of the slow-oxidative fibers, and it is grouped in large motor units. Some of these fibers are predominantly oxidative and some are predominantly glycolytic, but all have less speed and power than the fast-glycolytic fiber.

Endurance training can cause a shift from glycolytic to oxidative metabolism, i.e., the conversion of fast-glycolytic fibers to fast-oxidative-glycolytic through the development of mitochondria and myoglobin. This results in a slower contraction speed. Neither speed training nor strength training, however, can convert slow-twitch to fast-twitch or increase the speed or the number of muscle fibers.

The proportions of fiber type vary among the skeletal muscles of the body and in some cases among locations within the muscle, with more superficial regions containing more fast-glycolytic.[12] Muscles of the arm and shoulder typically have a higher density of fast-glycolytic fibers. Muscles of the neck, back, and leg that work against gravity to maintain posture have a higher density of slow-oxidative fibers. The gastrocnemius muscle of the lower leg, important for running, typically has about 50 percent slow-oxidative fibers, while the soleus muscle adjacent to the gastrocnemius has about 90 percent slow-oxidative.[13]

How do the natural proportions of the three fiber types affect the overall speed and power of the subscapularis muscle of a pitcher's rotator cuff? Two studies involving cadavers show the subscapularis to have an average of about 38 percent fast-glycolytic, 25 percent fast-oxidative-glycolytic, and 37 percent slow-oxidative fibers.[14] A method of estimating the relative muscle speed based on the cross-sectional area of each of the three fiber types multiplies the distributions by the relative shortening speed of each fiber type — 3.68 for fast-glycolytic, 1.07 for fast-oxidative-glycolytic, and 0.35 for slow-oxidative.[15] This calculation indicates that a pitcher whose subscapularis has the average distribution of 38–25–37 would have a muscle-shortening velocity of 1.6. A pitcher with slightly more fast-glycolytic, a distribution of 42–25–33 (and similar fiber diameters), would have velocity of 1.8, or 12 percent faster. It is likely that pitchers gifted with Bob-Feller-like arm speed have a larger percentage of fast-glycolytic fibers and a smaller percentage of slow-oxidative fibers.

The same can be said of the flexor muscles of the forearm that determine hand and finger speed — the flexor carpi radialis, flexor carpi ulnaris, flexor digitorum superficialis, and flexor digitorum profundus. A pitcher having a large number of fast-glycolytic fibers in these muscles will have a high wrist-and-finger-flexion velocity, beneficial for high linear velocity, rotational velocity (spin rate), and ball movement. A fast flexor carpi ulnaris gives the pitcher the ability to throw an exceptional curveball.

Fast-glycolytic muscle is white or pale in color because it has very little myoglobin. Slow-oxidative muscle is dark red in color because it is dense in myoglobin. This color difference allows one to see a general anatomical distribution of fast- and slow-twitch muscle fibers at Thanksgiving dinner. White meat is fast-glycolytic muscle, which is found in the turkey's breast, the muscle that powers the wings for short escape flights. Dark meat is slow-oxidative muscle, found in the postural muscles of the turkey's legs. If roast duck is on the menu, one sees that duck breast is dark meat. This is because ducks are adapted to long flights requiring the endurance provided by fast-oxidative-glycolytic muscles dense with myoglobin. A beef dish contains no white meat. Cattle apparently have no need for fast-glycolytic muscle. They rarely fly.

Most human muscles appear pink in color because they contain a mixture of the fiber types. Fiber-type proportions for a given muscle vary greatly from person to person. The quantities of fast- and slow-twitch fibers in the leg muscles are what differentiate sprinters from distance runners and thoroughbred racehorses from draft horses. Muscle biopsies are sometimes performed on leg muscles to determine the ratio of fast- and slow-twitch fibers. A top sprint horse, for example, may have six percent slow-oxidative, 54 percent fast-oxidative-glycolytic, and 40 percent fast-glycolytic fibers. Such testing is not known to have been done on pitching muscles, because of the difficulty of sampling tissue of the arm and shoulder muscles without damaging arteries or nerves. Consequently, there are no known data on the fiber-type distributions of the muscles that propel a major-league fastball.

Because muscle contraction is produced by enzymatic activity, the speed of contraction is affected by the temperature of the muscle. The heat generated in producing ATP increases the muscle temperature, which in turn increases the speed of the process and the speed of contraction. Hence, one benefit of warm-up pitches is to increase temporarily the speed of the pitching muscles.

Muscle fibers are multi-fuel engines. They can process glucose and fatty acids supplied directly from the bloodstream, as well as the glycogen, creatine phosphate stored within the muscle fiber. The explosive power needed for the major-league fastball comes mainly from glycogen, the storage form of glucose, after creatine phosphate provides the first shot of energy when a muscle is called to immediate action. Though it has more metabolic power than glycogen, creatine phosphate has less metabolic capacity; its quantity is relatively small and its replenishment is slow, so it mainly acts as a primer to get the molecular motors running quickly. Glycogen is rapidly converted to glucose and then to ATP. Viewed under a 250,000-magnification electron microscope, glycogen appears as tiny granules packed around the muscle fibrils. Muscle tissue normally contains about two percent glycogen by weight, and a strenuous bout of exercise may reduce this to about one-tenth this value.

Muscle fatigue is the inability of the muscle fibers to contract due to a shortage of available ATP. An ATP shortage may occur due to lack of stored glycogen or to a work rate too high to allow the glycogen-to-ATP process to keep up with the demand. The latter is usually not the case with the exertion cycle of the pitcher, with about one second of intense exertion every 10 to 40 seconds. Glycogen is the main source of ATP in periods of peak exertion, and with a high rate of energy consumption with each pitch, glycogen stores can diminish rapidly, particularly in the muscles bearing the heaviest workload. The higher the velocity of the pitches, the more rapid is the rate of glycogen depletion. A 100-mph fastball has almost 25 percent more kinetic energy than a 90-mph fastball, and this additional energy comes from glycogen stored in the fast-glycolytic fibers. Replenishing the glycogen in muscles normally requires one to two days[16] but can take much longer when there is damage, micro-trauma, to the muscle fibers. In pitching, this restoration period varies with the number and velocity of the pitches thrown, the extent of muscle fiber damage, and other factors addressed in Chapters 9 and 10. If a pitcher goes to the mound with less than 100 percent glycogen levels in the most heavily worked muscles of pitching, he may reach a point of diminished power output in those muscles. This is likely to result in differential fatigue and an early call to the bullpen.

4. The Four Elements of Pitching Power

Muscles can also lose power temporarily because of lactic acid, a product of inefficient glycolysis. Lactic acid interferes with the muscle's ATP synthesis process when it is produced more quickly than it can diffuse out of the muscle into the blood stream or be oxidized in mitochondria. Three common misconceptions propagated by the internet are that lactic acid is the only cause of fatigue, that it causes delayed-onset muscle soreness, and that it lingers in the muscles for several hours, requiring exercise to purge it. All are untrue. Lactic acid is taken away quickly and is converted to glucose in the liver and in the mitochondria of the muscle fiber in a recycling process that takes advantage of its remaining energy value. Lactic acid buildup causes the leg muscles to fatigue while running a 400-meter race, but it is not a significant cause of fatigue in the arm and shoulder muscles of a pitcher in his normal cycle of exertion and rest on the mound.

Which muscles bear the heaviest load in pitching and are thus likely to fatigue most rapidly? In 1991, a group of medical researchers, including Dr. Frank W. Jobe, the inventor of Tommy John ligament replacement surgery, published the results of a 12-year-long study in which they inserted electromyography sensors into muscles of the shoulder, arm, and torso to record the muscle-firing patterns of pitchers as they threw at game speed.[17] They repeated this on 56 college and professional pitchers while filming with high-speed cameras at 500 frames per second. The study yielded data on the coordinated sequencing of muscle firing during a pitch. It also showed that three muscles of the arm and shoulder worked at an exceptionally high intensity and were far more active than the other muscles used in pitching. The researchers presented the results as percentage of intensity of muscle firings measured in a "maximal manual muscle test," a static measurement of strength each pitcher performed with the sensors in place before pitching. These data show that the three muscles with highest activity in pitching are the:

- Flexor carpi radialis, which flexes the wrist — average value measured, 120 percent.
- Flexor carpi ulnaris, which also flexes the wrist — average 112 percent.
- Subscapularis (upper third), the prime mover of forward arm rotation — average 115 percent.

The researchers defined greater than 60 percent as "very high activity." The flexor digitorum superficialis, which flexes the fingers, was also found to have very high activity, 80 percent, during the acceleration phase. For comparison, the triceps, the prime mover for elbow extension, had an average value of 89 percent, and the biceps, which has little or no role in the arm-acceleration phase, 20 percent.

These forearm and shoulder muscles supply a large portion of the energy transferred to the ball in each pitch. A temporary power loss of these muscles due to glycogen depletion can manifest itself not only in loss of velocity but also in diminished spin rate and movement. Power loss in the flexor muscles of the forearm affects finger flexion and wrist flexion, and consequently control. The forearm flexors bear a large load despite their relatively small size. Each of the wrist flexors typically weighs less than an ounce, about 15 to 25 grams for the flexor carpi ulnaris, and about 10 to 20 grams for the flexor carpi radialis.[18] The finger flexors, the flexor digitorum superficialis and flexor digitorum profundus, are similarly small, with each fanning out into four tendons (one for each finger) and each weighing about 70 to 75 grams.[19] Another effect of power loss in these flexor muscles is that, when fatigued, they provide less stabilization of the elbow joint and less protection to the ulnar collateral ligament, as discussed in Chapter 8.

Relative to their workload and cross-section area, the forearm flexors and the subscapularis are the muscles most heavily stressed in producing a roaring fastball. Consequently, they are the muscles most likely to fail a pitcher and the ones that may require the most time for restoration and repair between starts. Because of their workload in pitching, they are the most in need of strengthening. They are the muscles most likely to yield the largest velocity gain from strength training, because they have the least internal load and therefore the highest rate of power transfer.

An issue for pitchers seeking greater fastball velocity is how best to strengthen the fast-glycolytic fibers to produce more power. How this can be achieved is apparent in the hierarchy of activation of muscle fiber types as workload increases. If a task requires little power, i.e., weak muscle contraction, then only the slow-oxidative fibers are forcefully activated. If a stronger contraction is required, the fast-oxidative fibers are activated next to assist the slow-oxidative fibers. As the power requirement increases further, the fast-glycolytic fibers are activated last.[20] Thus, strength training for the most powerful muscle fibers requires powerful exertions. A pitcher does not involve the fast-twitch muscles when playing catch from a short distance, but he does so when throwing a near-game-speed bullpen session or long-toss. He is likely to activate them when he performs weight/resistance training, calisthenics, or plyometric exercises.

Similarly, a sprinter preparing for the racing season does not build his speed by running long distances at a slow pace, because doing so significantly activates only the slow-twitch fibers. To prepare for racing, a sprinter regains the speed he has lost through the inactivity of the off-season by running short sprints at near-maximal effort, forcefully activating the fast-glycolytic fibers of the legs as well as the slower oxidative fibers. Both the sprinter and the pitcher temporarily lose velocity in the off-season because the strength of the fast-glycolytic fibers diminishes with inactivity. The arm and shoulder muscles that supply the power for pitching are not often used in routine activities; hence, when not throwing or performing strength training in the off-season, these muscles weaken. Lack of use in routine activities may also explain some of the person-to-person variability in the strength of the throwing muscles. Weight training, calisthenics, and farm work like Bob Feller performed in his youth can remedy a deficit of arm, shoulder, and core muscle strength. Feller's hay-bale tossing is not unlike the exercises performed with medicine balls for development of fast-twitch muscle strength in the shoulder and arms. Training with hay bales or medicine balls, however, does not provide the rigorous control and specificity that progressive overload weight training provides, as will be discussed in Chapter 10.

Transmission of Power—Timing

Though the pitching motion of most pitchers appears naturally fluid and efficient, the timing and coordination needed to ensure maximum transfer of power from the muscles to the ball is complex, requiring a large amount of practice to optimize. The ability to coordinate these movements precisely at high speed is a natural ability that resides in the brain and nervous system. It is this same ability that, for example, exceptional golfers have and typically exhibit at an early age and hone through thousands of repetitions. The repetitions program the motor cortex, the part of the brain that controls motor movements, by activating the muscle motor-units (groups of muscle fibers varying from a few fibers to several thousand fibers controlled by a single motor neuron). It produces precisely coordinated and powerful muscle contractions to propel the ball and stabilize the joints. Precise timing also ensures optimal recruitment of muscle motor units so that the workload and stress is shared efficiently among the muscles in the kinetic chain.

Pitching a baseball can be compared to launching an airplane from an aircraft carrier, because both apply four coordinated power sources. In pitching, the energy transferred to the ball comes from muscle contractions of four movements — trunk flexion, trunk-and-shoulder rotation, forward arm rotation, and wrist/finger flexion. The four energy sources of launching carrier aircraft are the steam catapult, the airplane's engine, the ship's engine, and the wind (natural energy that helps attain flying speed). The launch of a carrier plane is much simpler, however, than the launch of a baseball, because all four velocities are linear and aligned, and they reach their maximum at the same instant. In pitching a baseball, the coordination to achieve maximum power transfer is much more complex because:

- The power is provided through rotational motion around four different axes.
- Each of the movements of pitching has a different velocity range, with the fastest, forward arm rotation, being about 20 times faster than the slowest, trunk flexion. The points of maximum velocity for all four do not coincide at the point of release.
- Muscles do not apply a constant force. They generate less force at the extremes of their range of movement, where there is less overlap of the filaments that produce contraction. Muscles have a force curve somewhat like the torque curve of an automobile engine.
- Timing and coordination change as the intensity of the effort changes, due to the activation of the more powerful fast-glycolytic muscle fibers as the intensity increases.
- The pitcher controls the location and movement of the pitch at the same time he is generating the power for the pitch, and to do so may require attenuating the power of forearm flexor muscles controlling the wrist-and-finger flexion.
- The optimal timing changes as some muscles weaken or strengthen over time, or in the short term fatigue more rapidly than other muscles, producing differential fatigue in muscles of the kinetic chain.
- The optimal timing changes, and must be relearned, as a young pitcher grows in height and weight, producing changes in muscle strength, leverage, and rotational velocities.

The most troublesome aspects of timing for a pitcher involve large differentials in velocity between two coordinated movements. This often results in the slower of the two movements lagging behind the faster. For each of the three instances listed below, the faster movement has two to three times the velocity of the slower movement.

The Timing of Wrist-and-Finger Flexion

Pitchers' wrist-and-finger flexion velocity averages about 3,000 degrees per second, while their average is forward arm rotation velocity about 8,000 degrees per second. These are the two highest velocities among the pitching movements. Ideally, both should reach a maximum at the same time, at ball release, at a point of zero angle between the hand and forearm. That the precise timing between forward arm rotation and wrist-and-finger flexion is troublesome is apparent in the large variability in the angle between the hand and forearm measured in studies by three different researchers. In one study, the average wrist angle at release was three degrees with a standard deviation of 11 degrees, indicating that for 95 percent of pitchers, wrist flexion velocity ranges from minus 19 to plus 25 degrees.[21] Another study measured a mean release angle of minus 19 degrees with a standard deviation of eight degrees (a range of minus 35 to minus three degrees).[22] A third study showed a mean angle of four degrees with a standard deviation of four degrees (a range of minus four to plus 12 degrees).[23] The negative values for the angle indicate that the hand lags behind the arm; it does not reach alignment with the forearm when the ball is released, thus transmitting less-than-full power to the ball for linear and rotational velocity. The hand may lag behind the arm because of fatigue of the forearm flexor muscles, a lack of focus in finishing the pitch, or simply imperfect coordination. In any case, the full power of the forearm flexor muscles is not applied to the ball.

Most pitchers—including some who can top 100 mph—minimize the difficulty of wrist timing by keeping the wrist almost rigid, limiting the amount of wrist extension and flexion. In doing this, the final application of force in the pitch is provided mainly by finger flexion. This produces a shorter moment arm, resulting in a lower spin rate, a smaller contribution of the flexor muscles to linear velocity, and less late acceleration (further discussed in Chapter 6).

The Timing of Elbow Extension

There is also a large velocity differential between trunk rotation and elbow extension, with trunk rotation typically about 1,200 degrees per second and elbow extension about 2,500. Elbow extension is partially

The Science of the Fastball

driven by centrifugal force — the faster the trunk-and-shoulder rotation velocity, the faster the elbow extends. The importance of elbow extension is that it occurs near the point of maximum velocity of forward arm rotation, the movement that provides the greatest amount of energy to the ball. If elbow extension occurs as arm rotation is gaining velocity, it can be likened to downshifting as an automobile gains speed. To take advantage of this large pulse of power, elbow extension should occur as late as possible, and it typically occurs about 93 percent of the way through the pitch (from the point of stride-foot contact). Late extension is best achieved by having a very rapid rate of extension. Extending too early and extending to too great an angle, i.e., approaching 180 degrees, are two problems of elbow extension that affect ball velocity. To limit the angle of extension and maximize the moment arm during the arm rotation requires eccentric contraction of the biceps muscle working against the triceps and against centrifugal force. It is this force, the drag applied by the biceps, that probably governs the angle of elbow extension. Contracting eccentrically produces greater stress on the biceps, increasing the potential of injury to the biceps. Elbow extension is one of two movements in which antagonist muscles can affect velocity. The other involves the teres minor and infraspinatus of the rotator cuff slowing down the arm rotation, as will be described in Chapter 5. The average angle of extension in Fleisig's data is remarkably consistent across age groups, an average of 23 to 24 degrees from full extension. The standard deviation of the angle, however, ranges from five to seven degrees, indicating a range of nine degrees to 38 degrees for 95 percent of pitchers.

The Timing of the Trunk Rotation and Trunk Flexion

These two trunk movements cock the arm and accelerate the base of the arm. They have the same starting point, stride foot contact, and ideally should reach maximum velocity at the same time — at the point of maximum external rotation of the arm. Typically they do not, however, because one is about three times faster than the other: trunk flexion occurs at about 400 degrees per second and trunk rotation at about 1,200 degrees per second. Trunk flexion usually peaks later. Fleisig found this to occur as late as 25 percent after ball release in less-skilled pitchers. To make both movements peak at the same time, a pitcher can adjust his timing of

4. The Four Elements of Pitching Power

trunk flexion in three ways: (1) shift the starting point backward by arching the back, (2) increase the velocity of flexion with a longer, more powerful stride, or (3) increase the velocity of flexion with more powerful contraction of the hip flexors and abdominal muscles. The power generated by well-timed trunk flexion is transmitted to the arm in the cocking of the arm, storing energy momentarily in the biological springs of the arm and shoulder. Deriving greater power from the trunk flexion means that the arm can be cocked with less energy from the rotator cuff muscles that rotate the upper arm rearward. As will be discussed in Chapter 5, cocking the arm with little or no assistance of these muscles may reduce the damping on forward arm rotation to yield greater arm speed.

An oft-repeated adage in sports is that practice does not make perfect; only *perfect* practice makes perfect. To begin and sustain perfect practice, the pitcher must receive immediate visual feedback about his pitches in order to program the motor cortex for optimal timing and coordination. While visual feedback on control and movement of the ball is immediately available to a pitcher in all situations, feedback on velocity and timing is not. Information about velocity is available to professional pitchers in game situations — when it is least beneficial — but is not usually available to pitchers in practice sessions, when it is most beneficial. Feedback on timing usually comes from real-time observations by the pitcher or his coach or catcher regarding positioning, joint angles, relative angular velocities, and coordination. Feedback on timing and coordination can best be presented to a pitcher with slow-motion video. When combined with expert interpretation by a pitching coach, slow-motion video can provide the pitcher the best practical means for achieving perfect practice and for attaining and sustaining optimal timing and coordination.

The exact patterned practice that produces better timing and coordination can yield greater velocity. Such practice is best achieved by pitching at game speed, because muscle fiber recruitment and activation of fast-glycolytic motor units changes with the intensity of effort. The timing and motor-unit activation for a max-effort pitch differs from a 95-percent effort pitch, a 70-percent effort in the bullpen or side session, and easy throws while playing catch. This means that to increase top-end velocity, a pitcher must regularly pitch from the mound at maximal or near-maximal effort. This has been described succinctly as: to pitch faster, pitch faster. The main issues of pitcher training consequently relate to frequency and intensity. How frequently should max-effort training sessions occur and how many max-effort pitches should each session involve to be beneficial? At what point do the pitcher's efforts cease to be beneficial? How much max-effort pitching/throwing is too much? These issues are addressed in Chapters 9 and 10.

5

The Dalkowski Phenomenon
Under-Damped Biological Springs at Near-Resonance

"He [Steve Dalkowski] threw harder than anyone. I saw Nolan Ryan from the coaching box and, I know you might think I'm stretching the point, but Ryan didn't compare with Steve." — Cal Ripken Sr., quoted in the *Baltimore Sun*, August 11, 1996

No one has yet solved the puzzle of Steve Dalkowski's prodigious velocity. That there is plenty of incentive to do so is apparent in the annual money showers known as the amateur baseball draft and free-agent signings. To explain the Dalkowski phenomenon is to decipher the code of hypervelocity pitching, perhaps leading to the development of Steve-Nebraska-like pitchers who can liberate any team from the chains of baseball mediocrity. Perhaps Dalkowski's phenomenal ability cannot be replicated. Perhaps it simply requires natural talent that comes along as frequently as Haley's Comet. Perhaps there was no phenomenon at all, but simply folklore like that of John Henry, the pile-drivin' man. Anecdotes about the 5-foot-10, 170-pound left-hander from Connecticut abound and indicate that he may have been the fastest pitcher of all time. Though anecdotal data are sometimes unreliable, his phenomenal ability, first heralded by a strange noise when he was 15 years old, seems genuine.

His sister, Pat Cain, recalled the noise his fastball made when he was a high-school sophomore. "I can remember my father and I sitting at one of his tenth-grade games at the park, on the top bleacher," she said. "All of a sudden we heard this [loud] 'whhhhm' sound. Like that—'whhhhm.' At first we thought it was static from a radio or the wind in the trees or something, but it kept going and going and going every few seconds. It was the sound of Stevie warming-up."[1]

Even then, the effect of his fastball was remarkable. "In tenth grade.

The Science of the Fastball

I could strike everybody out," said Dalkowski, who set the Connecticut high school record of 24 strikeouts, a single-game record that remains unbroken 50 years later. In his second varsity start of that sophomore year, he struck out 18, walked 18, and needed 173 pitches to complete the nine-inning win, 11–3.[2]

In the annals of professional baseball, there are countless stories of young fireballers who never made the leap to the majors. These pitchers, some of whom could top 100 mph, were typically characterized as throwers not pitchers, a distinction based on skill and control. Dalkowski, a bespectacled left-hander of ordinary stature, stands out among the near-major-leaguers. He pitched in the minors from 1957 through 1965 and became perhaps the most famous minor-league pitcher of all time because of his fastball and inability to tame it. There are many Dalkowski fans who stoke the embers of his legend and hail him as the fastest pitcher of all time.

Cal Ripken, Sr., thought his top end might have been 110 mph, maybe 120 mph. Such speeds were never actually measured, of course. The only known scientific speed measurement to which his fastball was subjected occurred in June 1958 at Aberdeen Proving Ground, Maryland, where he threw 93.5 mph into a Lumiline on flat ground. Because of his deficiency of control, he had difficulty throwing through the opening of the timing device. He was also thought to have fatigued his arm while trying to do

Steve Dalkowski, believed by many to be the fastest pitcher of all time, was never able to tame his fastball before losing his power to an elbow injury at age 24 (National Baseball Hall of Fame Library, Cooperstown, New York).

5. The Dalkowski Phenomenon

so, and he was said to have thrown over 150 pitches in a game the day before the measurements were made. Still, if 93.5 mph was his plate speed that day, his release velocity would have been about 99 to 100 mph.

Feller and Ryan were tolerably deficient in control early in their careers. Dalkowski's wildness, however, was exceptional and marginally intolerable, abating only for brief periods in his career. When he was released from the minors at age 26, he had pitched 995 innings, struck out 1,396 batters, and walked 1,354. In one Appalachian League game in 1957, he struck out 24, walked 18, hit four batters, threw six wild pitches, and lost, 8–4. In one Northern League game, he struck out 15, walked 17, and gave up only one hit while losing, 9–8. In an extra-inning game in the Eastern League, he struck out 27 and walked 16, throwing 283 pitches. In another game, he walked 21 and struck out 21. In high school, he pitched a no-hitter while walking 18 and striking out 18.

His legendary feats are described in the book, *High Heat: The Secret History of the Fastball and the Improbable Search for the Fastest Pitcher of All Time*.[3] Testimonials from people prominent and highly respected in professional baseball provide credibility to stories about his speed:

- "He threw a lot faster than [Nolan] Ryan. It's hard to believe but he did," said former Orioles manager Earl Weaver, who managed Dalkowski in the minors and saw Ryan pitch many times.[4]
- "A lot of stories get embellished, but this guy was legit. He had one of those arms that come once in a lifetime," said Hall of Famer Pat Gillick, who was once his teammate and roommate.[5]
- "I've umpired for Koufax, Gibson, Drysdale, Maloney, Seaver, Marichal, and Gooden, and they could all bring it, but nobody could bring it like he could," said umpire Doug Harvey about Dalkowski. "In one season, he broke my bar mask, split my shin guards, split the plastic on my chest protector, and knocked me back 18 feet."[6]
- "Hearing him warm up on the sideline was like hearing a gun go off. I kept thinking: if this guy ever hits me, he'll kill me," said former Red Sox player Dalton Jones.[7]

Doug Harvey's empirical evidence provides credibility, but other stories about Dalkowski's phenomenal power are not similarly supported. He was said to have thrown a baseball through a wooden outfield fence and, on another occasion, through a backstop screen. Details about the type and structural condition of these barriers are not known.

The Science of the Fastball

In attempting to characterize a physical process or phenomenon for which there is little or no empirical data, a scientist typically proposes a model — a logical, simplified representation of the complex reality. Here, the phenomenon is Dalkowski's great velocity, and the key characteristic on which a model is based to explain his complex reality is his untamable wildness. For this analysis, the model is called the under-damped, near-resonance model. It involves the element of power about which there is a dearth of scientific data specific to pitching — elastic-strain energy storage and return by the biological springs of the arm and shoulder.

Elastic-strain energy storage and return is the source of explosive power in many sports — in jumping, sprinting, pitching, or throwing objects like the javelin for distance. Exceptional explosive power requires a combination of: (1) an exceptional number of fast-glycolytic muscle fibers in the prime movers, and (2) exceptional elasticity, biological springs with collective stiffness matched to both the power of the muscles in the kinetic chain and the weight of what's being propelled. High jumpers, basketball players, and ice skaters apply this explosive power to jump higher; long-jumpers to leap greater distances; sprinters to run at greater speeds; and distance runners to race with greater economy.

There is a substantial volume of scientific data on elastic-strain energy storage and return as it relates to locomotion.[8] Hence, such data relate to the leg, not the arm and shoulder of a pitcher. In locomotion, elastic components of the legs store and return energy with each step to make two-legged and four-legged animals faster and more energy-efficient afoot.[9] Assisted by gravity, the biological springs — collagen fibrils of tendons and ligaments and titin in muscle fibers — serve to increase the speed and efficiency of movement. These springs increase velocity because the recoil velocity of stretched tendons and ligaments is greater than the contraction velocity of muscle.[10] The spring-like elements release energy at a much higher rate than muscles do and consequently increase the power. This is especially beneficial because a muscle's power diminishes at the extremes of its range of movement, producing a power curve much like the torque curve of a standard automobile engine.

The spring-like elements in the arm and shoulder increase the velocity of a fastball through power amplification. Since power is defined as the rate of performing work, it is the amount of work or energy divided by the time it takes to do the work. Decreasing the time over which the same quantity of energy is delivered increases the power. A slingshot illustrates the concept of power amplification. In cocking the slingshot, energy from the muscles is transferred to the slingshot's elastic band as the band is stretched. This same quantity of energy is then released in milliseconds when the band is released. If it takes one second to cock the band, and one-thousandth of a second for the band to snap forward, the power is amplified by about 1,000.

The elastic components in a pitcher's body have more complex connections than a slingshot. They also have greater damping (suppression), and consequently there is less amplification of power, but their effect on velocity is substantial. In each pitch, arm-cocking occurs between stride foot contact and the beginning of the launching phase, the point at which the arm is fully rotated backwards. As noted in Chapter 3, the energy storage in the biological springs also bridges a timing gap between the first three and last three movements of a pitch. Arm cocking typically takes about 0.12 seconds from the point of stride foot contact. Recoil, the release of the stored energy, occurs in about 0.01 seconds. The ratio of cocking time to recoil time provides a rough estimate that the power is amplified by 12 (0.12 divided by 0.01). This is much less amplification than a slingshot, but a pitch involves more than just recoil; energy from the contraction of shoulder and arm muscles is released nearly simultaneously.

In running and jumping, gravity provides the force for cocking the biological springs. In pitching, however, gravity has only a minor contribution, one that results from the pitcher's short descent from the top of the mound. Cocking occurs mainly by: (1) momentum transfer, (2) prime movers working against inertia, and (3) antagonist muscles, those opposing the prime movers. Energy storage occurs in the following cocking actions, listed in order of importance:

- *Cocking the arm.* This involves a transfer of kinetic energy from the trunk as it rotates and flexes forward. This propels the elbow forward while the hand, ball, and forearm (starting in the near-vertical position) are held back by inertia. Assistance comes from two muscles on the back side of the rotator cuff, the infraspinatus and teres minor. Cocking the arm involves storing energy in five different sets of biological springs, stretching: (1) the anterior band of the ulnar collateral ligament, (2) the titin in the subscapularis muscle, (3) its tendon, (4) the titin in the forearm flexor muscles, and (5) their tendons.
- *Cocking the hand.* This also involves stretching the flexor muscles of

the forearm and their long tendons. This cocking is driven mainly by the inertia of the hand holding the ball as the arm rapidly rotates forward, and by the flexors contracting to begin wrist flexion about a hundredth of a second later.
- *Cocking the trunk in extension.* This involves stretching the muscles of the abdomen by the contraction of the back muscles. The back muscles must work against the momentum transferred to the trunk during the stride, which is assisted by gravity in pitching from the mound.
- *Cocking the trunk in rotation.* This involves stretching the oblique muscles as the trunk rotates sequentially, beginning with the pelvis.

In cocking the arm, how significant is the energy-storage role of the anterior band of the ulnar collateral ligament? Its effect has never been quantified, but it appears to be the most important spring for storing the substantial energy transferred from the trunk. The band is elastic, consisting of the same rope-like bundle of Type I collagen fibrils as tendons; it wears out, becoming more compliant with the cumulative effects of stretching beyond its elastic limit; and its absence causes a substantial decrease in pitch velocity. The indirect evidence that is most convincing about the band's importance is that ligament and tendon tissue has far more energy storage capability than the titin in muscle. One study found that muscle stores about 5 Joules of energy per kilogram, while tendon and ligament can store 2,000 to 9,000 Joules per kilogram, suggesting that muscle elasticity plays only a minor part.[11] Consequently, the two most important springs of the arm are the anterior band and the tendons of the subscapularis. These two springs are arranged in series — in a diagram, they would be shown connected end-to-end — while the springs of the forearm flexors are in parallel, side-by-side in a diagram. When springs of different stiffness are placed in series, their combined stiffness is less than the stiffness of the weaker spring, so if damage occurs either to the anterior band or to the rotator cuff tendon, the energy storage capability is reduced to less than that of the weaker of the two. This means that injuring either one will substantially reduce a pitcher's power. The forearm flexor muscles are in parallel with the anterior band; consequently, there is little effect on the total energy storage if one becomes weakened by fatigue or muscle damage. Fatigue of the flexors will have little effect on arm speed, but it will significantly reduce hand speed, and the flexors will be less effective in protecting the anterior band from injury.

5. The Dalkowski Phenomenon

The role of the anterior band is comparable to that of a jumper's Achilles tendon, which has been shown to release about two horsepower in the vertical component of a long-jumper's leap.[12] A band that is stiff and strong, but not too much so, is best. Having the right stiffness means that it is tuned to the weight of the arm holding the baseball for the velocity at which the pitcher has the speed and strength to pitch. Perhaps one reason pitchers who are large in stature, like Cy Young Award winner C.C. Sabathia of the Yankees, can pitch economically at high velocity is that they have thicker (stiffer) ligaments and tendons throughout the body, including the ligaments of the elbow.

A pitcher begins cocking the elastic components of his arm and shoulder once his stride foot is firmly planted. Arm-cocking is completed when the forearm is fully rotated backward to a near-horizontal position. Much of the energy stored in the cocking phase is transferred from the leg and torso. It is released in a brief slingshot-like pulse along with the energy of contraction of the muscles of the shoulder and arm. During the launching phase, there is a rapid, near-simultaneous delivery of energy from two sources — elastic recoil and muscle contraction. If the two releases of energy were to occur simultaneously, the pitcher would achieve the phenomenon known as resonance.

Galileo, the great Italian scientist who preceded Italian baseball by about four centuries, first recognized resonance while studying pendulums. Resonance can occur when a system, such as a pendulum or a weight on a spring, easily exchanges kinetic energy (energy of motion) and potential energy (stored energy). The arm, with its mass and biological springs, easily exchanges kinetic energy and potential energy, so it has a natural frequency. Resonance is the tendency of a system to oscillate with greater amplitude at its natural frequency. In pitching, resonance can occur only if the speed at which the muscles apply force (the forcing frequency) approaches the natural frequency of the arm.

The arm doesn't oscillate, of course. It moves through an arc limited by damping, mainly by the antagonist muscles. The arm's natural frequency is indicated by the speed at which the biological springs propel the forearm forward at the start of the launching phase. This could be called the natural speed; it is determined by the stiffness of the springs and the weight of the forearm with the ball. If the energy supplied by the muscles and the recoil energy released from the biological springs are not perfectly coordinated, some of the energy is wasted. This is most easily understood by means of

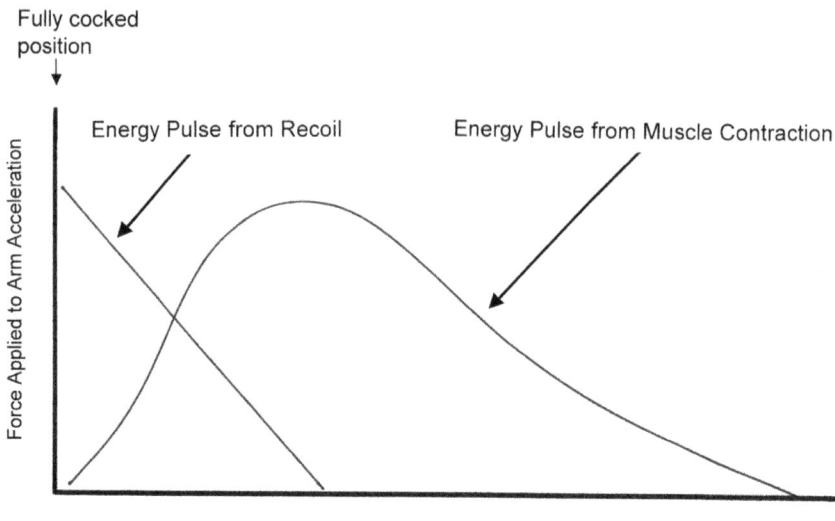

Figure 3: Qualitative graph representing the two energy pulses that accelerate the arm in the launching phase of a pitch. The elastic-recoil pulse is followed by the muscle-contraction pulse.

the analogy of pushing a child on a playground swing. If the push is made too early relative to the oscillation, the swing slows down. If the push is made too late, the swing does not go as high. If the push is perfectly timed at the point of maximum potential energy and zero kinetic energy — when the swing comes to a stop momentarily before changing direction — the swing goes higher, achieving resonance. This point of maximum potential energy and zero kinetic energy in the pitcher's windup is the point at which the arm is fully cocked.

As noted previously, the force curve of a muscle is like the torque curve of an automobile engine. *Figure 3 is a graph* illustrating the two pulses of energy that accelerate the arm during a pitch. As depicted in the figure, the height and width of these pulses are approximate, because these forces have never been measured in pitching. The curve on the right represents the force applied by the subscapularis muscle rotating the arm forward from the fully cocked position. This force is smallest at the extremes — at the cocked position and near the point of ball-release. Shown on the left side of the graph is a descending line that represents the release of energy from the biological springs. Its peak force occurs when the arm

5. The Dalkowski Phenomenon

is fully cocked. Because recoil delivers its largest force at the start of arm acceleration, it provides a catapult-like boost, a powerful push to begin the rotation while the force from the muscle is weakest. The higher the natural frequency of the arm, the greater is the speed of recoil as the arm starts to rotate.

With different shapes, the peaks of the two pulses naturally occur at different times, roughly one-hundredth of a second apart. This means that it is not possible to achieve resonance with the pitching arm. However, as the amount of energy stored in cocking the arm increases, there is more overlap between the recoil pulse and the muscle pulse, bringing the two pulses closer together to *approach* resonance. A pitcher who has exceptional speed of trunk flexion and trunk rotation and biological springs of appropriate stiffness in his arm and shoulder will achieve high arm speed without maximal effort from the muscles of the arm and shoulder. This is the key to pitching economically at high speed. With the normal timing of the two pulses shown in the graph, the application of muscle force to the arm is analogous to a slightly late push of the playground swing. And when the antagonist muscles of forward arm rotation—the teres minor and infraspinatus—don't relax rapidly enough, it is analogous to a too-early push of the swing.

Steve Dalkowski's phenomenal velocity was probably due to an ability to generate two exceptionally strong pulses. Compared to most pitchers, his two peaks were probably higher (more force) and narrower (greater speed), yielding more total power to the arm and more overlap with less time between peaks. Consequently, Dalkowski probably came closer to resonance than other pitchers.

Dalkowski was probably endowed with an exceptional combination of power and elasticity. This means he had: (1) a large number of fast-glycolytic fibers in the subscapularis and flexor muscles of the forearm; (2) stiffer-than-normal tendons of these muscles; (3) an anterior band of the ulnar collateral ligament having a larger-than-normal cross-section area, making it a stiffer-than-normal spring, and (4) superb coordination of his high-speed cocking and launching movements. Collectively, his biological springs gave him a high natural recoil speed of the arm, and the most important spring was likely the anterior band of his ulnar collateral ligament.

Except for surgical replacement of the anterior band, the pitcher has no means of improving the biological springs of his arm and shoulder. He can approach resonance only by increasing the velocity, and power, of all six movements of pitching.

- If the pitcher's natural frequency happens to be *higher than* his forcing frequency, he can approach resonance by strengthening all the prime movers of the kinetic chain of pitching. This is the process that occurs naturally in the growth spurt of adolescent pitchers. It also occurs as a result of strength training, as will be described in Chapter 10. Strength training can not only yield a more powerful pulse of energy from the subscapularis, it can also produce a more powerful recoil pulse by increasing the power transferred from the arm-cocking movements. Improved mechanics can help the pitcher transfer more energy from the trunk to the arm and shoulder.
- If the pitcher's natural frequency happens to be *lower than* his forcing frequency, he cannot approach resonance. He has a smaller recoil pulse, less of a jump-start capability, and he must derive most of the energy of the pitch from the muscles of his arm and shoulder. This is the situation when a pitcher loses elasticity with age and/or innings pitched. His anterior band becomes weaker and more compliant; his muscles lose elasticity. His response may be to try to pitch above his natural frequency, chasing radar-gun readings by applying more power from the arm and shoulder muscles. In doing so, the pitcher loses energy-efficiency because he wastes the kinetic energy of the trunk, transferring and amplifying less energy from the stride, trunk rotation, and trunk flexion. He then fatigues more easily, even with a high level of fitness.

In the sport of figure-skating, a skater can lose the ability to perform a triple axel by gaining weight, because the increased weight without an attendant increase in stiffness of the biological springs of the leg results in a lower natural frequency. In pitching, weight gain has little or no effect on the natural frequency of him arm because the weight of the forearm, hand, and ball in combination do not change significantly over time. The natural frequency of a pitcher's arm and shoulder thus varies only with elasticity, which diminishes with age and the accumulation of damage to muscle fibers or fibrils of tendons and ligaments, as will be discussed in Chapter 8. When elasticity diminishes, the pitcher is forced to pitch at a lower natural frequency or to over-throw and become energy-inefficient.

Strength changes can cause a shift away from resonance. When

5. The Dalkowski Phenomenon

strength diminishes temporarily through muscle fiber damage, fatigue, or off-season inactivity, the pitcher temporarily is forced to pitch further from resonance. Fiber/fibril damage can cause short-term loss of elasticity that can be ameliorated by rest and recovery — or by surgery to replace a worn or torn anterior band of the ulnar collateral ligament. Although such surgery is generally believed not to increase velocity, it is possible to achieve a higher natural frequency by replacing the band with one of greater stiffness. In Tommy John surgery, this is typically accomplished by using the gracilis tendon from the leg rather than the palmaris longus tendon from the opposite forearm. In some cases, the gracilis tendon can provide greater strength and stiffness.

How well does Steve Dalkowski's performance as a pitcher conform to the near-resonance aspect of the model?

- **Wildness.** Pitching near resonance means that a substantial amount of recoil energy is released nearly-simultaneously with the energy from the muscles. This complicates the pitcher's ball-release because a large part of this energy pulse is not directly controlled by the brain through the motor neurons. The brain controls the contraction of the muscles, but not the recoil of the biological springs. Consequently, pitch-control can be more difficult to achieve. Wildness is a characteristic of many high-velocity pitchers early in their professional careers, and it is likely due to an inability to accommodate the recoil pulse or to make changes to control the recoil pulse.
- **Pitching at high velocity without maximal effort.** Dalkowski said that he never threw as hard as he could. When a pitcher derives greater energy from recoil, he shifts workload toward the largest muscles of the kinetic chain — the muscles of the leg and torso — and in doing so reduces the load on the smaller muscles of the arm and shoulder. The pitcher thus distributes the work among all the muscles of the kinetic chain more efficiently, and develops exceptional power with less-than-maximal effort from each of the muscles. The burden on the arm and shoulder is reduced because the biological springs of the arm and shoulder allow more of the energy from the three cocking movements to be transferred to the launching movements.
- **Sustaining velocity through high pitch counts.** Dalkowski's ability to perform well after throwing more than 200 pitches in some out-

ings indicates that he was pitching economically. By deriving more of his power from the large muscles of the legs, hips, and trunk, he was forestalling fatigue of the smaller, normally overworked muscles of the arm and shoulder. Pitching near resonance allows a pitcher to achieve high velocity with the least amount of energy from the arm and shoulder muscles, and consequently with a slower depletion rate of glycogen from these muscles.

Walter Johnson and Nolan Ryan apparently began pitching more economically, near resonance, in their fourth major-league seasons. Feller and Ryan may have bettered Dalkowski in natural frequency, arm speed, and hand speed. But their wildness was not as extreme, indicating that Dalkowski may have been qualitatively different in a way that involves the third variable of resonance, one that has a substantial effect on both control and velocity — damping.

Sandy Koufax probably found near-resonance economy in 1961, and in doing so altered the trajectory of his career. Edward Gruver's biography, *Koufax*,[13] describes a spring training game in Orlando in which the Dodgers' left-hander walked the bases loaded on 12 pitches in the first inning. Gruver considers the first-inning visit to the mound by catcher Norm Sherry a seminal moment in Koufax's career.

"He threw a lot of fastballs up and out of the strike zone and guys wouldn't swing at them," said Sherry. "He was throwing each fastball harder than the one before." When he went to the mound, he asked Koufax, "why don't you take something off the ball and just let them hit it? We can get outs and get out of this inning, because nobody's going to swing at the rate you're going." Koufax complied and struck out the side. After the inning, Sherry told him, "I'm not blowing smoke up your rear end, but you just now threw harder trying not to than when you were trying to." Koufax finished the seven-inning game with a no-hitter in which he struck out 8 and walked only 2 more. He went on to have a breakout season, winning 18 games and striking out 269.

In that spring training game, Koufax may have reduced the power from his arm and shoulder muscles, relying more on the power from his legs and trunk and less on the arm and shoulder to pitch more economically without a loss of velocity. This may have been the same experience of Nolan Ryan in 1972, his first season with the California Angels. If so, why did Koufax and Ryan find better control at near-resonance, while

5. The Dalkowski Phenomenon

Dalkowski did not? The answer may lie in the amount of damping the antagonist muscles of the pitcher's rotator cuff provide during forward arm rotation.

One factor in controlling a pitch is the force applied in opposition (by the antagonists) to the prime-movers (the agonists). Just before the two bursts of energy accelerate the arm to high speed, the teres minor and infraspinatus are activated to apply force in the opposite direction. This co-activation serves to exert control on the pitch and stabilize the joint. In doing this, the antagonists produce a damping effect, like that of an automobile's shock absorber, dissipating some of the energy to protect the shoulder joint. This action, like dragging the brake, stabilizes the joint against what Smokey Joe Wood once said about his own max-effort pitching: "I threw so hard, I thought my arm would fly right off my body," Wood told the press after winning game one of the 1912 World Series, according to *Baseball Almanac*. Perhaps Wood perceived the possible result of under-damped near-resonance. The result of reduced damping is greater power amplification and greater arm speed. Dalkowski probably achieved under-damped near-resonance by naturally having less drag on his forward arm rotation.

Data from the electromyographic analysis referenced in Chapter 4 show the activity of the teres minor to be very high (average 71 percent) in cocking, high (54 percent) in acceleration, and very high (84 percent) in deceleration. For the infraspinatus, activity averaged 74 percent in cocking, 31 percent in acceleration, and 37 percent in deceleration. For both these muscles, the activity during a pitch thus changes from very high to moderate/high in the 0.02 to 0.03 seconds of the forward arm rotation.

How long does it take the muscles that oppose forward arm rotation to make the transition from contraction to relaxation, that is, how quickly does their force diminish? In research experiments, muscle relaxation is measured in terms of half-relaxation time, which for fast-glycolytic muscle is about 0.01 to 0.03 seconds. This indicates that the teres minor and infraspinatus still produce a large retarding force when recoil energy kick-starts the arm into its forward rotation, it also means that this braking force may not diminish to a low level when the subscapularis produces its peak force about 0.01 seconds later.

The implication is that the rearward rotators — the teres minor and infraspinatus — may have as much effect in determining fastball velocity as the subscapularis. When these antagonists do not quickly and fully relax,

Smokey Joe Wood was a max-effort pitcher who once said, "I threw so hard, I thought my arm would fly right off my body." At age 22 he won 34 games for the 1912 Red Sox, but a shoulder injury ended his pitching career at age 26 (Library of Congress, LC-DIG-hec-02659).

they produce a damping proportional to the force they apply in cocking the arm. It is therefore likely that the stronger these two muscles are and the more force they contribute to cocking, the greater is their negative effect on velocity. If the pitcher transfers enough power from trunk rotation and trunk flexion to cock the arm with little or no assistance from the rotator cuff, there is likely to be less damping, less energy taken away from the most powerful movement of pitching, forward arm rotation. The electromyographic data show the average activity of the teres minor to be about 47 percent of the activity of the subscapularis during forward arm rotation. This value is about twice that of the agonist-and-antagonist pair for elbow extension, for which the activity of the biceps is 22 percent of the activity of the triceps.

Perhaps Dalkowski's phenomenal velocity and wildness were due to a naturally weak teres minor and infraspinatus, because he played in an era when pitchers did no strength training. Perhaps he naturally did not activate the teres minor and infraspinatus but applied only exceptional trunk-flexion and trunk-rotation velocities to cock the arm.

The prevailing belief is that shoulder-strengthening exercises are necessary to prevent injuries to the back side of the rotator cuff, which is subject to muscle-damaging eccentric contractions during both the acceleration and deceleration of the arm. Like hamstring injuries in sprinters, such injuries are believed to result from a strength imbalance between the agonists and antagonists. The most significant strength imbalance, however, may result from differential fatigue, a temporary loss of muscle strength and speed as a result of sustained activity. One study involving 21 teenage pitchers measured the effect of fatigue on the force generated by the infraspinatus before and after a simulated game of 75 to 90 pitches.[14] Between pre-game and post-game measurements, the activation level of the infraspinatus dropped from 96 percent to 89 percent, and the external rotation force dropped an average of three percent. Fatigue of the infraspinatus and teres minor appears more likely to occur in a pitcher who derives less power from the cocking movements of trunk rotation and trunk flexion. Fatigue can also be hastened by ill-timed strength exercises. Pitchers are sometimes observed to perform rearward arm rotation exercises with elastic bands as part of a pre-game warm-up, predisposing fatigue of the rotator cuff muscles by partially depleting their glycogen.

So, it appears that strengthening the infraspinatus and teres minor has a positive effect for taming wildness, a negative effect on velocity, and an uncertain effect on preventing shoulder injury. Steve Dalkowski never suffered a shoulder injury. His managers and coaches tried many things to help him achieve better control, but apparently they did not try strengthening the back side of his rotator cuff. Dalkowski finally improved his control in his 1962 season. At age 23, his bases-on-balls dropped to just 6.4 per 9 innings, down from a career high of 28.8 three years earlier, possibly because of diminishing elasticity of the anterior band of his ulnar collateral ligament — and consequently a lower natural frequency. When this occurred, he probably no longer developed an exceptional pulse of energy from lightly damped recoil. The diminished elasticity was perhaps a harbinger of an elbow injury. In spring training with the Orioles in 1963, he developed elbow pain that severely affected his control. Diagnosed as a pinched nerve — not as a sprain or tear that in retrospect seems more likely — the injury occurred on the same day he was fitted for his first major league uniform. From that point on, his velocity and his great strikeout ability were never the same. He hung on for two more years in the minors before retiring in 1965 at age 26.

6

Triple Play
The Importance of Hand Speed

"I'm deceptive. I can look like I'm chillin,' and be haulin'. And I can look like I'm haulin' and be chillin'." — Seattle Seahawks running back Shaun Alexander, *Los Angeles Times*, "Quotebook," January 13, 2005

Though Shaun Alexander's quotation is about his ball-carrying style in the National Football League, it also describes how a pitcher can deceive a batter about the velocity of a pitch. Hall-of-Fame manager Connie Mack said it another way in providing a clue about Walter Johnson's strikeout ability: the ball "seemed to jump at them before they could get their bats into motion." What he meant was that Johnson appeared to be chillin' when he was actually haulin' — pitching at high velocity without appearing to do so. For Johnson, much of this effect was due to his hand speed, which was perhaps as exceptional as his sweeping sidearm delivery. The great Satchel Paige also possessed exceptional hand speed. "Satchel had the greatest right wrist I've ever seen on any man," said Buck O'Neil, who played with and against Paige in the Negro Leagues. "He'd snap that wrist and that ball would be up there at 90 miles an hour before you'd know it."[1]

Conversely, a pitcher can look like he is haulin' while he is actually chillin'. This is the intended deception in throwing a changeup or curveball. A deceptive speed change disrupts the timing of the batter, who judges the speed of the ball mainly by the speed of the pitcher's larger moving parts, his arm and trunk. The change in speed occurs about one-hundredth of a second before release, a point at which the batter is least able to perceive it. In the changeup, the ball's velocity is *less* than the velocity the arm and trunk indicate — an effect produced by the action of the hand at release in one of two ways. The first is by diverting most of the energy of wrist/finger flexion from producing linear velocity to producing topspin, for the curveball. The second is to reduce the moment arm of wrist flexion by moving the ball closer to the wrist, reducing the acceleration the hand produces by about one-third as it travels through its normal arc of motion. Theoretically, the curveball can produce a larger speed differential, but both produce a secondary benefit of causing the ball to drop more rapidly than normal as it slows near the plate, either because of magnus force from the topspin or sink from lack of spin.

This effect of hand speed is symmetrical. It is equally effective whether the ball velocity is *greater or less* than the perceived arm-and-trunk velocity. It defies the batter's cues about the ball's velocity with late deceleration or late acceleration, the latter being the effect Connie Mack described. Others have referred to the ball jumping out of the hand, exploding over the plate, zooming in on the batter, or to the pitcher having a lively arm. The effect is well known, although how to achieve it is probably not well understood. In the case of late acceleration, it may also be aided by a burst of energy from elastic recoil, as discussed in the previous chapter.

Exceptional hand speed is perhaps the most under-appreciated asset of a pitcher. It is powered by the flexor muscles of the forearm, which may be a pitcher's most important and under-appreciated muscles. The triple-play of benefits provided by exceptional hand speed probably had a substantial effect on the record strikeout numbers of Johnson, Feller, and Ryan. These benefits are: (1) late acceleration, (2) a higher spin rate producing greater movement, and (3) greater linear velocity. In combination with an outstanding, deceptive curveball, their roaring fastballs were whiff-producers because much of their velocity came from exceptional hand speed.

These three benefits are greatest when wrist-and-finger flexion is applied through the largest arc of motion, which is determined by the angle of maximum wrist extension. For pitchers with exceptional hand speed, the wrist rapidly hyper-extends when forward arm rotation begins, having been jerked backward during the rapid acceleration of the arm. The hand then snaps forward to provide a burst of energy to the ball at the instant of release. The arm's acceleration causes the long flexor tendons to stretch slightly, then recoil to amplify the power.

Scientific studies with high-speed photography have shown that wrist-flexion velocity is the most variable of the pitching movements. The coefficient of variance in one study is 26.7 percent, which is about five times the variance of trunk rotation. Assuming a normal distribution, the range of wrist flexion velocity for 95 percent of pitchers is about 1,500 to 4,500 degrees per second.[2] A second study, by Vaughn, indicates a range of 2,000 to 4,700 degrees per second. Converting these angular velocities to linear velocities using an average hand length of 7.7 inches means that the velocity contribution of wrist-and-finger flexion could range from about 11 to 36 mph. These estimates, however, are high because the force of wrist-and-finger flexion propelling the ball produces a reaction, a retarding force that slows forward arm rotation speed an instant before release. Some of the energy from the flexion also goes into spin. The actual contribution of wrist flexion to linear velocity has not been accurately measured.

A pitcher who derives, for example, 25 mph of his fastball velocity from wrist-and-finger flexion theoretically has a maximum possible differential of 25 mph between fastball and curveball speed. For the changeup, the differential is about one-third to one-half of this value, 8 to 12 mph, because it is determined by the difference in ball position relative to the wrist. Pitchers with a higher differential either have phenomenal hand speed, or they violate the cardinal rule of the off-speed pitch: don't change your arm speed, or any other aspect of the delivery visible to the batter. Johnson, Feller, and Ryan each threw change ups occasionally but found greater success with the curveball, possibly because of its higher speed differential.

This large range in hand speed may indicate differences in ability to learn the precise coordination of the two high-speed movements of forward arm rotation and wrist-and-finger flexion. Or it may be due to variability in the power of the flexor muscles — the proportion of fast-glycolytic muscle fibers and their strength. It takes about one-tenth horsepower to spin the fastball at 1,800 rpm. This increases to about four-tenths horsepower for 3,600 rpm, a spin rate more likely to produce a fastball hop, a large break from its normal vertical descent, or with a tilted axis of spin like Walter Johnson's fastball, a large lateral movement. The effect of spin on movement is discussed in Chapter 7.

Hand speed is difficult to measure, even in a laboratory setting, but there is a visual indication that does not require a slow-motion camera. It is the angle between the wrist and forearm during the arm acceleration phase. The angle of wrist extension (away from the palm, *as shown in Figure 4*) during forward arm rotation is more easily perceived than the angle of flexion (toward the palm) at the point of ball release. Two studies

The Science of the Fastball

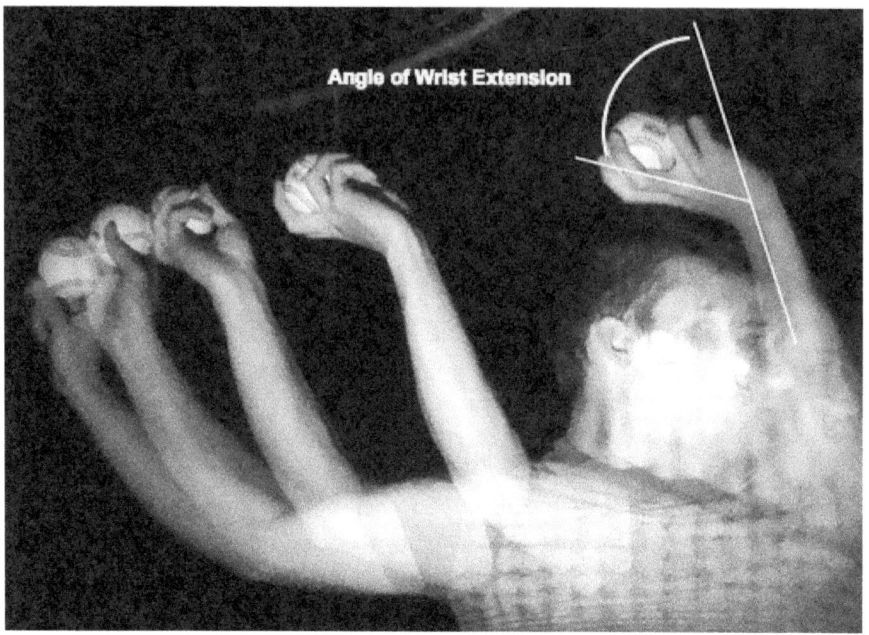

Figure 4: A time-exposure photograph taken with a strobe light shows a maximum wrist-extension angle for this pitcher to be about 55 degrees.

found the angle of extension to average 41 to 42 degrees with a range from 25 to 56 degrees based on two standard deviations from the average. A large wrist extension angle can also provide the benefit of hiding the ball part of the way through the arm acceleration phase, obscuring it from the batter's view momentarily as the arm moves forward. Sandy Koufax pitched with a very high angle of wrist extension, as did another strikeout record-setter, Tom Seaver. Both were three-time Cy Young award winners who apparently had exceptional hand speed. Koufax in 1965 set the single-season post–1900 strikeout mark with 382. Seaver, Nolan Ryan's teammate on the 1969 World Series champion Mets, tied the single-game record with 19 strikeouts on April 22, 1970. In doing so, Seaver struck out the last 10 batters in succession.

The second indication of hand speed is the angle of wrist flexion at release. This is the angle between the wrist and forearm at the completion of the pitch, which indicates whether the timing of the wrist flexion is optimal or whether the hand lags behind the arm. Data collected with

6. Triple Play

Tom Seaver pitched with a high wrist-extension angle indicative of a high spin rate. With the Mets in 1970, he tied the major-league single-game strikeout record of 19. Note that the ball is momentarily obscured by the wrist angle as his arm accelerates (National Baseball Hall of Fame Library, Cooperstown, New York).

high-speed photography show that the hand may lag behind by as much as 35 degrees at ball release, as noted in Chapter 4.

A small wrist extension angle is common among young pitchers, but it is also seen in many major-league pitchers, including Aroldis Chapman of the Cincinnati Reds, whose fastball in 2011 was timed at 105 mph by PITCH f/x. A puzzling aspect of hand speed is that some of the fastest fireballers pitch with a small wrist extension angle. A pitcher with the smaller angle locks the wrist by isometric contraction of the forearm flexor and extensor muscles. This does not limit the extension angle to zero because the force of acceleration causes some extension to occur. The isometrically contracted flexor muscles act as struts for the long tendons. As the arm accelerates, the inertia of the ball slightly stretches the tendons and muscles, which then recoil as acceleration decreases. Isometric contraction of prime movers is the same principle applied in running and hopping except that the tendons are stretched by the force of gravity. The wallaby, for example, applies this principle to hop great distances with great speed and energy efficiency. In pitching, it is the inertia of the ball and hand that produces the stretching. One problem with this approach to pitching is that if the extensor muscles, the antagonists of the flexors, are also isometrically contracted, they may damp the recoil and minimize the power-amplification effect.

This isometric-contraction (rigid-wrist) approach has two advantages. First, it uses less energy in that fewer muscle motor units are activated in isometric contraction, thus fatiguing the forearm less rapidly. Second, it eliminates the need for precisely timing the wrist flexion. There are, however, three disadvantages. First, it derives less power from the forearm flexor muscles, so there is less late acceleration; the final push to the ball is provided by finger flexion, which has about half the moment arm of wrist flexion. Second, it results in a lower spin rate and consequently less movement, and third, it may slightly increase the strain on the flexor muscles and anterior band of the ulnar collateral ligament. With a high wrist extension angle, the hand stays back during the acceleration of forward arm rotation, and the ball is then as much as five percent closer to the elbow; consequently, at the point where the torque is greatest, there is about five percent less torque at the elbow with a high wrist extension angle.

How is a pitcher with a small wrist extension angle able to exceed 100 mph with his fastball? He compensates for less-than-full power from the forearm flexor muscles with more power from the subscapularis and

6. Triple Play

from elastic-strain recoil, that is, greater arm speed. As noted in Chapter 3, forward arm rotation speed varies widely among pitchers. For 95 percent of pitchers, this range is estimated to be 5,600 to 9,800 degrees per second. An implication is that a pitcher possessing both exceptional arm speed and exceptional hand speed has the potential to achieve the extreme velocities of Feller and Ryan.

If a pitcher with this mode of limited wrist action also lacks the ability to throw a good curveball, it may be due to below-normal power from the flexor muscles or to having never learned the specific coordination for the curveball. Barrentine's data indicate that wrist-flexion velocity for the curveball is about 12 percent less than wrist-flexion velocity for the fastball.[3] The difference between the two pitches is the side of the ball to which the fingers apply torque and the flexor muscle that is dominant. The flexor carpi ulnaris does most of the work of spinning the curve because the palm is on the side of the ball in snapping off the 12-to-6 curve. All the flexors contribute to the spin of the fastball, making more power available for generating spin. Off-season strengthening of the flexor muscles with wrist curls can improve hand speed by increasing the available power. If the deficiency is in coordination, the pitcher may be able to improve his wrist extension angle and the power he derives from his forearm by modifying his technique. The hand-speed connection between the curve and fastball is sometimes apparent when a pitcher "loses" his curveball at the same time he experiences deficiencies in his fastball — a temporary inability that may result from differential fatigue involving the flexor carpi ulnaris muscle. As will be addressed in Chapter 13, performance outliers are likely caused by differential fatigue involving the flexor muscles.

There are no data on a baseball's rate of spin from pitching performances of the 20th century. The advent of PITCH f/x in 2007, however, made it possible to see how performance on the mound can be affected by spin rate. There is a caveat with regard to this spin data, however. PITCH f/x measures the ball position in three planes just after release and calculates spin rate based on some simplifying assumptions. Consequently, PITCH f/x calculates spin rate much less accurately than linear velocity. With this limitation, the *range* of spin rate, rather than the average spin rate, may better predict the success of a given outing; that is, a wider range in spin rate means more pitches are delivered in the no-man's land of spin — more fastballs with little movement, more hanging curveballs and sliders, more easily hittable pitches.

A second caveat is that there are far too many variables in pitching, including the skill of the catcher in calling for pitch type and location, to yield definitive conclusions about how one independent variable, spin rate, affects one dependent variable, whiff rate (swing-and-misses per total pitches). Nevertheless, the spin data of David Price, an outstanding young left-hander of the Tampa Bay Rays, provides an example of the apparent effect of spin rate. Price, who has been compared to Sandy Koufax, averaged 13.3 percent swinging strikes during the months of August and September 2010 when his average fastball spin rate was 2,600 rpm and his average velocity was 95.8 mph. This whiff rate was much higher than the major-league average for swinging strikes, 8.6 percent, during the 2010 season. Against Boston on July 7, 2010, Price achieved a 23 percent whiff rate with his four-seam fastball when his average fastball spin rate was 2,800 rpm. He induced no whiffs with his curve or changeup. In that seven-and-two-thirds inning performance, he struck out 10 and maintained a spin rate between 2,300 and 3,500 rpm on his fastball. In a game against the Yankees 11 days later, Price's fastball whiff rate decreased to 4.5 percent when his average spin rate dropped to 2,200 rpm (range 1,400 to 2,800), though his average velocity was slightly higher at 95 mph. He gave up seven earned runs in five innings.

Could it be that Price, in his best games, discovered the combination of velocity and spin rate that produces a late hop in the flight of a fast-spinning four-seamer, the same niche Koufax frequently found almost 50 years earlier? This niche is the subject of the next chapter.

7

The Fickle Flight of Koufax's Fast-Spinning Four-Seamer

"It isn't often a man can win a World Series deciding game with only a fastball, but that's exactly what Sandy Koufax did at the expense of the power-laden Twins here yesterday." —Paul Zimmerman, *Los Angeles Times*, October 15, 1965

The benefit of an off-speed pitch, the quiet complement of the roaring fastball, is well known. It upsets the batter's timing. It introduces uncertainty. It makes the batter delay his decisions on whether to swing and when to swing, forcing him to overcome the bat's inertia too quickly for precise bat-control. A fastball alone, even one that tops 100 mph, does not introduce uncertainty. A pitcher without reliable off-speed pitches might as well give the backhand glove flip, the fastball signal used in the bullpen. With a curve or changeup unlikely, the batter simply prepares for a fastball. If it's a three-ball count, the pitch is likely to be a four-seam fastball. In any pitcher's repertoire, the four-seamer has the straightest trajectory and is easiest to control. It is also the easiest to hit — unless it is thrown the way Sandy Koufax threw it.

Koufax at times defied conventional wisdom and succeeded with only a fastball. Most notably and remarkably he did so in the 1965 World Series, winning Game Seven on only two days of rest by throwing almost all fastballs; he couldn't throw his curve for a strike that day, possibly because his flexor carpi ulnaris was still fatigued from his previous game. His line in that momentous victory: 9 innings, 3 hits, 3 walks, 10 strikeouts — with only a hummer. This remarkable feat came at the end of a season in which he threw 335 two-thirds innings and won 26 games after being advised by his doctor not to throw between starts because of a severely arthritic elbow.

Understanding the Koufax four-seamer provides some insight into

The Science of the Fastball

Sandy Koufax's fastball had the right combination of linear and rotational velocities to produce a late hop. Note the extremely high angle of wrist extension as his arm begins to accelerate (Getty Images).

the record strikeout numbers of Bob Feller and Nolan Ryan. Yes, they had outstanding curveballs that gave them an exceptional whiff-producing combination. But the quirky aerodynamics of the four-seamer spinning rapidly around a near-horizontal axis added an effect well beyond speed differential. Though Koufax's four-seamer was not the fastest in baseball history, it may have been the most difficult to hit. It combined great velocity — close to 100 mph — with an exceptional spin rate that produced baffling movement. As thrown by Koufax, the four-seamer was not merely a high-velocity fastball but a niche pitch.

In his relatively short career, Koufax pitched four no-hitters, set a post–1900 single-season strikeout record with 382, and recorded 18 strikeouts in a game on two occasions. The left-hander from Brooklyn threw with a distinct over-the-top arm action and usually relied on two pitches, a four-seamer and a curveball, a combination that was probably as effective in generating swinging strikes as any in major-league history. Batters said that his fastball appeared to rise and to have late movement. Some claimed

7. The Fickle Flight of Koufax's Fast-Spinning Four-Seamer

that it moved two or three distinct times during its flight to home plate. His curve was almost as good as his fastball. He occasionally threw a changeup and slider.

Conventional wisdom says that it is more difficult to succeed in the major leagues pitching from a high arm slot. Koufax did so in six brilliant seasons from 1961 to 1966. With the right combination of variables, a Koufax-quality four-seamer hops as it approaches the plate, with movement that is late and sharp, though relatively small. The movement is not visible from the dugout or the stands, but it is to the batter and catcher. Although it is called a hop, it is not a hop. It breaks downward, not upward. There is no aerodynamic perturbation on the brief trip to the plate that could cause the ball to rise abruptly, no effect like an airliner bouncing up and down near a thunderstorm. The hopping four-seamer simply drops abruptly.

What causes the drop? It stalls. The four-seamer with its high rate of backspin produces lift. It flies, but it is a marginal flyer, not an efficient flyer like an airplane wing. A 3,000-rpm four-seamer at 100 mph has about the same lift-to-drag ratio as the Space Shuttle in its landing mode, another marginal flyer. This is in contrast to a two-seamer, which does not fly as well, and a sinker, which does not fly at all. Sinkers in the optimal range of vertical deviation generate a lot of ground balls.[1] But they generate no lift. Walter Johnson's fastball had sink because his sidearm delivery produced spin around a vertical axis, producing no lift.

When the lift is interrupted, the ball ceases to fly and breaks downward. This stalling effect has never been demonstrated in a scientific laboratory, but in the strange aerodynamics of a baseball, it has a logical explanation. The pattern of airflow around the ball changes as its velocity, rate of spin, and orientation of the spin axis change. In a certain velocity range, the drag coefficient drops rapidly as the flow around the ball changes and becomes turbulent.[2] This change is called the drag crisis, and it causes, the drag coefficient to drop from about 0.5 to 0.2. It occurs around 60 to 70 mph. The knuckleballer pitches in this range, using the drag crisis to make the ball dance left, right, and downward. The velocity of the fastball puts it far beyond the drag crisis, but if its rate of backspin is high enough, the fastball can back itself into the drag crisis. When the ball spins at 3,000 rpm, it is rotating with a surface velocity of about 25 mph. With backspin, the upper surface is thus retreating at 25 mph; consequently, if the ball's velocity is 100 mph, the flow *over* the ball relative to its surface is reduced to 75 mph, very close to the drag crisis. There is very little change in the rate of spin between the release and the plate.[3] But there is a significant change, about five mph, in the linear velocity. As the ball decelerates en route to the plate, it is likely to enter the critical flow regime. If so, the drag rises sharply, the flow pattern changes abruptly, and the ball ceases to fly momentarily. It breaks sharply downward, transforming itself in mid-flight from a straight fastball into a sinker.

The downward break does not appear on the screen with PITCH f/x because the computer fits a smooth, curved trajectory to the predicted ball positions based on the measured velocities as soon as the pitcher releases the ball. From the pitcher's perspective, the best location for the stall to occur is close to the plate, since that makes it most difficult for the batter to adjust to the late drop. If it stalls 10 feet from the plate, it may drop only 2 inches, but that amount of drop is enough to induce a whiff or a ground ball. The stall won't occur if the spin rate is too low, so if the pitcher's forearm flexor muscles become fatigued in the later innings, his fastball is likely to become more easily hittable.

When a pitcher finds the niche, the aerodynamic sweet spot, in which all the variables are favorable for stalling near the plate, his four-seamer can bless him with an exceptional number of swinging strikes, perhaps even a record number of strikeouts. When he doesn't find it, and he relies heavily on the four-seamer from a high arm slot, he may have one of those inexplicably short outings known as "getting shelled."

The whiff rate of the four-seamer is usually less than that of the slider, changeup, and curve. However, the hopping four-seamer has the potential to be a more reliable out pitch because it is easier to control. When the spin rate is not high enough to produce a late hop, its lift can still produce a large upward deviation from the normal trajectory. The lift prevents the ball from dropping as rapidly as it would with no backspin. Without any lift from backspin, a 95-mph fastball on its 0.45-second trip to home plate can drop 40 inches from the straight line on which it is launched.

Can a fastball thrown from an overhand delivery actually rise, as those who saw the roaring pitches of Koufax and Dalkowski claim? Scientists say no. One scientific study concluded the rising fastball to be a perceptual illusion.[4] Mathematical models calculate the lift a baseball produces as a product of spin rate, velocity, air density, and a coefficient of lift that is experimentally determined. A lift of five ounces, which theoretically would make the ball fly level most of the way to home plate, can be achieved at

7. The Fickle Flight of Koufax's Fast-Spinning Four-Seamer

sea level by a ball traveling about 100 mph and spinning at 4,400 rpm, by one traveling 130 mph and spinning at 1,800 rpm, or with another combination of velocity and spin rate that produces the same lift. It seems certain that no pitcher, not even Dalkowski, has ever thrown 130 mph. It is not certain whether a pitcher can spin a 100-mph fastball at 4,400 rpm. The issue of whether a fastball can actually rise thus becomes: can someone throw a 100-mph fastball that spins at 4,400 rpm? PITCH f/x data indicate that spin rates of about 3,500 rpm have been achieved. The limitation is in the total amount of power a pitcher's muscles must generate to deliver a fastball at 100-mph and 4,400-rpm spin rate. With the power amplification achieved by pitchers possessing exceptional hand speed and arm speed like Koufax, Feller, Ryan, Paige, and Dalkowski, it is perhaps possible. Walter Johnson is not included here because his sidearm delivery produced a near-vertical axis of spin. He achieved a great deal of horizontal movement and an effective amount of sink. But no rise and no hop.

8

The Band and the Gap

Tommy John is the only athlete in the history of sport to be immortalized for replacing a worn-out body part.

Jamie Moyer's 24-year career as a major league pitcher makes a convincing statement that velocity is not the most important attribute of a fastball. As of 2010, the left-hander from Pennsylvania had started more than 500 games, striking out 2,405 batters in 4,020 innings. In the season after he turned 41, he won 21 games and was selected to the All-Star team. At age 46, he earned his 267th major-league victory. In his 40s, he averaged 81 mph on his fastball, a lightly humming hummer about as loud as a barn owl in flight. His fastball had about one-third less kinetic energy than Walter Johnson's, making Moyer a low-energy pitcher, or more accurately, an energy-efficient pitcher who applied precise control, movement, deception, and intelligence to keep batters off the base paths. Moyer's long career illustrates not only Ryan's assertion about the importance of speed but also the second law of thermodynamics as it applies to pitching — all things eventually wear out, including the elbow ligament of an energy-efficient pitcher. Moyer's elbow ligament reached the point of failure near the end of his 2010 season with the Philadelphia Phillies. Four months later, at age 48 and still planning to pitch again, he underwent Tommy John ligament replacement surgery.

Moyer earned a salary totaling $82 million in his first 24 major league seasons, so one could easily characterize his left arm as golden.[1] But all arms, no matter how valuable, have a critical component of the elbow that, ounce for ounce, is far more valuable than gold to a pitcher — sinew, the same type of tough, elastic material from which Native Americans once made bow strings. This piece of sinew is the anterior band of the elbow, which is so important in producing a roaring fastball that it should be called "The Pitching Ligament." It is a tough, rope-like bundle of Type I collagen fibrils that amplifies the power in pitching in the same manner the Achilles tendon does in leaping.

8. The Band and the Gap

The Pitching Ligament, about the size of a stubby pencil, is usually referred to as the ulnar collateral ligament (ulnar relates to the longer of the two bones of the forearm, the ulna). The anterior band, which bears the primary load when the elbow is flexed more than 30 degrees, is one of three bands or bundles. The other two are the posterior and transverse bands. Dr. Frank W. Jobe of California developed the first procedure for replacing it, surgery commonly referred to as medial elbow ligament reconstruction (medial describes its location on the side of the elbow toward the body). He performed it first on Los Angeles Dodgers pitcher Tommy John, giving the surgery its popular name and immortalizing the pitcher for his torn ligament rather than his outstanding career.

When he performed that first surgery in September 1974, Jobe felt that it had only one chance in 100 of being successful. After 18 months of rehabilitation, however, John returned to the mound and proceeded to win 164 more games, running his career total to 288 major-league victories. A left-hander with a mid- to upper–80s fastball and an outstanding curveball, he pitched until he was 46 years old. He amassed 26 seasons in the major leagues, with 14 of those seasons and three of his four All-Star Game appearances coming after the surgery.

In all sports, ligaments and tendons, the dense connective tissues of the body, have a major effect on the success and duration of an athlete's career. Muscles provide the power, while tendons and ligaments provide a decisive difference in performance by transmitting power, amplifying power, and stabilizing joints. Muscle strength can be increased greatly through training, but tendon and ligament strength peaks in early adulthood and does not increase significantly with training.

Ligaments connect bone to bone. Tendons connect muscle to bone, transferring the power from the muscles to the bones to produce movement. In the case of overhand pitching, it is a ligament—the anterior band—that transmits the force of muscles even though it connects bone to bone. Ligaments and tendons have the same structure, bundles of fine collagen fibrils that have a wavy or crimped appearance under an electron microscope. These individual fibrils are only 20 to 150 nanometers thick. Some tendons have a sheath, a tough membrane around them to ensure that they move freely and smoothly. In Tommy John surgery, a tendon without a sheath is used to replace the anterior band.

The velocity of Jamie Moyer's fastball was much higher than 81 mph when he came into the majors in 1986. It had to be; no pitcher in the radar-gun era ever gets past the gatekeeper of professional ball without the consent and express digital approval of the radar gun. So what happened to his velocity as a result of 4,020 innings of pitching? His biological springs wore out, his energy storage and return capability diminished, and he accepted pitching with an arm having a lower natural frequency. He could have resisted this change by pitching above his natural frequency, but the additional energy costs would have hastened the decline without providing a performance benefit.

The springs familiar to most of us never wear out — hardly ever does anyone replace the springs of the family automobile. Why did Moyer's biological springs wear out when the stresses on his elbow were probably the least among major league pitchers, outside of a few knuckle-ballers? It is because the spring-like collagen fibrils bundled into tendons and ligaments are not actually elastic but viscoelastic. This means that when stretched beyond a certain point, they permanently deform or break. That point, referred to as the elastic limit, is about 105 percent. Damage can occur when the fibrils are stretched five percent beyond normal length.

During major league spring training of 2001, a team of medical researchers from Philadelphia's Jefferson Medical College used high-resolution sonography to study the cumulative effect of repeated stretching of pitchers' anterior bands. They examined the elbows of 26 major-league pitchers ranging in age from 21 to 39. Their ultra-sound images revealed micro-tears in the bands of 69 percent of their pitching arms. In 35 percent, they also found calcifications, which often accompany ligament injuries. Published in 2003, the study showed that the anterior bands of the pitching arm were thicker and had more looseness of the joint under pressure, an indication of joint instability. When pressure was applied, the gap or joint space in the pitching elbow was significantly greater than the gap in the non-pitching arm — measuring 4.2 mm on average, compared to a 3 mm gap on the non-pitching arm. A wider gap indicates a more compliant band and less transmission, storage, and return of energy to accelerate the arm. A conclusion of the study was that elbow ligament degeneration strongly correlates with the number of years in professional baseball.[2]

The widening of the gap indicates one of two conditions of micro-trauma. Either fibrils have been permanently stretched (deformed), or a significant portion of the fibrils have broken. The result is a band that is less stiff and returns less energy when stretched. The thickening of the lig-

8. The Band and the Gap

ament highlights another problem with the collagen fibrils. Although the body slowly repairs the broken fibrils with new connective tissue, it does not organize the tissue into the original structure of long bundles of fibrils. Instead, it wraps new tissue haphazardly around the broken fibrils to produce a dense scar that thickens the ligament. The healing process thus creates a structure with less strength and elasticity because the new tissue does not align in the direction of force. As such, the damage is not completely reversible, and consequently *the healing process does not halt the degradation of ligaments/tendons as it normally does in muscle and bone.* Unlike damage to muscle fibers, which the body repairs in a matter of days, the less-than-perfect repair of broken fibrils takes two to three months. These facts are key pieces in the puzzle of elbow ligament failure. Once the first fibril is permanently stretched or broken, there is a progression toward complete failure as long as the stresses of pitching continue. This progression may alternate between two phases — one of deformation and one of breaking — with the transition between the two marked by acute injury involving inflammation and pain so severe that it is not possible to pitch.

How could a low-energy pitcher like Jamie Moyer exceed the 105 percent elastic limit without throwing high heat? The answer is muscle fatigue. The anterior band does not work alone. Unlike the Achilles tendon, which is in series with muscle, the band works in parallel with several muscles of the forearm. It shares the load. Tests on bands removed from cadavers indicate that without sharing the load, the band would likely fail under the normal, expected stresses of pitching.[3]

The right arm of R.A. Dickey, a knuckleball pitcher for the New York Mets, illustrates this load-sharing. Dickey was a hard-throwing righthander at the University of Tennessee when the Texas Rangers selected him in the first round of the 1996 amateur draft. Before he signed his contract, the Rangers found that Dickey did not have a complete ulnar collateral ligament in his pitching arm, a discovery that reduced his signing bonus substantially. Apparently, he was born without the ligament, or his body absorbed the remnants of it after he tore it while pitching as a teenager. Whatever the reason, his fastball was in the 90s in college and in the upper 80s early in his pro career. Diminishing velocity led him to develop an outstanding and career-saving knuckleball.

Having no anterior band, or a compliant one, in the pitching arm is like having a worn clutch in an automobile. The band not only transmits power from trunk flexion and trunk rotation, it also amplifies it. In the absence of the band, the titin strands in the forearm flexor muscles collectively act as the main biological spring in the arm; however, the titin is more easily damaged because of its weak links, the Z-disks on the ends of each sarcomere. The titin is also far less effective in storing strain energy than the collagen of ligaments and tendons. A study published in 1977 showed collagen to be capable of storing about 1,000 times more strain energy than active muscle.[4] Less energy is stored and returned, more is lost in transmission each time torque is applied, and the flexor muscles become more susceptible to damage. Fastball velocity is typically reduced by five to 10 percent when the anterior band becomes worn or torn. Becoming a knuckleballer is a logical progression, not only because less power is available, but also because knuckleballers have a smaller potential for injury to the forearm flexor muscles.

Muscles are also important to the stability of the shoulder joint. Loss of velocity can occur if the labrum, the fibrous cartilage ring that retains the head of the humerus, is frayed or torn. Strengthening exercises for the arm and shoulder muscles are considered insurance against injury, and they are the essence of rehabilitation once an injury occurs. Ligaments and tendons heal most effectively with a gradual resumption of load-bearing, which may help the collagen fibrils align with the direction of tension. There are limitations, however, in applying strength training for joint stability. Strengthening exercises can be counter-productive when performed between pitching outings during the season. As will be discussed in the next two chapters, resistance exercises between appearances can make the muscles fatigue more quickly if the exercises are too intense.

When these muscles are fatigued due to glycogen depletion or cumulative micro-trauma to the fibers, they produce less force during a pitch and have diminished ability to share the load and protect the joint. For the elbow, the result is that the band is subjected to greater forces and may stretch beyond 105 percent of its normal length. It appears that the flexor carpi ulnaris and flexor digitorum superficialis, because of their proximity to the band are the most important in bearing the load,[5] although experiments to verify this based on electromyography have been inconclusive.[6]

The time it takes the band to tear to a point requiring replacement surgery is determined by the stress to which it is subjected after the first point of failure is reached. Excessive stress occurs as a result of: (1) pitching with fatigued flexor muscles of the forearm, and (2) pitching above the

8. The Band and the Gap

natural frequency, i.e., at maximal effort. For the fibrils of Jamie Moyer's anterior band, the transition between deformation and breaking took a quarter century, much longer than most pitchers. As his velocity gradually declined, he was presented with two alternatives: pitch at a lower natural frequency — a lower velocity — or allow the progressive degradation to occur at a faster pace. These are the alternatives whether there is a gradual loosening of the band or an acute injury accompanied by inflammation and pain. The acute injury gives the pitcher a choice of surgery or rehab, the latter being a two-month rest to allow scar tissue to bind the broken fibrils. Rehab usually returns the pitcher to near full velocity, but it may be only a temporary amelioration, forestalling the band's eventual catastrophic failure unless the pitcher ignores the radar gun and pitches at a lower natural frequency.

It is of course best to protect and preserve the band. As long as the collagen fibrils stay within the elastic limit, they can better withstand stress than muscle fibers can. Muscle fibers are repaired quickly because they have great plasticity and an abundant blood supply. Ligaments and tendons do not; their metabolic rate is about one-seventh that of muscle.[7] Though muscle fibers heal faster, they are more fragile, which means that it is the muscle fibers that determine the acceptable duration of a pitching outing. So, the essence of protecting the band is protecting the muscles around the band from a temporary loss of strength. On the mound, this means avoiding fatigue of the forearm flexor muscles. Between starts, it means ensuring that damage to these muscles heals fully and that glycogen is restored to them.

As was discussed in Chapter 4, the electromyographic activity of the flexor carpi radialis and flexor carpi ulnaris indicates that differential fatigue would likely affect the flexor muscles of the forearm because their activity level is the highest among the arm and shoulder muscles used in pitching. In a practical sense, the early onset of differential fatigue in a game can sometimes be a self-resolving problem. Fatigue of the flexors results in a reduced control and spin rate, which leads to more hits and/or walks, which in turn usually results in a short outing and less likelihood of injury. While this oversimplified sequence of results may occur in professional baseball, the problem may not self-resolve in amateur ball where fastball phenoms can overwhelm batters with speed, even without their best control and movement. Differential fatigue may thus be more likely to sow the seeds of elbow injury in teenage pitchers — particularly when there are differential growth rates among muscle, ligament, and tendon during adolescence.

Because Nolan Ryan pitched in the radar-gun era, his career provides some insight into the rate at which velocity loss occurs as the elastic stiffness of the anterior band diminishes and/or muscle strength declines. Ryan experienced acute elbow injury three times in his career. First, there was inflammation in his second season in the majors. He underwent elbow surgery to remove four bone chips in 1975, and he was bothered by elbow soreness throughout the 1986 season. His anterior band finally failed in 1993, at age 46. Unlike Moyer, he did not seek to extend his long career with Tommy John surgery. The progression of his fibril deformation may be apparent in the very gradual decline of his fastball velocity from the 97 to 98 mph range in the early 1970s to the range of 92 to 93 mph in the early 1990s. "I figure I've lost a couple of miles per hour off my fastball every 10 years," said Ryan in his 1992 autobiography.[8]

Based on the number of innings he pitched in the majors and an estimate of 15 pitches per inning on average, Ryan probably threw more than 80,000 pitches in facing over 22,500 batters in his 27-season career. Using the same method of approximation, Walter Johnson threw about 88,000 pitches in 5,914 innings in 21 seasons; Bob Feller, about 57,000 in 18 seasons; and Jamie Moyer, about 60,000 in 24 seasons.

Every machine has a finite service life defined by the durability of the irreplaceable component that wears out most quickly — and the mechanisms designed to protect it. In the arm of a pitcher, this critical component — now replaceable with about a 12-to-18-month hiatus — is that small piece of sinew on the medial side of the elbow. The mechanisms that serve to protect it are the muscles of the forearm.

9

Diminishing Velocity
Five Effects That Link Eccentric Contractions to Power Loss

"Pitching is a most unnatural motion." — Dr. George Bennett, orthopedic surgeon

When Dr. George Bennett offered this assessment to a *Sports Illustrated* writer in 1956, he was explaining that the shoulder is not constructed to resist the stresses of pitching a baseball.[1] An eminent orthopedic surgeon at Johns Hopkins Hospital, Dr. Bennett specialized in mending injured shoulders. Though his observations on pitching injuries were unquestionably factual, his observation on the pitching motion was more of an opinion. In truth, overhand pitching is no less natural than walking or running. One can easily find illustrations of ancient hunters throwing spears overhand. One cannot find, however, depictions of underhand spear throwing, ancient or otherwise. To find a pitching motion that *seems* unnatural takes only a visit to a fast-pitch softball game. The standard delivery in softball, underhand pitching, has an unnatural appearance, but it does not produce large demand for orthopedic services. Collegiate softball pitchers sometimes pitch two or more games in a day or pitch as starters on consecutive days. On average, they pitch twice as many innings per month as baseball pitchers, and they do so without ill effects. No baseball pitcher can match their routine and retain the ability to brush his hair.

The difference? It is not the "unnatural" motion. Rather, it is eccentric muscle contraction that makes overhand pitching injurious to the shoulder and arm. In an eccentric contraction, a muscle is forced to lengthen while producing tension. The "normal" muscle action is concentric contraction, which involves shortening under tension. A third type of contraction, isometric, involves no length change under tension. Eccentric contraction causes far more strain than the other two, more stretching of muscle fibers beyond their elastic limits, and consequently more damage to muscle fibers. This effect was first recognized in the 1950s.[2] Researchers have found that it is the magnitude of strain during lengthening contractions — not simply the force itself — that causes muscle damage.[3] Among the many experiments conducted on mice and men to study muscle damage and repair, almost all involve eccentric contractions. It is an approach of experimental convenience and control because it takes relatively few repetitions of lengthening against force for damage to be subsequently apparent under an electron microscope.

In pitching a baseball, the most damaging eccentric contractions occur with two abrupt changes in momentum in the arm-acceleration phase — one at the beginning and one at the end. At these two points, muscles are overmatched by the momentum of the arm. First, the subscapularis muscle and the flexor muscles in the forearm absorb kinetic energy of the arm, rapidly reversing its direction as it rotates backward to the fully cocked position. Electromyographic readings taken in the late cocking phase show very high activity of the subscapularis and high activity of the flexors, indicating that these muscles contract before the point of full cocking to reverse the momentum while they are still lengthening.[4] At the cocked position — which indeed looks unnatural when captured in a photo — the subscapularis, the flexor muscles of the forearm, their tendons, and the ulnar collateral ligament anterior band, are stretched to store energy transferred from trunk rotation and trunk flexion. It is this stretching, this elastic-strain energy storage and return, that gives overhand pitching its velocity advantage over underhand pitching.

The second point of eccentric contraction occurs when the pitcher releases the ball. The infraspinatus and teres minor of the rotator cuff absorb the kinetic energy of the arm, abruptly decelerating it from its maximum velocity. In contrast, the underhand softball pitch produces far less strain in decelerating. It has a slower rotational velocity, and after ball-release, the arm continues on a rotational path that dissipates its kinetic energy more gradually. In baseball, statistics show that the incidence of injury to the rotator cuff is about twice as high as injury to the elbow, probably because of the much higher velocity of the arm when the rotator cuff acts like a brake.[5] There are, however, indirect effects of muscle damage to the forearm flexor muscles that make it at least as troublesome as damage to the rotator cuff. These effects relate to glycogen restoration and are addressed below and in the next chapter.

9. Diminishing Velocity

Muscles have built-in biological springs, elastic strands of titin that have the same purpose as the collagen fibrils of ligaments and tendons. Titin stores and returns energy, but in muscle fibers, titin is not a long continuous spring like the collagen fibril of a tendon. Each titin strand runs only half the length of a sarcomere and is anchored at the middle and the end of the sarcomere. The end of the sarcomere, the Z-disk, is consequently the weak link in the muscle's biological spring and the point at which fiber damage is usually seen in research experiments involving eccentric contractions. The Z-disks of fast-glycolytic fibers are thinner (about 60 nanometers thick) and thus more susceptible to strain damage than the Z-disks of slow-oxidative fibers, which are about 2½ times thicker.[6] Damage also appears inside the sarcomeres as broken filaments, the sliding threads of protein molecules that are 10,000 times smaller in diameter than a human hair. More severe damage involves ruptures of the muscle fiber membrane, leading to a leaking of fluid from the fiber.

These weak links in the muscles' biological spring are the main reason that muscle fibers do not withstand excessive strain of the eccentric contractions in pitching. As a rule, however, muscle fibers are repaired rapidly when there is little damage. Damage varies with the amount of stretching beyond the fibers' elastic limit and — because each fiber contains millions of weak links — damage varies with the number of times the stretching is repeated. Repair time varies with the extent of damage and the number of sarcomeres damaged. The repair time determines how frequently a pitcher can perform routinely without injury.

The time needed to repair damage produced by eccentric contractions governs the performance schedule in many sports. Consider the champion distance runner, for example. The leg muscles that propel a runner contract eccentrically with each stride, absorbing energy and lengthening against tension each time a foot strikes the ground. A runner's center of gravity rises and falls two to three inches with each step, and this short but jarring descent produces eccentric contractions with significant strain. A runner's leg muscles sustain more damage in a 26-mile marathon than in a one-mile race, and even more damage if the marathon involves a lot of downhill running, which increases the amount of strain. Full recovery from a world-class marathon performance can take two months or more. Full recovery from a world-class mile race takes about a week.

Why do some thoroughbred horse trainers consider it too stressful and too risky to compete in all three events of horse racing's triple crown?

The Kentucky Derby, Preakness, and Belmont are each about 2 to 2½ minutes in duration and are two and three weeks apart, plenty of time for a two-legged runner to recover. The reason is that a 1,500-pound horse induces strain of far greater magnitude in the eccentric contractions of the leg muscles than does a 150-pound man. Over-racing or overtraining a horse can bring an abrupt end to its racing career, or its life. In pitching, the variables of strain quantity and strain magnitude are better known as pitch count and pitch velocity, respectively. The product of these two variables is strain energy, and damage to the eccentrically contracting muscles varies with the total amount of strain energy applied to them during an outing on the mound. From this perspective, it becomes apparent that the disadvantage of maximal-effort pitching is in the magnitude of strain it produces and the increased muscle damage that goes with it. To minimize the injurious effects of excessive strain energy, a pitcher must control the magnitude of strain, i.e., the power applied to each pitch, as well as the number of repetitions, i.e., the number of pitches. A closer can survive routinely throwing max-effort for one inning; a starter cannot expect to do so for seven, eight, or nine innings.

To worsen matters for the pitcher, the muscle fiber type that is most susceptible to the damage of eccentric contraction because of its thin Z-Disks is the fast-glycolytic, the fiber that makes the fastball roar.[7] The durability of fast-glycolytic fibers is of little concern to the marathon runner, because he relies on slow-oxidative muscle fibers throughout most of his 26-mile ordeal, forcefully activating the fast fibers only when he goes up or down hill. Thoroughbred racehorses rely on fast-glycolytic and fast-oxidative-glycolytic fibers to win races on flat tracks, and are thus more susceptible to injury than marathon runners.

The Effect of Incomplete Repair

Skeletal muscle is the most adaptable tissue of the human body. With an abundant blood supply and an army of stem cells stationed on each muscle fiber awaiting a call to action, muscle is the most quickly repaired component of the pitcher's power train. When muscle damage occurs, the body responds with an incredibly complex maintenance process to quickly restore millions of damaged micro-engines to full working order.

The process begins with the cleanup of broken parts. First-responder

9. Diminishing Velocity

cells, the white blood cells called neutrophils and macrophages (meaning big eaters) arrive and begin vacuuming up and digesting the debris. Their arrival initiates an inflammation phase, which begins from one to 12 hours after the damage occurs and lasts up to about four days. Debris removal usually occurs in the first two days after injury. During the third and fourth days, a different type of macrophage plays a key role in regenerating muscle cells,[8] secreting growth factors, hormones (chemical messengers) and cytokines to attract and regulate the satellite cells.[9] Once the debris-clearing is complete, the process of rebuilding the muscle fiber structure and restoring its function begins when satellite cells, stem cells residing on the periphery of the muscle fibers, are activated by growth factors. These cells multiply and migrate to the site of the damage, peaking in quantity three to four days after the fiber has been damaged. They rebuild by fusing together and/or fusing to existing fibers. This is when a pitcher who uses anabolic steroids gains an advantage over pitchers who do not. Use of these illegal hormones increases protein synthesis within cells, accelerating the repair and regeneration process to produce a more rapid recovery after a pitching performance.

Though inflammation has an important purpose, it is not completely beneficial. It can inflict additional damage, probably as a result of the white blood cells injuring healthy regions of injured fibers or damaging adjacent uninjured fibers. It is important to note, however, that debris removal is a necessary phase that precedes the actual rebuilding, just as it is for a structure in the aftermath of a fire or a natural disaster. This cleanup work takes a substantial portion of the recovery period, delaying the actual rebuilding. Thus, if a pitcher returns to the mound only two to three days after his last outing, he may have allowed only enough time for cleanup of muscle damage, not for rebuilding. When muscles are stressed repeatedly without time for repair, damage accumulates and strength diminishes.

Such was probably the case in 1884 with Charles "Old Hoss" Radbourn, a hard-drinking 5-foot, 9-inch right-hander who compressed a 4,500-inning major-league career into 11 seasons between 1880 and 1891. Midway through his '84 season with the Providence Grays, Radbourn agreed to pitch every game for the remainder of the season in exchange for a pay raise and reserve-clause exemption the following year. He then pitched 40 of his team's next 43 games and registered 36 wins. He set a single-season major-league record with 59 wins that year, pitching 678 two-thirds innings, striking out 441 batters, and winning the National League's triple crown of pitching. He also pitched 73 complete games, the

The Science of the Fastball

second most in baseball history. What was his body's response to this softball-like pitching schedule? His shoulder became so sore that he was unable to comb his hair. He had to apply hot towels and liniment each night to ease the aching so he could sleep.[10] On game day, his warm-up routine took hours to complete, beginning with short tosses at home plate, increasing in distance gradually until he was pitching from second base and, finally, as his dead arm came to life, from short center field.[11] After the '84 season, his strikeout numbers dropped, his ERA rose, and his pitching was never the same. By the time he retired from baseball to open a bar in Bloomington, Illinois, he had accumulated 309 wins. Aside from being enshrined in the Baseball Hall of Fame, his legacy was to define the limits imposed by the eccentric contractions of pitching a baseball.

Radbourn's soreness was apparently what is now known as delayed-onset muscle soreness (DOMS), a condition first studied and described as ruptures within the muscle about a decade after Radbourn's transition from ballplayer to bar-owner. DOMS is a result of muscle damage caused by eccentric contractions, either from a single bout of exercise or the

Old Hoss Radbourn, shown in a Boston Beaneaters uniform, endured unrelenting shoulder pain to pitch 678 innings and win 59 games for the Providence Grays in 1884 (National Baseball Hall of Fame Library, Cooperstown, New York).

accumulation of minor damage from several bouts with inadequate recovery. "There is no question that DOMS is uniquely related to eccentric exercise and not to exercise itself," writes Dr. Richard L. Lieber, a noted research scientist.[12] DOMS is marked by a loss in strength of the damaged muscles. Other symptoms are soreness or tenderness, stiffness, swelling, and inflammation. In causing soreness, the body sensitizes pain receptors, producing pain to limit the functioning of the injured fibers. Swelling involves increased blood flow to the site to facilitate recovery, which normally takes about seven days. When damage is extensive, however, it can take much longer.[13] It is likely that the degree of soreness and the time needed for recovery from it are proportional to the number of sarcomeres damaged. If few are damaged, there may be no pain. If many are damaged, then both the pain and the time needed for recovery will be substantial.

During the season, pitchers have little control over the damage routinely inflicted on the arm and shoulder muscles, because there is little flexibility in pitching schedules outside the disabled list. Pitchers also have little control over the rate at which their body recovers from muscle damage. Individual differences in age, genetics, fitness, and general health may affect the rate of recovery, but the repair process works at a steady pace. There are no legal ways to speed up the repairman cells, not even to help a Hall-of-Fame-bound ace return to the mound on two-days' rest in the World Series. For a pitcher, muscle repair is governed by: (1) the extent of damage, (2) the body's natural rate of repair, (3) the time available for repair, and (4) what the pitcher does between starts to hinder or aid the repair process. Pitchers can control only the last of these, and they do so by adjusting the intensity of training between starts or, typically, by taking anti-inflammatory pain medicine.

Inflammation and soreness are the bio-molecular motors' warning lights, indicators about the extent of damage and the time needed for repair. Unfortunately, these signals are not always accurate. The threshold for significant damage can be less than the threshold for DOMS; the absence of soreness does not equate to an absence of damage. A 130-pitch outing, for example, may not cause soreness but is likely to require a longer recovery period than a 100-pitch outing. DOMS does not occur with minor damage, and it does not always occur with more severe damage, so it is not a reliable indicator of damage. DOMS peaks in one to three days but does not subside completely for a week to 10 days. The repair work continues after pain subsides.

The Effect of Anti-Inflammatory Drugs

There were no anti-inflammatory pain medicines available to Old Hoss Radbourn in 1884, about a decade before aspirin, the first non-steroidal anti-inflammatory drug (NSAID), became available in the U.S. This was probably to Radbourn's benefit, despite the intense pain he endured and the difficulty of his warm-up routine. More than a century after his rotator cuff suffered under the strain of eccentric contractions, professional pitchers have become routinely reliant on NSAIDs such as Ibuprofen and Naproxen to suppress inflammation and pain. A loss of strength is one result of muscle damage, and NSAIDs produce what appears to be a more rapid return of strength. Studies of the repair process, however, indicate that by turning off inflammation, NSAIDs inhibit the production of a certain signaling molecule necessary for muscle regeneration.[14] This delays the rebuilding of the muscle fibers. Results of experiments performed in 1995 on the leg muscles of rabbits show that the quick return of strength that NSAIDs produce is only temporary and probably a result of simply reducing the protective response of pain. In these experiments, a *decline* in strength was observed four weeks after the muscle-damaging bout of exercise and three weeks after the last NSAID was administered, leading to the conclusion that NSAIDs provide a short-term benefit and long-term detriment.[15] The implication is that chronic use of NSAIDs during the baseball season inhibits muscle repair, causing damage to accumulate and leading to a gradual loss of pitching power. This presents a quandary for the pitcher — to pitch with soreness or postpone the healing of routine muscle damage until the end of the season. Postponing recovery means that a longer recovery period is necessary to fully repair muscle damage. Extensive muscle damage can take months to be fully repaired, and postponement creates a risk that the repair will not be fully completed before pre-season training resumes or the pitcher begins play in a fall or winter league.

The Effect of Muscle Damage on Muscle Fatigue

A loss of strength and speed can occur not only through muscle damage but also muscle fatigue. Though these two pathways to power loss might seem to be independent, they are not. Each affects the other, a link that is critically important in pitching.

9. Diminishing Velocity

Muscle fatigue is defined as the short-term, reversible loss in the strength and speed of muscle contractions during sustained, repetitive activity. As was discussed in Chapter 4, the main fuel for the fastball is glycogen stored in the muscle, and depletion of glycogen is the primary cause of fatigue for a pitcher. The rate of glycogen depletion varies with muscle fiber type as well as the level of exertion. Fast-glycolytic fibers use glycogen much more rapidly than the other fiber types because anaerobic glycolysis is very inefficient. Slow-oxidative fibers produce 36 molecules of ATP from one molecule of glycogen, while the anaerobic process of the fast-glycolytic fibers produces only two molecules of ATP from one glycogen molecule. This inefficiency is somewhat like an automobile engine operating with the choke stuck in the "on" position, wasting fuel because of incomplete combustion due to lack of oxygen.

Damage to fast-glycolytic fibers can occur in the fatigued state because they become very stiff, entering a state of rigor when they can no longer generate ATP from glycogen.[16] That is, fatigued fibers can neither contract nor relax, and in this rigid state they are susceptible to damage when stretched in contractions that continue under the power of muscle fibers not yet fatigued. This effect may be minor and imperceptible when only a few muscle fibers are affected, but in unusually high pitch counts, it may affect a large portion of the fibers in a muscle, leading to DOMS, and the power loss that goes with it.

The Rechargeable Arm

With regard to energy storage, the anaerobic energy system of the fast-glycolytic fiber is much like a rechargeable electric battery. This type of fiber draws its energy from glycogen stored within the fiber. With intramuscular storage, the capacity for storing glycogen is limited; the stored glycogen is available only to the muscle fiber in which it is stored, and the stored energy is consumed much more rapidly than it is replenished. How long does it take to recharge the arm, to restore glycogen to the muscle fibers? No data on the glycogen levels of pitchers' arms are known to exist; however, muscle biopsies from other athletes show that glycogen is restored in one to two days after a typical workout.[17] As muscle damage becomes more extensive, however, restoration takes much longer.[18] The white blood cells are likely responsible for this longer restoration period. In the inflammation phase, macrophages sweep up the glycogen particles with other cell-damage debris. "Glycogen particles disappear," writes one researcher who documented this process by observing it under an electron microscope.[19] This macrophage-produced delay in glycogen restoration is one reason that baseball pitchers can pitch far fewer innings per week than softball pitchers. The underhand pitchers' routines are governed by the normal restoration period. Overhand pitchers' routines are governed by the longer restoration period required when fibers are damaged by eccentric contractions.

An unrepaired fiber gets recharged more slowly, and a partially recharged fiber is more likely to be damaged. One condition leads to the other, initiating a cycle of further damage and depletion. In this cycle, glycogen levels in the pitcher's arm and shoulder muscles remain low, and the recovery period necessary to end the cycle becomes longer. Muscles fatigue more quickly, possibly leading to damage to other parts of the kinetic chain, such as the anterior band of the ulnar collateral ligament.

A pitcher can terminate this cycle by resting the arm and shoulder, but rest is not always taken when needed. Pitchers tend to ignore or conceal soreness, pressing onward with NSAIDs and even working harder between starts to ensure job retention. The result is a condition well known in sports medicine — overtraining, repetitive overloading without sufficient recovery. As described in a study called "Overtraining Injuries in Athletic Populations," overtraining retards muscle repair.[20] Research has shown that overtraining causes satellite cells to decrease in number, resulting in the slower formation of new fibers and slower regeneration of damaged fibers.

One would expect the radar gun to be an aid in recognizing the condition of overtraining of pitchers. Loss of fastball velocity, however, is not the first symptom of pitchers' overtraining, because the effects of overtraining usually appear initially in the most heavily worked muscles of the kinetic chain, which are the flexor muscles of the pitcher's forearm. The first sign of overtraining in any sport is inconsistency. Frequent poor performances are indicative of insufficient recovery between performances, as discussed further in Chapter 13. Inconsistent group performance can be a sign of collective overtraining of a pitching staff. On the team level, institutionalized overtraining becomes apparent in short outings by starters, above-normal injury rate, lack of progress in development, or pitchers' finding greater success when dealt to other clubs. A culture of overtraining can yield a team pitching deficiency.

When the pernicious cycle of muscle damage and glycogen depletion leads to sustained poor performances, a pitcher requires a longer postseason recovery period to fully heal and re-strengthen the arm and shoulder. But pitchers who end a season poorly tend to view a late-season slump as a mandate to work harder, rather than to rest the arm and shoulder for two months. Pitching in fall or winter leagues after the season ends, a common practice in baseball, shortens or eliminates the rest period necessary for full recovery and can ultimately shorten a pitcher's career.

Differential Fatigue

Fatigue, the temporary power loss in muscles, produces the most profound effects as *differential* fatigue, a condition in which one muscle loses power before other muscles in the kinetic chain do so. Differential fatigue can be a problem in any sport, with the most common effect being increased injury potential. In pitching, differential fatigue is likely to affect performance when it involves muscles for which: (1) the workload is high, (2) the power-transfer rate is high, and (3) coordination is critical. The flexor muscles of the forearm meet these criteria. Pitching requires explosive power combined with surgical precision — and endurance. It demands fine control of the fingers at high speed, and when fatigue slows the muscles that control the hand and fingers, the precise coordination necessary for control and pitch movement is disrupted.

As indicated by electromyographic activity data shown in Chapter 4, the wrist flexors — the flexor carpi ulnaris and flexor carpi radialis — are two of the most active muscles in pitching, and the finger flexors, particularly the flexor digitorum superficialis, are also highly active. Differential fatigue involving these muscles of the forearm can affect control, movement, and velocity. These relatively small muscles are stressed and highly active during the 0.02- to 0.03-second launching phase of each pitch. They first are stretched during the cocking of the arm and then again in quick succession in the cocking of the wrist. Next, they contract rapidly, in about 0.01 seconds, during the flexion of the wrist and fingers. When these muscles begin to fatigue, some of their fast-glycolytic fibers cease to contract and relax because of their inefficient use of glycogen and variations in the distribution of glycogen among fibers. If the less-powerful oxidative metabolism takes up the load, the result is diminished power and diminished speed of contraction. If other prime movers, remain at full power, the hand and/or fingers lag behind, disrupting the critical timing of wrist flexion and finger flexion relative to forward arm rotation.

The effect of differential fatigue of the flexor muscles is similar to the effect of differential cooling of the arm. This temperature effect is probably responsible for some of the four-pitch walks that occasionally occur with the leadoff batter of an inning, particularly after the pitcher has sat for a long period. This involves the arm muscles cooling faster than the shoulder muscles between innings on the mound, and as such is more common in cool weather. Cooling of the muscle fibers slows contraction time substantially.[21] If the pitcher does not insulate the forearm to keep it warm between innings, the flexor muscles close to the skin, particularly the flexor digitorum superficialis, lose heat more rapidly than the rotator cuff muscles, which are deep in the shoulder and naturally better insulated. The result is that the wrist/finger flexion can lag behind the arm, causing a temporary deficiency of control until the pitcher fully warms up his forearm again.

Although the greatest effects involve fatigue of the forearm flexors and rotator cuff, differential fatigue can increase the potential for injury to other muscles involved in pitching, particularly the antagonists. Because the antagonist muscles contract eccentrically during each pitch, they are susceptible to muscle fiber damage and glycogen depletion. Since these muscles are not prime movers, this typically manifests itself as muscle soreness. Though this may not directly cause a power loss, it may produce an indirect effect on performance in the following movements:

- The stride: eccentric contraction of the groin and hamstring.
- Trunk flexion: eccentric contraction of the back muscles.
- Trunk rotation: eccentric contraction of the pitching-side oblique muscles.
- Elbow extension: eccentric contraction of the biceps.
- Wrist flexion: eccentric contraction of the extensor muscles of the forearm.

While injury-prevention measures for these muscles typically involve strength training, injury often occurs in pitchers who perform strength training during the same period as pitching or hard throwing, indicating

9. Diminishing Velocity

that the short-term effects of glycogen depletion and differential fatigue may lead to the injury.

The Effect of Muscle Fatigue on the Elbow

As was described in Chapter 8, the anterior band of the ulnar collateral ligament is a component of the power train likely to be affected in the chain of power loss. When fatigued, the muscles of the forearm share less of the load placed on the elbow. The result can be damage to the ligament fibrils, breaking or stretching that causes the band to become more compliant and reducing its power transmission and energy-storage-and-return capability. If the radar gun provides feedback to the pitcher that his velocity is diminished, he may respond by pitching with greater exertion, deriving more power from the subscapularis through faster arm rotation and placing even greater stress on the weakening ligament.

The anterior band marks the end of the chain of power loss. Injury to this band often marks the end of the season, or even a career. In summary, the chain of power loss that begins with eccentric contractions has five links:

- The strain of eccentric contractions in pitching produces muscle fiber damage routinely. The most significant effect of this damage occurs to the flexor muscles of the forearm and the muscles of the rotator cuff, which are eccentrically loaded on each end of the arm-acceleration phase.
- Excessive strain produced by maximal-effort pitches can cause muscle fiber damage greater than the body can repair within the recovery period allowed by a five-man pitching rotation. Training exertions involving the fast-glycolytic fibers between starts serve to lengthen this recovery period.
- Incomplete repair of muscle damage retards the full restoration of glycogen, the primary energy source of the fast-glycolytic fibers important in pitching. This causes differential fatigue to occur sooner on the mound and can lead to further muscle damage, initiating a cycle commonly referred to as overtraining.
- Taking NSAIDs to suppress inflammation and soreness delays the repair of damaged muscle fibers and may delay glycogen restoration.
- Pitching beyond the onset of fatigue of the forearm flexors and rotator cuff increases the stress on the connective tissue of the elbow and

shoulder joints, leading to power-transmission losses and the incremental failure of the connective tissue in both joints.

A sixth effect leading to power loss is one of omission — failing to regain, after the season ends, the muscle strength lost to the stresses of pitching 30 to 50 innings a month with less-than-complete recovery. The first step of re-strengthening is rest, allowing perhaps two months to repair cumulative damage to fast-glycolytic fibers accrued during the season. The second step is progressive-overload resistance training, strength training that applies and maximizes the benign effect of muscle damage caused by eccentric contractions. This effect is examined in the next chapter.

10

Building Strength and Velocity with the "Magic" of Eccentric Contractions

> *"Just watch your scrawny chest and shoulder muscles begin to swell, those spindly arms and legs of yours bulge, and your whole body start to feel alive, full of zip and go."*—Charles Atlas muscle-building ad from the 1940s

Strength training is a pitcher's sure path to greater velocity. Though better timing and coordination of the pitching movements can improve velocity, strength is the element of power from which the largest gains are possible. The velocity of the ball is determined by the amount of power transferred to it between stride-foot contact and release.

The baseball weighs only five ounces; consequently, there is a common perception that strength is of little importance in pitching. This perception, however, does not recognize the leverage of the rotator cuff and forearm flexor muscles and the relatively large internal resistances—i.e., the weight of the body's moving parts. Leverage trades force against movement and multiplies the ball's load on the arm and shoulder muscles. The weight of the arm also contributes substantially to the load these muscles bear.

Consider the subscapularis, on the forward side of the rotator cuff. The prime mover in the arm-acceleration phase, this muscle applies its force on the short side of a long lever. Its tendon wraps around the head of the humerus bone, so its moment arm for rotating the humerus is only about three-quarters of an inch, half the diameter of the bone at its head. The other end of the lever is the tip of the middle finger, roughly 18 inches from the humerus, which gives the final push to the ball as it is released. When the arm accelerates from the fully cocked position, leverage increases the load on the muscle by a factor of about 24 (18 divided by 0.75), not

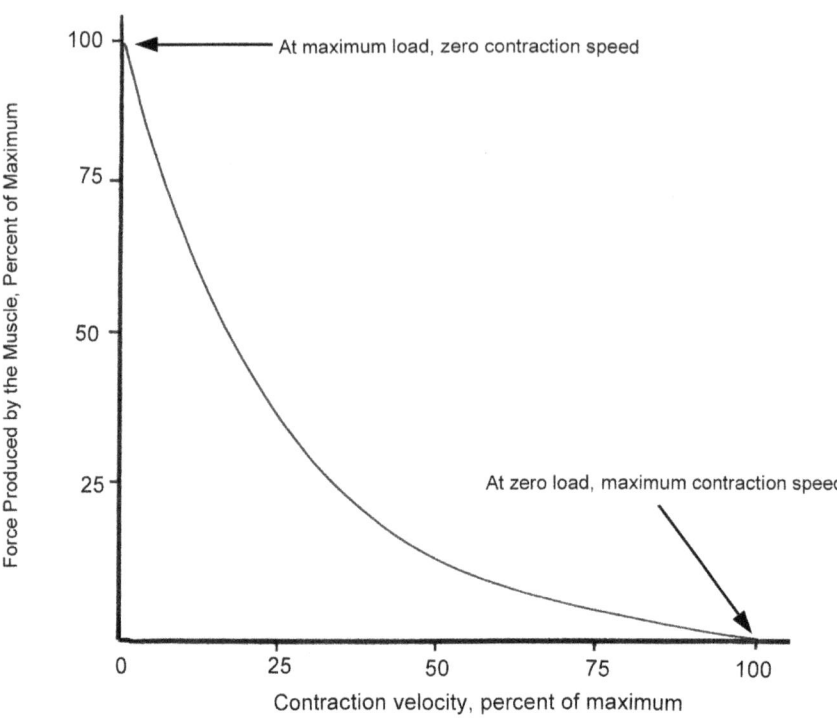

Figure 5: **Load versus Contraction Velocity of a Muscle.**

including the weight of the forearm and hand. It is this leverage that produces arm-rotation speeds as high as 10,000 degrees per second.

The subscapularis consequently bears a sizeable load with or without the baseball in hand, which means that it contracts at a speed less than its natural maximum contraction speed. This maximum speed can be measured by removing muscle fibers from the body and activating them with electrical impulses. With no resistance to contraction, this maximum speed is analogous to an automobile's tachometer reading when the accelerator pedal is floored with the transmission in neutral, engine running of course. Anchor one end of the muscle fiber and apply a small load on the other, and it contracts more slowly. Apply a larger load, and it slows down further. The relationship between the speed and load of a muscle fiber is *shown in Figure 5*, illustrating what seems intuitive — as the load on a motor (the muscle fiber) increases, the motor slows down. What this graph implies is that reducing the load on each fiber allows the muscle to contract faster.

10. Building Strength and Velocity

Walter Johnson's off-season strength work consisted of chopping wood, milking cows, and other farm work. He is shown working on his farm in 1938, after retiring from baseball (Library of Congress, LC-DIG-hec-24259).

With strength training, the muscle adapts by increasing the number of contracting protein filaments in each muscle fiber, enlarging the fiber diameter to achieve greater contraction force so that it contracts more rapidly under load. Even though a pitcher cannot increase the natural speed of his muscles, he can increase the speed of his fastball with strength training. A pitcher can demonstrate this to himself by throwing a lighter baseball, about half the weight of a standard ball, toward a radar gun. The velocity will be greater than his velocity with a standard five-ounce baseball, and it will tell him where along this ski-jump-shaped curve of *Figure 5* his personal speed-strength relationship of pitching lies. The velocity difference at release between a standard baseball and a two-ounce ball represents his potential for velocity improvement with strength training.

Off-season strength training for pitchers existed in an unfocused, unstructured form for most of the 20th century. Walter Johnson, for example, built the strength of his rotator cuff, wrist flexors, abdominals, obliques, triceps, latissimus dorsi, and other muscles by chopping wood in the off-season. He exercised his finger-flexors by milking cows. Bob Feller did similar work on the farm between seasons, including pitching hay and tossing hay bales. "Pitching hay, which many of us did in those years, helped us in pitching baseballs later," said Feller, looking back on his career after retirement.[1]

Along with calisthenics and rope-skipping, Feller included light weight lifting in his regimen throughout his career, even when he was aboard ship during World War II. But he stayed away from heavy weights and from progressive-overload weight training, fearful of the effects of having large muscles. "You need long, lean muscles. Therefore, you shouldn't use heavy weights," he wrote in 2001. "Once you become muscle-bound your ability to throw a baseball if you're a pitcher, or to hit a baseball if you're are a hitter, diminishes."[2]

Feller's belief about excessive muscularity was shown to be suspect by an opinion he offered about Jackie Robinson in 1946. During Feller's postseason barnstorming tour that autumn, a reporter asked him if he thought Robinson, one of the players on the tour, would be able to hit major league pitching. Robinson had just completed a season with the AAA Montreal Royals and would make his historic ascent to the Brooklyn Dodgers the following year. Feller's reply, published in *The Los Angeles Times*, was that Robinson might be too muscle-bound to hit the fastball pitchers of the American League.[3] Robinson had starred in football, basketball, and track while at UCLA, but had a batting average of just .097 in his only season with the varsity baseball team. Feller's judgment might have been based on a correlation between Robinson's muscularity and his collegiate batting average, but it was wildly off the mark. Three years later, Robinson was voted the National League's Most Valuable Player after leading the league with a .342 batting average.

10. Building Strength and Velocity

Apprehension about big muscles wasn't limited to Bob Feller. It was baseball's collective belief that pitchers should have loose muscles, a condition not formally defined by medical science but probably the opposite of toned muscles. Muscle tone is the continuous, passive, partial contraction of muscles, a tightness produced by unconscious nerve impulses while resting. Whatever the focus of the muscularity concern, it was probably derived from images of body-building pioneers like Angelo Siciliano. Once a bullied, 97-pound weakling, Siciliano began displaying his muscular physique in body-building advertisements on the back cover of comic books in the 1940s under the name of Charles Atlas. After transforming his body with the "dynamic tension" exercise program he devised, he promoted himself as the world's most perfectly developed man. His program, which required "no apparatus, pills, or diet," included isometric exercises and indeed succeeded in increasing strength and muscle size. He wasn't a star in any competitive sport, so he probably contributed to the perception that large and prominent muscles were superfluous, suitable for display on the beach but not for practical application on athletic fields.

It took several decades to change baseball's outlook, but during the 1960s and '70s the value of weight lifting finally began to be recognized. One of the pioneers was Nolan Ryan. In 1972, his first year with the Angels, he began his own weight-training program on a little-used 12-station Universal Gym beneath Anaheim Stadium. He considers this personal initiative a transitional point in his career. He did not cause a rush of pitchers into weight lifting; rather, he became part of a shift in baseball's perception of strength training.

"When I signed back in 1965, the standard approach to training for pitching was quite simple: just throw off a mound, do some sprints, and you're all set," wrote Ryan in his 1991 book about strength training. "In those days, of course, it was unheard of for a pitcher to train with weights. There was a great fear among old-line baseball people then that weight-lifting would make you muscle-bound."[4]

The term muscle-bound didn't merely imply that large marquee muscles were without benefit. It implied that they were a detriment. To be sure, arm biceps of 22-inch circumference like those of Arnold Schwarzenegger can adversely affect pitching, but not merely by limiting one's range of motion. The biceps is not a prime mover of pitching; it is the antagonist in the elbow-extension movement. So, if there is a problem in being muscle-bound, it is not in having too much strength. It is in having too much strength in the wrong muscles.

The Science of the Fastball

The muscles a pitcher needs to strengthen are the prime movers in the kinetic chain of pitching. Listed in priority, these are the:

- Wrist flexors and finger flexors of the forearm.
- Subscapularis of the rotator cuff.
- Obliques of the torso.
- Abdominals and glutes.
- Leg muscles.

This ranking coincides with the sequence — in reverse — of the kinetic chain diagrammed *in Figure 6*. As noted in Chapter 4, the power transfer rate is higher for the muscles listed higher in the ranking. That is, the leg muscles at the beginning of the chain transmit much less energy to the ball than they exert in moving the body and its limbs. As a result, the best way to increase fastball velocity is to build strength toward the end of the kinetic chain. Relative to the muscles at the beginning of the chain, these have:

- A higher rate of power transfer to the ball.
- Greater leverage to amplify speed, as with an automobile transmission operating in high gear.
- A higher activity level during a pitch.
- Smaller size and less power.

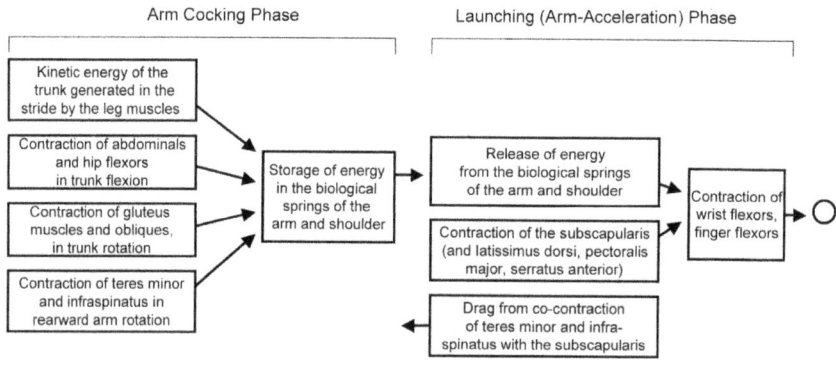

Figure 6: **Flow of Energy from Muscles to the Ball in the Kinetic Chain of Pitching. Note that a portion of the energy from the trunk bypasses energy storage if trunk flexion or trunk rotation is not fully completed by the time the arm is fully cocked.**

10. Building Strength and Velocity

Consequently, it is most beneficial for a pitcher to increase the strength of his wrist- and finger-flexors and his subscapularis. The flexors and the subscapularis have short fiber lengths, averaging about 2½ inches, suitable for accelerating the short side of the lever to achieve high rotational velocities of the arm and hand. With its short fiber lengths, the subscapularis has, relative to its weight, a large cross-section area. Because it is hidden behind the ribcage, it is typically overlooked and does not present visual feedback about the results of strength training. No one has ever gawked at a super-sized subscapularis on the beach.

A muscle becomes stronger as it develops a larger cross-section area. In doing so, it develops greater mass, placing additional force generators in parallel. Rather than adding new muscle fibers, strengthening means adding new fibrils within the fibers or new filaments within the fibrils.

As the sport of baseball began to allay its cultural fear of being musclebound, players appropriated two items from the tool kit of the bodybuilding industry: (1) progressive-overload weight lifting and (2) anabolic steroids — the former being beneficial to players, the latter being ultimately detrimental to players and to the sport. These two tools are not a packaged pair, contrary to what may be a popular perception. Each one causes the body to markedly increase the synthesis of protein, resulting in muscle growth. With patience and a methodical approach, body-builders and weight-lifters develop large, strong muscles without anabolic steroids. They do so by applying progressive overload, a principle pioneered about 540 B.C. by six-time Olympic wrestling champion Milo of Croton.

The story of Milo, a man known for superhuman strength, illustrates the benefits of a patient, methodical progressive-overload weight-lifting program. Young Milo began building his strength by picking up a newborn calf, placing it on his shoulders, and carrying it about a mile each day. As the calf grew larger, it subjected Milo to gradually heavier loads over a period of many months. Details of his bovine-transport program may have been embellished over the centuries, but the story seems credible. A calf may weigh 80 to 100 pounds at birth and may gain one to two pounds per day on average. This rate of progression isn't far from that of modern-day weight-lifters' dead-lifts and squats, which employ the large muscles of the legs, hips, and back. Aside from the steadily increasing difficulty of gripping the animal to lift him, Milo's progressive-overload regimen differed in two ways from that of modern lifters. First, he apparently repeated his routine every day, stressing the same muscles daily, not on every other day per conventional weight lifting practice. Second, his single exercise lacked muscle specificity; it placed too much strain on some muscles and not enough on others. This contrasts with modern lifters who use barbells, dumbbells, and pulley machines that can be adjusted in one- to two-pound increments over a range of weight, each appropriate to a specific muscle or muscle group, large or small. Milo's regimen was obviously inappropriate for baseball players, as was his diet. He was said to have eaten 20 pounds of meat and 20 pounds of bread each day, a diet that might have been qualitatively sound — assuming he also ate some fruits and vegetables — but excessive. Strength training requires protein, the building block for muscle tissue, but not 20 pounds of it daily. And walking a mile with a 1,000-pound load each day would surely deplete glycogen stores from the muscles of Milo's legs, requiring more than 24 hours for complete restoration, even with the abundance of carbohydrates supplied by the bread.

Muscle strengthening is a complex process involving satellite cells and growth factors that reside in the muscle fibers, and white blood cells and hormones supplied through the blood. One important factor to Milo's success was probably higher-than-normal levels of testosterone, a hormone essential to muscle growth. A hormone is a chemical messenger that carries a signal from one cell to another. If the nervous system can be characterized as the hard-wired communications network of the body, hormones are the transmissions of its cell-phone system. The cellular transmissions have a delay in producing a response, but the responses are typically prolonged. Testosterone is a male sex hormone whose main effect, its androgenic effect, is promoting growth and developing male organs and masculine characteristics such as a deep voice and body hair. Testosterone also has an anabolic effect, which is to help muscle and bone tissue grow by increasing the rate of protein synthesis. Testosterone is the "original" anabolic steroid, a term commonly applied to many of the man-made hormonal substances similar to testosterone. The Anabolic Steroid Control Act that the U.S. Congress passed into law in 2004 lists 59 different substances as anabolic steroids — including synthetic testosterone — and defines them as controlled substances. Anabolic steroids have many beneficial medical uses; however, their use in enhancing sports performance typically results in blood concentrations well above natural levels, and these concentrations poorly controlled over time can produce serious side effects.

Hormones other than testosterone also play a major role in building muscle tissue. They signal the satellite cells that lie dormant on the muscle fibers to activate, multiply, migrate to the site of muscle damage, and fuse together. Growth factors, which include hormones secreted by the muscle fibers, instruct the satellite cells to divide and take on characteristics different from the original satellite cell.

Testosterone has been used by sprinters to build leg strength and consequently to improve sprint speed. After Canadian sprinter Ben Johnson won the 1988 Olympic 100-meter dash in world record time, his medal was taken away and his record deleted when tests showed that he had taken stanozolol, an anabolic steroid. The most obvious effects of steroids in baseball are the strength gains that produce game-changing results by extending long fly-outs into home runs. This effect has been obvious in hitters, and steroid effects are substantial but less obvious in pitchers. Anabolic steroids not only help pitchers become stronger quickly, they hasten the repair of the muscle damage that occurs routinely in pitching.

Magical Results from Progressive Overload Strength Training

It is not unusual for the word "magic" to appear in commercial advertisements for muscle building and strength training. Hyperbolic claims can be expected regarding dietary supplements, growth stimulants, or revolutionary training programs. It *is* striking, however, to find the word "magic" used on the pages of *Skeletal Muscle Structure, Function, and Plasticity*, a textbook on the science of rehabilitation written by a noted research scientist, Dr. Richard L. Lieber.

"The idea that eccentric muscle contractions are 'magic' is an important concept in exercise prescription," writes Lieber. "If the ultimate goal of an exercise intervention is to improve muscle strength, at the muscle tissue level the evidence suggests that progressive overload (including eccentric muscle actions) should be used. Eccentric contractions ... provide a potent stimulus to increase muscle strength. This is sort of a two-edged sword: eccentric contractions can not only produce strengthening but also injure the muscle."[5]

Lieber's use of the word magic is powerful in view of his prominence in the science of muscle rehabilitation. It illuminates the scientific basis of a core principle sometimes overlooked by practitioners of strength training—that the stimulus for muscle growth is muscle damage, a stimulus best applied with progressive overload training involving eccentric contractions. The two-edged sword analogy is an important one. In order to achieve strengthening, muscle damage must be carefully handled.

The human body repairs muscle damage routinely, whether it is caused by overload or by trauma such as a cut or contusion. The healing process, which is continuous in response to minor damage, involves regeneration of partially damaged muscle fibers. Research indicates that, in order to be regenerated, remnants of the original fibers must exist and macrophages must participate in the process so as to stimulate the satellite cells. Damage initiates cell-signaling, which in turn activates the satellite cells, leading to repair, growth, and overcompensation. Minor damage does this without a long delay imposed by DOMS; the regeneration process can begin within hours.[6] The period during which satellite cells become activated and multiply lasts up to 48 hours after the damage to muscle fibers has occurred.[7] Yet the more muscle fibers damaged, the greater the delay, which means that the key to achieving benign damage is to limit the debris cleanup work the big-eater white blood cells have to do. Thus it is important to minimize inflammation, not by using NSAIDs, but by subjecting the muscle fibers to a limited amount of strain energy.

This implies that there is a narrow path to optimal strengthening, one that lies between two broad avenues leading to a loss of muscle strength — under-use and overuse. Under-use is the gradual use-it-or-lose-it dissipation of muscle mass that occurs without regular exercise. Overuse is most commonly seen in endurance sports such as marathon running. Damage varies with the intensity of the exercise, but not in a linear way; doubling a workout does not double the benefit and may yield no benefit at all without additional recovery time. Because the relationship is non-linear, there exists a point of optimal intensity, a level of strain that maximizes muscle growth within the time and the body's resources available for repair. This point between overuse and under-use is a region on a curve that represents the narrow path to strength gain, the region of optimal, benign damage.

Criteria for Pitchers' Maximum Strength Gains

These principles lead to seven criteria for optimal strength training. To produce the maximum stimulus for muscle growth and the maximum benefit to a pitcher, strength-training exercises must:

- Involve eccentric contraction of the muscles used in pitching.
- Recruit the same muscle motor units used in pitching.
- Involve sufficient load to activate the fast-glycolytic fibers of these muscles.
- Focus overload strain specifically on each of the muscles used in pitching.
- Provide a means of regulating the strain to the realm of benign damage.
- Provide a means of incrementally increasing the strain at a rate that matches the strength gains.
- Provide adequate time for muscle repair and glycogen restoration between bouts of exercise.

Among the many different approaches available to the pitcher for building strength and velocity, no single exercise meets all these criteria. Optimal strengthening of the muscles used in pitching requires a combination of multiple exercises properly phased. There are several different exercises for building strength in pitchers, each with different advantages and disadvantages.

Long-Toss and Max-Effort Pitching. Max-effort pitching meets the first four criteria, but it lacks a means of controlling the overload and increasing it over time to provide a near-constant stimulus for growth. Strength and velocity gains consequently cease once there is no longer an increasing overload. Long-toss partially overcomes this limitation. By establishing a throwing distance for each workout, for example 120 feet, long-toss provides a means of controlling and gradually increasing the strain. At shorter distances, however, the strain on the fast-glycolytic fibers may be below the optimal range. Pitching and long-toss involve eccentric contractions for all the pitching prime movers except the drive leg of the stride. The eccentric contraction occurs in the opposite leg, the forward leg, when it plants and stops the linear movement. Max-effort throwing ensures that the fast-glycolytic fibers are activated, which may not be the case when playing catch or pitching batting practice at moderate speed. This builds strength primarily in the forearm and shoulder, where the power-transfer rate and the muscle activation is highest. However, it provides little strengthening benefit to the cocking muscles. Worse, it can rapidly deplete glycogen from the arm and shoulder, a detriment if done extensively during the season. Both long-toss and max effort bullpens can increase injury potential during the season if there is in adequate time for repair of muscle damage before or after pitching performances.

Throwing Balls of Various Weights. Varying the weight of what's being thrown, an approach that was used in the former Soviet Union for training javelin throwers, produces varying loads on the muscles of the arm and shoulder. It has been found to increase fastball velocity. A scientific review article entitled "Effects of Throwing Overweight and Underweight Baseballs on Throwing Velocity and Accuracy" published in 2000 supports training with overweight baseballs, concluding that a regimen of throwing heavier and lighter baseballs produces significant improvement in velocity.[8] The review evaluated three studies of duration between six and 12 weeks, with three sessions per week of varying intensity. Overweight balls ranged in weight from 5.25 to 17 ounces. Such throwing of course involves eccentric contractions of the arm and shoulder muscles, and it is likely to recruit the same motor units used in pitching the five-ounce baseball until subtle changes in mechanics occur with increases in ball weight. The methods applied in these studies have three shortcomings relative to the criteria for optimal strength gains. First, they do not provide a means of incrementally and continuously increasing the strain at a rate matching strength gains, and the means of regulating the strain to the realm of benign damage is limited. In addition, they do not focus significant, controlled overload on each prime mover. Findly, because the weight differences among the balls typically used are small, the effects on the muscles in the cocking phase of the pitch—the legs, abdominals, obliques, and glutes—are probably negligible.

Exercises with Elastic Bands. Popular for its convenience, the use of elastic bands allows the pitcher to closely duplicate the arm motion from the standing position while applying resistance. Use of bands, however, typically lacks a rigorous means of steadily increasing the load. Resistance can be increased by stretching the band further; however, there is typically no guidance about regulating the resistance.

Calisthenics. Exercises that apply one's own body weight or strength to produce resistance have the shortcoming that body weight cannot be easily varied incrementally to allow progressive overload. Body weight also cannot be easily varied downward to ensure a starting resistance within the range of benign strain. Typically, progression is a matter of increasing repetitions rather than resistance, which does not allow similar control or produce the same stimulus for growth as a steadily increasing load.

Plyometrics. Plyometrics, exercises involving high-speed lengthening

10. Building Strength and Velocity

and shortening of the muscles, produce very rapid transition between eccentric and concentric muscle loading during what is referred to as the stretch-shortening cycles. Because of the rapid movement, plyometrics induce greater strain on muscle fibers than calisthenics by increasing the momentum available at the eccentric-to-concentric switch. With greater strain, there is potentially greater stimulus for strengthening than with calisthenics; however, plyometrics lack controls for limiting the strain and a means of incrementally increasing it over time. There are plyometric progression models in which loading increases from minimal to high in stages over a period of years as a young athlete matures. These, however, increase loading too infrequently to optimize the gains.

Physical Labor. Bob Feller performed physical labor in his teen years on the farm, but likely derived more strength benefits for the pitching muscles from chin-ups, push-ups, and throwing the baseball on his field of dreams. Physical labor is the least disciplined approach to strength building because it does not focus on and recruit the same muscle motor units or involve the same eccentric contractions as pitching. In addition, it provides no means of regulating the strain to the realm of benign damage or increasing the strain incrementally over time. When one works five days per week at the same routine, there is likely to be inadequate time for muscle repair and restoration of glycogen to the most heavily worked muscles.

Weight lifting. Weight lifting fulfills all the criteria for optimal strength gains if the set of exercises duplicates each of the pitching movements closely enough to recruit the same muscle motor units, and if it involves resistance great enough to limit the number of repetitions. Training with light weights falls short on two criteria: activating fast-glycolytic fibers and producing enough strain for benign muscle damage. Conventional progressive-overload weight-lifting methods, however, include several practical controls on the magnitude, repetitive quantity, and incremental increases of strain, controls that do not typically exist in other exercises.

These controls yield a reliable approach to increasing the physiologic cross-section area of pitching's prime movers to produce faster contractions in each movement of the kinetic chain. Without such controls, strengthening exercises tend to produce limited gains, quickly reaching a plateau in strength and velocity. The controls allow the pitcher to find the zone of benign damage with gradual, methodical increases in load over weeks and months while keeping the number of repetitions nearly constant.

- **Controlling the Strain of Eccentric Contractions.** The key word in progressive-overload training is strain. Force produces strain, a stretching of the muscle fibers during eccentric contractions. It is not the large force of the barbell that produces the stimulus for muscle growth; it is the amount of strain the large force produces in the muscle fibers.[9] Muscle tissue must be subjected to this strain in order to begin the biochemical steps for adaptive growth.[10] The strain and subsequent damage must be limited to a benign amount, and the practical means of regulating strain is to limit the resistance applied in eccentric contractions (lowering the weight) to the resistance applied in concentric contractions (lifting the weight). Each repetition involves lifting and lowering, and if the weight is too heavy to lift, it is too heavy to produce the right amount of strain during the eccentric contraction.

- **Controlling the Progression of Overload.** This is the key to continuous improvement in strength. To maintain the same level of strain as the muscle becomes stronger, the weight must be increased, ideally at the same rate at which the muscle strengthens. Doing so may involve increasing the weight perhaps 10 pounds per week in performing squats or only one pound per week in wrist curls. The rate of increase is governed by the rate of strengthening and is defined by the ease — determined by lactic acid accumulation — with which the same number of repetitions can be performed. Weight increments as small as a pound can provide a near-constant strain and consequently a near-constant rate of damage as the muscle strengthens.

- **Controlling the Number of Repetitions.** Achieving maximum strength gains requires lifting weights heavy enough to produce strain in the muscle fibers. In progressive-overload weight lifting, the repetitions are kept to a small number, with the conventional approach being three sets of 10 or fewer repetitions for each muscle or muscle group in each workout. The weight cannot be too heavy to allow completion of the repetitions before resting one to two minutes for lactic acid clearance. Lactic acid temporarily interrupts proper muscle function and, by doing so, defines the limit on repetitions in the set. Lactic acid accumulates at a rate varying with the work rate, i.e., the amount of weight lifted and the distance the weight is lifted, cumulatively over the repetitions. As the weight increases, lactic acid production increases proportionately if the repetitions are completed in the same amount of time.

- **Focusing Controlled Strain on Prime Movers.** With regard to specificity, weight-lifting lies at the opposite end of the spectrum from farm work. It allows the strain to be focused and controlled on the prime movers of pitching, which would be over-trained or under-trained with other types of exercise. The use of dumbbells, barbells, or weight-and-pulley machines allows for precise loading of the prime movers with the optimum resistance and progression.

- **Allowing Adequate Time for Muscle Repair.** In weight lifting, the time allowed for muscle repair and regeneration is controlled by convention, with a recovery period of at least 48 hours in the typical every-other-day weight-lifting routine. This convention works well, apparently matched to the amount of muscle damage that occurs in a normal weight-lifting workout. Perturbations in the routine that result in muscle soreness may indicate the need for a longer recovery period. A person may have diminished ability to recover as he grows older, and consequently may require 72 hours between weight lifting workouts involving the same muscles or muscle groups.

Strengthening the Pitcher's Hidden Powerhouse, the Subscapularis

The subscapularis is the rotator cuff muscle that directly drives the fastest movement of pitching, forward arm rotation, accelerating the forearm to rotational velocities of up to 10,000 degrees per second after a kick-start from the elastic-strain energy stored during arm cocking. A welterweight muscle that typically weighs about as much as a standard baseball, the subscapularis gets the least individual attention in strength training because it is hidden behind the rib cage. It is one of the muscles that articulate and stabilize the complex joint of the shoulder. You can't put a tape measure on the subscapularis or flex it in the mirror to check whether it is growing stronger. Consequently, its strength training can be characterized as group training in the dark — exercises that affect several muscles at once, each of a different size, configuration, and role, without individual feedback on the effectiveness of the exercise.

The chin-up is the long-enduring standard for strengthening the muscles of the rotator cuff, including the subscapularis. Some physical therapists prescribe "chin-ups, chin-ups, and more chin-ups," for doing so. But the chin-up has its shortcomings in specificity, strain control, and incremental increases. Its specificity is roughly on par with Milo's calf-carrying, being imprecise in duplicating the pitching motion and in recruiting the same muscle motor units used in pitching. Triangular in shape, the subscapularis has longer muscle fibers on the side away from the torso, which allows it to accommodate elevating the humerus when raising the arms above the shoulder. Beginning with the arms elevated, the chin-up involves the muscles of both sides of the rotator cuff contracting together rather than in sequence. These muscles work to pull the humerus downward to a horizontal position. In doing this, the outer third of the subscapularis, because it is farther from the shoulder joint and consequently has better leverage, does more of the work than the inner portion, where the muscle fibers are shorter. During a pitch, however, it is the inner portion that does more of the work of rotating the humerus. This is apparent in the electromyographic activity data cited in Chapter 4. The outer third of the subscapularis averages 56 percent activity during the arm-acceleration phase, while the inner third averages 115 percent.

Strain on the rotator cuff during chin-ups can vary with the arm positions and hand orientation. Due to its obscurity and wide range of motion, the rotator cuff can be easily under-trained. But it can also be very easily over-trained, making its zone of benign damage more elusive than those of other muscles. A resistance exercise involving two or more muscles of varying size, leverage, and load can produce excessive localized strain and differential fatigue, both of which increase the potential for overtraining and injury. When a muscle is subjected to strain in multiple exercises of a workout, this potential increases further. And when the starting point of the exercise is at or near the single-repetition maximum — because the body weight cannot be adjusted downward — excessive muscle damage, which shows up as delayed-onset soreness, becomes more likely. Such is the case with the rotator cuff and chin-ups or pull-ups.

One variation referred to as the subscapularis pull-up is particularly stressful for this important pitching muscle. It involves pushing away from the bar when starting the descent from the bar. This exercise is said to guarantee soreness, indicating it is likely to result in excessive strain. In performing other conventional strength exercises involving the shoulder — bench presses, pull-downs, pullovers — the rotator cuff is subjected to strain. Consequently, controlling the total strain energy to the rotator-cuff muscles is extremely difficult. Overtraining becomes apparent in the frequency of rotator cuff injuries, which often affect weight-lifters. This is not to say that chin-ups are undesirable for rotator cuff strengthening, but that the chin-up for pitchers is a double-edged sword at its sharpest, with strong potential to yield poor results or injury when performed with inadequate controls to limit the amount of strain and the use of other exercises involving the shoulder within the recovery period of pitching or training.

The issue of duplicating the pitching movement for precise motor-unit recruitment with weight lifting favors pullovers performed lying down, with a dumbbell. As a weight-lifting exercise, pullovers provide control over strain and accommodate incremental increases. But as noted above, the benefit of the pullover can be easily lost if other exercises such as pulldowns and pull-ups are also part of the training routine.

Strengthening the Wrist- and Finger-Flexors

In contrast to the four muscles of the rotator cuff, which are obscure, the four flexors of the wrist and fingers are prominent, with the muscles and tendons on visual display. Gains in muscle size can be estimated with a tape measure around the forearm. Progressive-overload weight training is easily applied to the wrist and finger flexors with wrist curls around a horizontal axis, usually performed with dumbbells of adjustable weight. An offset dumbbell can also be used to strengthen the flexor carpi ulnaris along the curveball axis, but this tends to work the muscle doubly because the flexor carpi ulnaris is also worked in the fastball (horizontal) axis. Like the rotator cuff, the forearm flexors become involved in several different weight lifting exercises — and in calisthenics like pull-ups and chin-ups — because they supply the force to grip and hold the bar. The effect of this extra duty is likely to become apparent in glycogen depletion, more so than muscle damage, because the grip is isometric. Still, the effect can be significant, particularly if weight lifting is done during the season. Weight lifting on days opposite throwing days can hasten fatigue of the forearm flexors and slow the repair of the muscle fibers affected by both weight lifting and throwing.

Strengthening the Obliques and Glutes

The strength and speed of these muscles determine the velocity of the trunk-and-shoulder rotation movement, which involves rotating the pelvis, trunk, and shoulder. This sequential rotation, along with trunk flexion, cocks the arm. The gluteus minimus and gluteus medius initiate this rotational movement at stride foot contact by turning the pelvis rapidly toward home plate. Then the obliques twist the trunk and shoulders toward home plate. The most common methods of strengthening the obliques involve calisthenics and twisting the trunk against the resistance of elastic bands or medicine balls held at arm's length. Neither approach supports incremental increases in resistance. To apply progressive-overload to the obliques requires a rotary torso machine, which presents an adjustable resistance to rotation with the pitcher in the sitting position. Common methods for strengthening the glutes are similar but less precise, with a multi-hip machine providing an incrementally increasing load.

Strengthening the Abdominals

Sit-ups, crunches, and leg lifts have long been used to strengthen the abdominal muscles. These have the same shortcomings as other calisthenics, primarily that they do not usually allow progressive overload. Weights can be held to increase the load, but typically this is not done in a progressive manner. There are, however, many types of weight machines with the capability to incrementally increase resistance for abdominal strengthening.

Strengthening the Legs

Nolan Ryan's initial weight routine in 1972 included bench presses, military presses, leg extensions and other exercises to build leg strength. The leg muscles can also be strengthened with sprinting and hill-running, but they are not strengthened significantly in throwing or jogging. Consequently, weight training is ideal for the legs, and large gains in size and strength can be achieved with squats and toe-raises. Strength training of the legs ultimately provides more power to cock the arm, benefiting a pitcher who has a strong, stiffly elastic ulnar collateral ligament to transmit the power from the trunk to the arm. Strengthening the legs also produces greater sprint speed.

Strengthening the Triceps

The strength of the triceps muscle of the arm affects velocity indirectly. Like the rotator cuff and the forearm flexor muscles, the triceps works against a high leverage, so strength gains can increase the speed of elbow extension. Greater speed allows the elbow extension to occur later, giving the ball a longer ride on longer moment arm during the arm's high-speed rotation. The triceps curl, a conventional weight-lifting exercise, is likely to recruit the same muscle motor units that are used in pitching, so this exercise meets the criteria for progressive-overload training.

Strengthening the Latissimus Dorsi

Latissimus dorsi is the Latin term for the widest muscle of the back. This muscle has very high activity in the arm-acceleration phase of a pitch, with average electromyographic readings of 88 percent recorded in the study cited in Chapter 4. The pull-down using a weight machine is the exercise of choice for strengthening the latissimus dorsi. This exercise, however, has the same drawbacks as the pull-up and chin-up: it works the muscles of the rotator cuff along with the latissimus dorsi. If performed with heavy weights and with other exercises that work the muscles of the rotator cuff, such as the pull-over, it can produce the adverse effects of overtraining in those muscles.

Off-Season Versus In-Season Strength Training

Many athletes perform strength training concurrently, overlapping the recovery period with the primary activities of the season. Concurrent weight lifting is problematic, however, with regard to muscle repair and glycogen restoration. Concurrent training increases the difficulty of finding the range of benign damage, the middle of three zones of training intensity. The first zone is one of too little damage, in which strength neither increases nor decreases significantly. The second zone is one of optimal damage, in which strength increases. In the third, too much damage occurs and strength diminishes because there is insufficient time for the body to repair the damage. Even in periods when strength training is the only exercise, the zone of optimal damage can be elusive, because a perceptible gain in strength can take weeks or months to manifest itself. A strength gain is the ideal feedback from a training regimen, but because strength accrues slowly, the pitcher may be unable to perceive a difference between the three zones of intensity. All appear to be equally effective—or ineffective—in the short term, making it difficult to achieve benign damage. During the season, pitchers usually dwell in the zone of excessive damage due to the stresses of pitching alone, particularly with max-effort pitching. Damage is based on total strain energy applied during the cycle of exercise and recovery—usually two to seven days in length—so all strain-producing exertions during this period contribute to cumulative damage. Lifting weights heavy enough to provide strengthening benefits adds substantial strain and damage and must be counted along with other strain producers in the pitcher's routine, such as long-toss and bullpens, making the pitcher even less likely to dwell in the zone of optimal damage during the season. In-season training that activates the fast-glycolytic fibers in the pitching prime movers tips the scale away from benign damage.

A pitcher may feel compelled to continue strength training during the season in the belief that strength will diminish without it. Strength loss can indeed occur during the season, but it is commonly the result of over-use rather than under-use. Muscle fibers synthesize protein continuously to replace proteins as they degrade. The rate of synthesis slows during extended periods of muscle inactivity, causing the muscles to become smaller. Referred to as disuse atrophy, this occurs in muscle with prolonged reduction in use, for example when a broken leg is placed in a cast for six weeks.[11] The activity of the muscle sustains the rate of synthesis, which means that a deficiency of activity for the muscles of the kinetic chain of pitching is unlikely to occur during the season. As discussed in Chapter 9, strength loss during the season is likely to be the result of inadequate recovery between outings, with damage accumulating through the end of the season. If a pitcher does not reverse the resulting strength loss with an off-season strength-building program and instead pitches in a fall and or winter league, he may experience a season-to-season loss of velocity.

The solution to the dilemma of excessive muscle damage is periodization, performing strength training before and after the season. Periodization breaks the training into segments, time-shifting the muscle-damaging exercises to ensure adequate recovery. Periodization balances training intensity over a year-long cycle and thereby prevents overtraining during the season and under-training during the off-season.

The second detrimental effect of in-season strength training is that it contributes to the depletion of glycogen, which can lead to a temporary loss of power from the muscles bearing the heaviest load in the kinetic chain of pitching. The effect on glycogen levels, further discussed in Chap-

10. Building Strength and Velocity

ter 12, is substantial. One experiment in which muscle biopsies were taken from weight-lifters found that three sets of 10 repetitions of elbow-flexion curls produced a 25 percent reduction in bicep muscle glycogen.[12] A similar percentage reduction in forearm flexor muscles' glycogen would be expected with wrist curls of similar intensity, that is, using a similar percentage of single-repetition maximum weight). The reason this effect is large is that progressive-overload weight training involves relatively heavy weights, which means relatively large amounts of work (work is weight times distance lifted times number of repetitions) and relatively large expenditures of the energy stored in the muscle performing the work. A workout with lighter weights, light dumbbells for example, would deplete less glycogen with the same number of repetitions. Light weights with few repetitions is indeed less detrimental, but it is also less beneficial. Light weights may fail to activate the fast-glycolytic fibers and to produce the strain necessary to achieve strengthening.

When a personal trainer stands next to a protégé struggling to complete a final weight lifting repetition and urges, "One more rep! You can do it," the trainer is conveying the message, "A little more damage, a little more damage!" The trainer, of course, has no means of knowing how much damage has been accrued, how much more would be optimal, how much more would be too much, and whether there will be soreness the following day. This is the essential problem in all strength-training programs—finding the range of benign muscle damage. The controls of progressive-overload weight training, however, can keep a pitcher from entering the zone of excessive damage. Unfortunately, misconceptions can override the best of controls, reducing weight lifting workouts to uncontrolled, iron-slinging exercises of testosterone-induced exuberance. A common misconception is that more is better, that one additional set of repetitions will provide more benefit. Strength building in many sports is hindered by this perception, which leads to excessive damage and requires a longer recovery period than is available. The more-is-better culture can ultimately lead to smaller strength gains, no strength gains, or even strength loss.

It is often easier to over-train than to under-train. Overtraining through workouts that are too frequent and/or too intense prevents the overcompensation that must occur for the muscle to become stronger. The process that produces muscle growth is a remarkable one, but it has little tolerance for overtraining. Overtraining can occur in the regulated conditions of weight lifting if pitching or high-intensity throwing is done between weight lifting workouts. Over-training can occur when the athlete performs extra sets or repetitions or increases the load too rapidly. The tendency to over-train is often driven by culture, and the culture in many sports is one of impatience, of trying to become stronger quickly. Bodybuilders and competitive weight-lifters, the developers of effective strength-building techniques, understand the process and the patience it requires. One noted body-builder described the optimal weight-lifting process as *coaxing* the muscles to accept the progressive overload in small, easily handled increments rather than forcing them.[13]

Long-Term Investment

Bob Feller once wrote: "In the game of baseball, when players get muscle-bound, they get injured."[14] Feller, who possessed and readily shared strong opinions about many things, wasn't always right. Regarding this assertion, he possessed neither empirical data nor criteria for muscle-bound baseball players. His perception was that, "it is not advantageous to become so muscular that you can't bend your elbow back far enough to give your ear a gentle tug." Whatever the criterion, there have been so few baseball players who could be considered muscle-bound that any conclusion about their injury rate is mere speculation. Biceps were the focus of Feller's disapproval, but baseball players don't seek to build big biceps. The biceps are not prime movers in pitching, hitting, fielding, or base-running. Biceps enlargement is an unavoidable result of chin-ups, which strengthen the shoulder. The biceps are antagonists in baseball and like other antagonists such as the hamstring, groin, and back muscles, they can cause pain for a pitcher and become injured if overworked.

Feller was half right about weight lifting's effect on injury. The risk does not come from being muscle-bound; rather, it is lifting weights during the season that can lead to injury. What he probably observed from his perspective of seven decades around major-league baseball was that when players lift weights, they increase their potential for injury. This is true in many sports, and it is true in baseball. Lifting weights heavy enough to produce strength gains while recovering from a strenuous outing on the mound takes the pitcher out of the realm of benign muscle damage and into the realm of excessive damage. It also depletes glycogen, particularly from the muscles of the arm and shoulder. This leads to the condition known as overtraining, which causes inconsistent performance, loss of pitching power, and injury.

Successful weight lifting is a process that requires careful control of the stimulus for muscle growth. It is not a scattershot process, but a finely tuned one that must be focused on the prime movers of pitching's kinetic chain. It is much like a conservative, long-term financial investment in that each workout yields imperceptibly small gains that become cumulatively significant over a period of months.

Major league baseball, however, provides little time for long-term investment in strength. The 162-game season, with six weeks of spring training and four weeks of post-season play, works against the principles of progressive overload training.

The off-season is but 3½ to 4½ months long, and a portion of that is best allocated to rest and recovery of the arm and shoulder from the stresses of the season. This leaves but two to three months to re-strengthen the muscles in which unrepaired damage has accumulated. Given the short off-season, strength training in baseball has evolved into an in-season program. Consequently, baseball has never gained full benefit from pitcher's strength training. The players who have benefited most are those with exceptional natural recovery ability and those who have cheated by using the drugs of athletic impatience, anabolic steroids.

It is extremely difficult to combine the strain-producing activities of pitching and weight lifting to yield an effective strength-building program. Attempting to do so brings a great risk of achieving no gains at all and often leads to losses. Strength training is a sure path to greater pitching power and greater fastball velocity, but it is a narrow one that has not yet been fully opened to pitchers.

11

The Wild Card of Pitching Power

> *"I am embarrassed to say it, but this is a testosterone sport."*—University of Arizona baseball coach Andy Lopez, quoted in *The Arizona Republic*, March 2009

A dugout-clearing fight that erupted during an otherwise mundane college baseball game led to this declaration about the influence of testosterone in baseball. Though other sports — boxing, ice hockey, football, rugby, and wrestling in particular — are more commonly viewed as testosterone sports, this coach's observation on baseball is an accurate one. In baseball's history there are many embarrassing episodes attributable to the dual powers of testosterone — its androgenic (masculinizing) effects and its anabolic (muscle-building) effects. Ty Cobb best illustrates the androgenic effects, earning a reputation for aggressive play and volatile behavior throughout his Hall-of-Fame career. His violent assault on a heckler in the stands, his post-game fistfight with an umpire, and his attack on night watchman George Stansfield are just three acts of aggression that went far beyond embarrassing. Baseball's prominent icons of the anabolic effects are Barry Bonds and Mark McGwire. With the alleged aid of synthetic testosterone, they toppled home-run records long held by baseball's greatest heroes, setting records that reside in an embarrassing realm of uncertainty.

"Throughout his life, a man's manliness — physically and psychologically — is most exclusively dictated by the quantity of a magical substance in his body, the hormone called testosterone," writes noted endocrinologist Dr. Herbert Kupperman.[1] Most sports are tests of physical and psychological manliness; consequently, most sports are testosterone sports. Testosterone is the wild card in the hand of natural talent dealt to an athlete. It is the wild card because its value is variable, consisting of whatever the athlete wills it to be through assiduous training; because its value is ultimately determined by the other natural talents he is dealt; and because it offers a short-cut to a winning hand through the use of artificial testosterone.

11. The Wild Card of Pitching Power

Among testosterone's androgenic effects are personality traits apparent in many pitchers — aggression, dominance, and sensitivity to the status threat of being beaten in competition. To pitchers, however, the anabolic effects — increased muscle growth rate — are far more important. Success on any playing field requires muscle plasticity, the ability of muscle to adapt to its functional demands and repair the damage that occurs routinely in training and competition. Testosterone is the pace-setter of muscle repair, regeneration, and remodeling. A naturally high level of testosterone is one of the genetic gifts that determine a pitcher's power and the velocity of his fastball. Potentially, it is as valuable as the other genetic gifts, which are: an abundance of fast-glycolytic muscle fibers, strong stiffly elastic ligaments and tendons capable of storing and returning large amounts of energy, and a neurological system that quickly learns and perfectly coordinates complex movements at high speed.

Satellite cells are the main players of muscle plasticity. They are the stem-cells-in-waiting that lie dormant on each muscle fiber, ready to build new tissue once they are activated in response to muscle damage. Satellite cells and their role in muscle plasticity were discovered in the 1960s, about the time Sandy Koufax was redefining the power of the fastball while badly in need of greater elbow-ligament plasticity. Testosterone and other hormones are the messenger molecules that orchestrate the complex process, instructing satellite cells about what to do. Scientific studies have shown that testosterone affects muscle growth by increasing muscle protein synthesis.[2] Testosterone's routine instruction to the cells is thus to manufacture protein, the building block of muscle tissue that must be replaced in a continuous cycle with or without strenuous exercise. There is a constant turnover of protein in muscle tissue as muscle filaments, the chains of protein molecules that produce contraction, wear out. These protein chains have a short useful life, normally degrading in days to weeks. As the protein degrades, more must be synthesized to replace it. As the demand increases, as more damage occurs to muscle fibers in training and competition, the body must respond with increased production.

The concentration of free testosterone circulating in the bloodstream determines the magnitude of the response, the rate of muscle growth. This concentration changes between morning and night each day and varies with several factors, but ultimately the dose, the average concentration over time, determines the rate at which the muscle fibers repair and regenerate, increasing muscle strength in a dose-dependent way.[3] The average man produces about seven milligrams of testosterone per day, but some men naturally have far more testosterone circulating in their bloodstream than others — as much as five times more within the range considered normal. Consequently, when there is stimulus for muscle growth, they have higher growth rates.

When the hormonal gift produces growth at a rate an athlete believes to be inadequate, he may feel compelled to cheat with doses of anabolic steroids. The commonly known effects of such doses provide strong evidence of testosterone's power to build power by the dose. A 1996 study in *The New England Journal of Medicine* describes the strength gains achieved by men with testosterone levels well above normal, both with and without 10 weeks of weight lifting.[4] Forty men participated, ten of whom were injected with 600 mg of testosterone each week, resulting in levels of testosterone about five times higher than normal. The experiment involved progressive-overload weight training three times per week. Those given testosterone injections achieved twice the strength gains of those who performed the same weight lifting exercises without injections. During the 10-week period, the group without the testosterone supplement improved their maximum lift in leg squats an average of 19.8 percent, and their bench press by 9.2 percent. The testosterone-injected group, however, improved by an average of 37.2 percent in the squat and 22.7 percent in the bench press. The study also included measurements of aggressive behavior but found no significant effects on mood or behavior over the 10-week period with the levels of testosterone used in the study, although a correlation between testosterone levels and aggression has been shown in several other scientific studies.

The male body deals the wild card naturally at puberty when sex glands start to function and secondary sexual characteristics begin to appear. When prodigious pitching talent emerges early in adolescence, heralded for example by a 94-mph fastball at age 15, it is because of this surge, which typically involves at least a tenfold increase in testosterone levels. This big dose propels the growth spurt, with muscle growth generally lagging behind bone growth by a year. If the exercise-induced stimulus for growth — benign muscle damage — occurs regularly to the pitching muscles during the delivery of the big dose, there is the possibility of a fastball prodigy developing. The beneficiaries of the big dose can often be identified by the androgenic effects of testosterone — dark facial hair, body hair, and a deepening voice. These markers are often seen in exceptional

11. The Wild Card of Pitching Power

young pitchers — like the thicket of black chest hair peeking from the collar of Steve Dalkowski.

A pitcher develops the power for a high-velocity fastball in two stages. The first stage begins in his mother's womb. The second begins at puberty with delivery of the big dose. Before and soon after birth, muscle twitch speed is established genetically by the type, quantity, and distribution of muscle fibers. The nervous system develops rapidly in the first stage, leveling off in childhood. At puberty, muscle strength increases rapidly, developing at a rate that varies from person to person over a period of months to years. The strength gain, like puberty itself, separates men from boys in pitching power. Exceptional pitchers in Little League sometimes become unexceptional pitchers at puberty because of a smaller or delayed presentation of the gift of testosterone.

Tendons and ligaments, important for elastic-strain energy storage and return, grow slowly at a near-constant rate, reaching their full strength late in the second stage, at about the end of the teen years. In adolescence, muscle strength increases much more rapidly than tendon and ligament strength; consequently, a strength differential can develop, producing a latent defect that leaves the pitcher's most important ligament, the anterior band of the ulnar collateral ligament, deficient in adolescence for transmitting, storing, and returning energy of the trunk to the arm and shoulder. This imbalance relative to rapidly increasing muscle strength may be the initiator of gradual, progressive failure of the anterior band.

The time of delivery of the big dose varies among male adolescents. When it arrives early and coincides with a strength-building program for pitching, there can emerge a prodigy like Bob Feller, who signed his first major-league contract at age 16. When the big dose comes later, a Billy Wagner emerges. Wagner developed much later than Feller, registering a top speed around 83 mph on his fastball as a high-school senior, about the age at which Feller was probably topping 100 mph. Wagner's velocity increased rapidly during two years at Ferrum College in Virginia, where he elevated his radar readings into the mid–'90s.[5] In his sophomore year at Ferrum, he set a national collegiate record of 19.1 strikeouts per nine innings. The Houston Astros picked him in the first round of the 1993 amateur draft, the year he turned 22. He reached the majors at the end of the 1995 season, and in his first full major-league season two years later, he set a record of 14.4 strikeouts per nine innings as a closer. Wagner's natural speed manifested itself along with a strength gain that followed a growth spurt of six inches in height the year after high school. Deriving exceptional power from trunk flexion — apparent in his angle of trunk flexion at the point of full arm cocking — he found long-toss to be his most effective strengthening exercise. "If I can name one thing that contributed most to my increase in velocity, it would be long toss," he said.[6]

The career trajectories of Feller and Wagner were quite different in their teen years, but they were more divergent in their thirties. Wagner sustained his power past 30, and at age 32 led the major leagues with 159 pitches of 100 mph or faster during the 2003 season, 147 more than any other pitcher that year.[7] The 5-foot-10 left-hander eventually pitched in 16 major league seasons before retiring in 2010. He sustained exceptional

Billy Wagner developed later than most fastball phenoms. As an All-Star closer, he sustained his power well into his thirties. Note his high angle of trunk flexion at the point his arm is fully cocked (photograph by Alex Kim, Wikimedia Commons).

11. The Wild Card of Pitching Power

power through his last season at age 39, despite a 12-month hiatus for Tommy John surgery. High testosterone levels may well have been a factor in the relatively short recovery period after the surgery. He struck out 26 in 15 two-thirds innings and registered a 1.72 ERA when he returned to the majors in late August 2009. A year later, pitching for the Phillies in his final major league game, he struck out the last four batters he faced to earn the 422nd save of his career, closing with a season ERA of 1.43.

By the time Feller turned 33 in 1952, he had begun a downward slide with little respite. His decline was apparently due to a loss of power, but the cause of the power loss was never determined. There are several possible explanations for why Feller went into decline while Wagner soared after age 30. A likely one is a shifting in the dose-demand balance, though it is, of course, impossible to know the testosterone levels of the two pitchers. Their muscle protein-synthesis demands, however, can be compared by looking at workload, the number of innings pitched. Feller pitched 1,850 innings in the seven seasons before he turned 33, not counting the innings he pitched in each of the month-long barnstorming tours after the 1946 and '47 seasons. Wagner pitched 452 innings in the seven seasons before he turned 33, a normal load for a closer but just one-fourth the load Feller carried as a starter. This comparison assumes that Feller continued to deliver max-effort fastballs routinely, that both applied about the same amount of power per pitch, and that demand consequently varied only with the number of innings pitched. Feller probably did continue as a max-effort pitcher; there is no indication that he rationed his most powerful offerings as Walter Johnson, Nolan Ryan, and Sandy Koufax began to do early in their major-league careers. His demand consequently remained high, and his testosterone dose may have begun to decline, as it normally does in men over the age of 30.

Generally, testosterone levels peak in the late teens to early twenties and decline at about one percent per year after age 30. While the circulating dose of free testosterone determines growth rate, the muscle damage that occurs on the mound and in training determines the demand. As the dose diminishes with age, the pitcher recovers more slowly and experiences a performance decline if his workload remains constant. A longer recovery period becomes necessary to sustain muscle strength and power. Dose must equal demand to maintain muscle strength in the continuing cycle of protein turnover. Dose must exceed demand for strength to increase. When repair lags behind in the cycle of damage and repair, the pitcher exceeds the ability of his body to recover, with the result that power diminishes.

One implication of the dose-demand balance is that testosterone is one of the differentiators between starters and relievers. Although athletes with lower levels of testosterone may ultimately attain strength equivalent to those with higher levels, doing so takes longer. It requires more patience and freedom from the rigid pitching schedule of the baseball season, meaning that strength building is best done in the off-season. The distinct advantage that higher testosterone levels provide a pitcher is in a more rapid recovery within the normal schedule constraints of pitching. The workload of the reliever in terms of innings is typically about half that of a starter. For this and other reasons, relief pitching is less arduous than starting pitching. In an analysis of the performances of 291 major league pitchers spanning 50 years, *Hardball Times* writer Steve Treder found that relievers have an eight percent lower ERA, 15 percent more strikeouts and give up 14 percent fewer home runs and five percent fewer hits.[8] Proceeding from starter to reliever is apparently a logical path for pitchers as they age.

This dose-demand balance shifts with aging but it is also likely to shift when workload on the mound changes substantially or when injury occurs. The effect of a workload increase can be seen when a pitcher advances from collegiate to professional baseball, thereby transitioning from a seven- to a five-day pitching cycle. The effect can manifest itself in inconsistency that sometimes affects pitchers upon entering professional ball, exhibiting symptoms of overtraining and early- or mid-season slumps. When injury occurs, muscle plasticity works in both forward and reverse. Adaptation consists of atrophy in response to lighter demands, just as muscles strengthen in response to greater demands. It can also help a pitcher return from surgery more quickly. Testosterone level not only separates men from boys, it can separate disabled-list pitchers from active roster pitchers.

A high level of testosterone is a gift that can keep on giving throughout a pitching career. It helps the gifted ones recover more quickly, preventing inconsistency, slowing or preventing the progression of injury, helping to regain strength quickly, maximizing gains in strength training, providing a cushion in times of dose-demand shift, and giving the pitcher the appropriate quantities of aggression, dominance, and competitiveness he needs to win ballgames. The wild card can and often does provide the winning margin.

12

Endurance, Durability, and Longevity
Amos Rusie vs. Pedro Martinez

> *"I would speculate that an average game in 1966 included 30–40 fewer pitches than one today. That's the difference between going seven and going nine (innings). It's not the pitcher, it's the game."*—Joe Sheehan, *Baseball Prospectus* writer, 2003

The complete game, emblematic of good pitching, has become an anachronism in major league baseball. In the century between 1904 and 2004, the percentage of complete games fell from 87 percent to a mere 3 percent.[1] Writer Joe Sheehan analyzed this trend in a *Baseball Prospectus* article in 2003, finding that strikeouts and walks as a percentage of outcomes have increased substantially since the 1920s, particularly since World War II.[2] "There are 65 percent more strikeouts and walks than there were in games 80 years ago, and 15 percent more than there were 20 years ago," he reports. More strikeouts and walks result in more pitches. His analysis also shows that power at the plate has improved over the years, particularly among players in the middle infield, shifting the balance between pitching and hitting. "The need to treat every hitter as a dangerous one may manifest itself in more maximum-effort tosses, which may cause a pitcher to tire sooner," comments Sheehan. Tactics too have changed; the definition of a successful at-bat now includes — if all else fails — forcing the pitcher to deliver at least eight pitches in the at-bat. Sheehan concludes that there are two trends driving the decline in the complete game — a baseball game requires more pitches, and each pitch requires more power. Not only is the road on which a pitcher travels longer, it is steeper. It demands a quality that was never sought in the training of pitchers a century ago — endurance.

Endurance is commonly measured in the number of innings pitched. It is more precisely measured in the number pitches thrown in an outing. An outing typically ends when there is a loss of power — detectable in diminished control, velocity, or movement — or an unfavorable outcome to an at-bat. Although pitchers are not considered endurance athletes, they are expected to perform at a high level of exertion for up to 2 hours, with a pulse rate around 140 beats per minute on the mound.[3] The rest pauses are generous, but the stresses on the body and mind are great. Conventional wisdom states that short outings are caused by lack of fitness, and that outings grow shorter as a season progresses because of diminishing fitness and strength.

Endurance is the ability to sustain power long into a game; durability is the capability to sustain power long into a season; and longevity is the capacity to sustain power long into a career. Relative to pitchers of the late 19th century, pitchers of the 21st century are trained to have greater endurance, durability, and longevity. But despite better science, better training, better fitness, better nutrition, better salaries, and more time between starts, they do not. Why? The game has indeed changed, requiring more pitches and more power. With it, the energy dynamics of pitching and pitcher training have changed, requiring greater energy expenditure per pitch and greater energy expenditure between outings.

Cy Young, the man for whom pitching's most coveted award is named, established high standards for endurance, durability, and longevity in his remarkable career. Between 1890 and 1911, he pitched 749 complete games, going nine innings in a remarkable 92 percent of his starts. Walter Johnson pitched 531 complete games, 80 percent of his starts. He led the American League in complete games six times between 1910 and 1916, pitching between 29 and 38 complete games in each of those seasons. Bob Feller pitched 279 complete games in 18 seasons, going the distance in 66 percent of his starts during his first 12 major league seasons. Nolan Ryan completed 54 percent of his starts from 1972 through 1979, about twice the average for that period in baseball. His complete games ranged in number from 10 to 26 per season in this eight-year period, but then dropped sharply. The problem, however, was not a lack of endurance. In Ryan's next nine seasons, with the Houston Astros, he completed just 13 percent of his starts, affected by injury and the imposition of pitch limits for the first time. The decline in complete games from Cy Young to Nolan Ryan follows the general downward trend of complete games in the major leagues, a trend that accelerated after 1970, about the same time power per pitch

12. Endurance, Durability, and Longevity

trended upward and other significant changes occurred in baseball. As the percentage of complete games declined, the number of pitches thrown per game became a better measure of endurance.

Ryan threw about 125 to 130 pitches per complete game. In 1988, his complete games required an average of 124 pitches, ranging from 116 to 141. In 1989, he averaged 127 pitches in all 31 starts, ranging from 99 to 164 pitches. Sandy Koufax averaged 135 pitches in his 11 complete games in the 1962 season, and 133 pitches per complete game in 1961, not including a 205-pitch, 13-inning win in which he struck out 15 batters. Koufax and Ryan were of course strikeout pitchers, and their pitch totals per compete game may have been higher than those of other pitchers. Greg Maddux, for example, required an average of only 106 pitches for his 11 complete games in the 1994 season, the year he won the third of his four Cy Young Awards. Curiously, his exceptional efficiency in getting batters out with few strikeouts and walks did not translate into a high rate of complete games. Throughout a 23-year major-league career in which he won 355 games, Maddux completed 15 percent of his starts. He did, however, last at least eight innings in almost 30 percent of his starts.

As the game has changed, the issue of endurance has become an issue of pitch count. Why can't pitchers routinely sustain their power and effectiveness beyond 130 pitches in a game? It is a question that relates to power and energy, and its answer lies in the difference between the two energy systems that power the muscle fibers — aerobic and anaerobic — and how energy is supplied and stored within each.

Pitching, like the Olympic events that feature sprinting, jumping, and throwing, is an anaerobic exercise, which means that oxygen is not required in the fast-twitch muscles' energy conversion process, glycolysis. Pitching differs from other anaerobic exercises, however, in that a single pitching performance requires repeating the explosive exertions many times. In a single track-and-field meet, a sprinter may run two or three dashes; a javelin thrower may make a half-dozen throws; and a high-jumper, a dozen leaps. A starting pitcher, however, must typically deliver 100 or more pitches, each requiring a substantial expenditure of stored energy to cause the rapid acceleration of both the baseball and the pitcher's whole body.

Anaerobic endurance is defined as the length of time that fast-twitch muscle contractions can be sustained by stores of glycogen and very limited quantities of creatine phosphate. The creatine phosphate is used up quickly; muscle maintains a small reserve of creatine phosphate but not

The Science of the Fastball

enough for sustained activities. The limiting factor for pitching endurance is the quantity of glycogen available to each muscle fiber.

An important characteristic of the anaerobic metabolism is intramuscular storage of energy. Glycogen is stored within each muscle fiber where it can be mobilized rapidly. As seen through an electron microscope, glycogen granules are nestled between and among the fibrils in each fiber. The granules are not shared among other muscle fibers, and once they are consumed, more granules are loaded into the muscle at a slow rate. Fat (triglycerides) are also stored within the muscle. Though fat has a higher energy content than glycogen, it is mobilized and oxidized at relatively slow rates. Only the glycogen can be mobilized rapidly enough to meet the energy requirements of pitching. The pitcher's anaerobic endurance is determined by the amount of glycogen stored in the pitching muscles when he takes the mound.

If a muscle sustains only minor damage during the pitcher's outing, the recharging of the muscles with glycogen takes about 24 to 48 hours. If there is significant muscle damage, enough to produce soreness and significant inflammation, it takes longer, perhaps a week, because the macrophages and neutrophils must do their work, and in doing so they

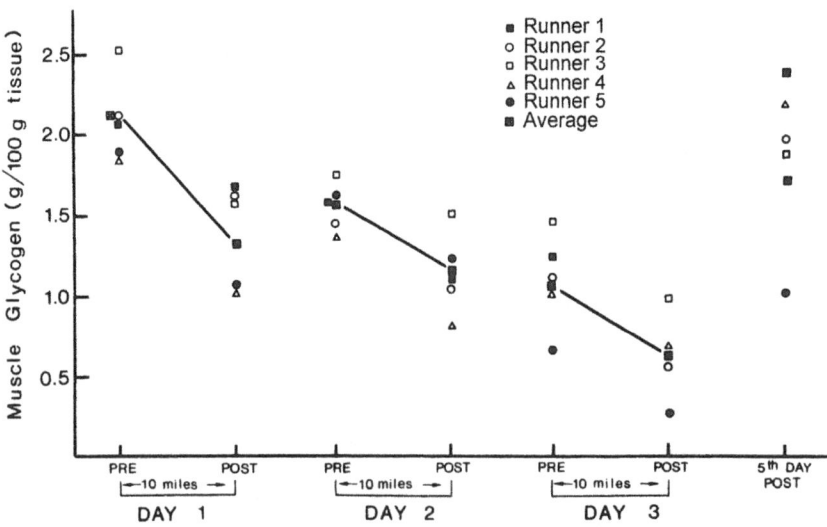

Figure 7: Glycogen levels measured in the leg muscles of runners before and after three exercise bouts of 10 miles each (reprinted with permission of TAFNEWS Press from *A Scientific Approach to Distance Running* by David L. Costill).

may scavenge remaining glycogen granules as they remove debris. *Figure 7 is a graph* showing the depletion and restoration of glycogen from the leg muscles of runners (who likely had no significant inflammation) over a five-day period in which they ran 10 miles per day for three days. Similar data is available on swimmers and weight-lifters showing a one-to-two-day restoration period, but there are no known data on the arm and shoulder muscles of pitchers. Note on the extreme right of the graph that on the fifth day, two days after the last workout, glycogen levels of four of the runners returned to the normal two percent of the muscle weight. For two other runners, the levels did not, indicating a substantial variability from person to person. With runners, this variability is high because they rely more on their aerobic energy system than their anaerobic; aerobic efficiency and the portion of energy the aerobic metabolism provides are likely to vary from runner to runner more so than anaerobic efficiency.

How can a pitcher, particularly a max-effort pitcher, improve his anaerobic endurance? He can do so by increasing the availability of energy to the fast-glycolytic fibers of his pitching muscles. There are four ways to do this: (1) increase the glycogen storage capacity in the muscles, (2) increase the rate at which glycogen is restored to the muscles, (3) add a significant second energy source to the fast-glycolytic fibers by adding aerobic capacity, and (4) conserve glycogen both on and off the mound.

The fourth method includes an approach that might seem impractical in the era of maximal-effort pitching — to pitch at less than maximal effort. Doing so reduces the workload of the fast-glycolytic fibers. In the hierarchy of activation, this places more of the load on the fast-oxidative-glycolytic fibers, which consume glycogen less rapidly. This yields a double benefit: (1) less energy is required for a sub-maximal pitch because of its lower velocity (energy is proportional to velocity squared), and (2) more of that energy comes from the aerobic process, less from the glycogen stored in muscle fibers. This double benefit was probably significant for pitchers like Christy Mathewson and Cy Young, who routinely pitched complete games and threw for more than 300 innings in a season at the turn of the 20th century.

Increasing Glycogen Storage Capacity

The anaerobic energy system can be improved by high-intensity exercise of short duration. High-intensity exercise, i.e., strength training, ensures the fast-glycolytic fibers of the pitching muscles are forcefully activated to stimulate muscle-fiber growth. This activation occurs in resistance training and high-intensity throwing/pitching. As the fibers grow larger in cross-section area with this training, it appears likely that muscle fibers' capacity for glycogen will also increase, maintaining the maximum glycogen level at about 2 percent of muscle weight.

Exercise for the anaerobic energy system involves high resistance and short duration, unlike exercise benefiting the aerobic system, which involves low resistance for long duration. For pitchers, this training is most beneficial when performed in the off-season to avoid the adverse, short-term effects on pitching performance, namely glycogen depletion and muscle damage. Avoiding these effects is also the reason that anaerobic training sessions are kept to a short duration.

Increasing the Restoration Rate of Glycogen

Studies have shown that athletes who train heavily and eat low-carbohydrate diets (about 40 percent of total calories) experience a day-to-day decline in muscle glycogen. When the same athletes eat high-carbohydrate diets (about 70 percent of total calories) glycogen replenishment is achieved more rapidly and without decline.[4] This means pitchers should avoid low-carb diets. A high level of fitness is also likely to enhance the rate of restoring glycogen, with trained athletes being better able to store glycogen than people of average fitness levels. This reinforces the benefits of maintaining a running program year-around. Maintaining fitness can also slow the effects of aging. Aging is known to adversely affect the ability of the body to produce and store glycogen. In general, recovery from stressful exercise is known to take longer as a person ages, even at a high level of fitness.

Adding a Second (Aerobic) Energy Source to Fast-Glycolytic Fibers

The fast-glycolytic fibers have little or no aerobic (oxidative) capacity. Consequently, these high-power muscle fibers have no significant back-up energy source to prevent them from entering a state of rigor if glycogen becomes depleted. Endurance training involving repetitions of long duration provides the stimulus to remodel the fast-glycolytic fibers into fast-oxidative-glycolytic fibers. This develops a second source of energy for the fast fibers, one that requires an efficient, on-demand supply system — the cardiovascular system — to deliver both oxygen and energy at the pace the muscles demand. It allows muscle fibers to generate force for longer periods by consuming glycogen stores less quickly. The cardiovascular system is the direct energy and oxygen supplier for the aerobic metabolism, but it is capable only of supporting slower-paced, steady endurance activities such as distance running. It does not supply energy at the same rate as glycolysis; consequently, it does not produce the level of power needed for a major-league fastball.

Adding aerobic capacity to the fast-glycolytic fibers means adding mitochondria, myoglobin, more capillaries, and oxidative enzymes to these fibers. Mitochondria are the microscopic powerhouses in the muscle fibers that process oxygen and energy from the blood. Myoglobin provides temporary oxygen storage in the muscle fiber. Mitochondria and the other aerobic components can be developed rapidly in response to endurance exercise, and a significant increase can occur during just a few weeks of training. Both go away in a few weeks as well, once the season ends and pitchers take a post-season break from throwing. Mitochondria also disappear during periods of strength training.[5] The conversion of fast-glycolytic fibers to fast-oxidative-glycolytic fibers is not completely beneficial for pitchers. Since mitochondria take up as much as 20 percent of the space in the slow-oxidative fiber, the oxygen-producing components take up space in the muscle fiber that could otherwise be used for storing glycogen. The conversion also reduces the twitch speed of the muscle fiber. At peak exertion, mitochondria can supply ATP at only one-third the rate that glycolysis does. The capability this adds can be compared to the small auxiliary gasoline engine in an electric automobile. It allows the car to reach a recharging station if the battery charge is drained, but to do so at a reduced power level. The aerobic capacity prevents the fast-glycolytic muscle fiber from entering a state of stiffness that leads to damage to the glycogen-depleted fibers.

This training takes the same approach as "suicide sprints," a term used to describe multiple short, fast runs with 180-degree turns that provide only a brief rest. These are popular in baseball and basketball for conditioning the legs. Running builds aerobic capacity into the leg muscles.

To build this capacity into the muscles of the arm and shoulder requires repetitive throwing or pitching in order to involve the fast-glycolytic fibers used in pitching. For pitchers, however, this is a double-edged sword. It can deplete glycogen from the arm and shoulder muscles just as rapidly as suicide sprints can from the leg muscles. More throwing means more muscle-damaging eccentric contractions, raising the potential for the effects of overtraining and making anaerobic endurance training difficult to optimize during the season. At its practical best, building aerobic capacity into the pitching muscles of the arm and shoulder requires perhaps a six-week pre-season throwing program of gradually increasing repetitions. The gradual resumption of throwing after an off-season break benefits the pitcher mainly by protecting him from injury. This effect is illustrated by an injury that sometimes occurs to pitchers in the early season. Nolan Ryan experienced such an injury in spring training a few months after his major-league debut.

"In 1967, I was in pretty decent shape, but in no condition to throw at full speed," reported Ryan in his strength training book. "As soon as I arrived at Jacksonville, Florida, I started overextending myself, going full tilt before I was physically ready to pitch. My forearm tightened. I kept throwing, but then — sure enough — I felt something pop. A tendon popped in my forearm in much the same way a rubber band snaps if you stretch it too far. I really thought my career was over. I figured I'd be back in Alvin, Texas, doing something besides playing baseball for a living. I returned to Alvin to rest my arm all summer. I couldn't even throw a ball three feet, let alone pitch."[6]

More specific details of Ryan's injury are unknown, but such an injury can be initiated by the depletion of glycogen from the fast-glycolytic fibers. It can occur when the arm is overworked before there has been sufficient time for the muscles to adapt to the heavier workload. The injury occurred in one of the forearm flexor muscles, which, as noted in Chapter 4, are the most heavily worked muscles in the kinetic chain of pitching. The adaptation is a gradual one, because the building of mitochondria and the strengthening of the muscle fibers is a process that takes weeks, not days. Throwing programs aimed at building endurance that fail to apply a patient, gradual approach usually produce undesirable results.

This type of injury can occur at any time during the season as a result of fatigue, the depletion of glycogen. Billy Wagner experienced a partial tear of a flexor muscle/tendon in the middle of the 2000 season. The injury

12. Endurance, Durability, and Longevity

occurred in June, during his 28th appearance of the season. Uncharacteristically, he gave up four walks and one hit without registering an out, then was placed on the disabled list, where he ended his season.

Pitching to fatigue, to a point at which one or more of the fast-glycolytic muscle fibers can no longer contract or relax, risks injury at any time during the season, particularly for the small, heavily worked flexor muscles of the forearm. This is true even when done in the well-intentioned pursuit of endurance. One college coach's impatient attempt to prepare his starting pitchers for the upcoming season was to have them throw three full-speed 120-pitch bullpen sessions with one rest day after each. This amounted to 360 game-speed pitches in five days. It was an attempt to squeeze six weeks of anaerobic endurance training into five days, and it was worse than simply unsuccessful. In a single season, two of the starting pitchers who completed the three bullpen sessions suffered elbow ligament injuries before mid-season, suggesting that the excessive workload depleted glycogen and caused muscle fiber damage in the forearm flexors, which ultimately led to a sprain of the anterior band of the ulnar collateral ligament.

The fast-glycolytic fiber has a fuel-supply problem the other two types of muscle fiber do not have. At heavy workloads, it relies solely on intramuscular storage of glycogen; it has no backup from the aerobic energy system. This problem is worsened by the difficulties of large-scale distribution — evenly distributing glycogen to the millions of molecular motors, the sarcomeres of the muscle fibers that work in series and in parallel to power each pitch. Fuel distribution can be a problem for any power system having multiple motors or multiple power generators, such as an eight-cylinder automobile engine. If the fuel supply to one cylinder of the V-8 engine is interrupted, that cylinder produces a drag on the other seven and creates potential for damaging the engine. Fast-glycolytic muscle fibers have, in essence, millions of separate fuel tanks of non-uniform size, which usually require at least two days to refill. This distribution system is far less efficient than providing fuel on demand for the muscle fibers that have aerobic capacity, supplying the fuel without delay to all sarcomeres from a common, immediate source, the bloodstream.

The result is that the threshold for fatigue is variable, and spot outages are likely to occur in the fast-glycolytic fibers once glycogen levels become low. This can shut down individual fibers, with fibers of motor units bearing a heavier workload shutting down first. As the fiber runs out of stored energy, it loses its ability to contract or relax and develops rigor, the state of high stiffness. As the fibers around the stiffened fiber continue to contract and relax, they cause it to stretch and become damaged. If the exertions continue, other fibers reach this state of fatigue, and the extent of damage increases, eventually leading to delayed-onset muscle soreness.

Conserving Glycogen

It becomes apparent that in order to increase a pitcher's endurance, his training during the season and pre-season must find the level of effort that prevents severe depletion of glycogen and allows time for repair of muscle damage. How effective is conventional pitcher training in increasing endurance, controlling glycogen levels, and minimizing muscle damage? A comparison of Amos Rusie and Pedro Martinez, two major leaguers who starred a century apart, provides some insight. Martinez's velocity was measured by radar. Rusie's was measured subjectively by the responses of batters he faced. His velocity was implied, validated in a way, by a rule change that he probably influenced with his exceptional velocity and wildness.

At 6-foot-1, 200 pounds, Rusie was one of the beefier pitchers of the 1890s. He was one of baseball's first great power pitchers, the prototype of intimidators who would come along decades later. His phenomenal fastball drew large crowds in New York when he pitched for the Giants from 1890 to 1898. "Words fail really to describe the speed with which Rusie sent the ball. He was a man of great height, great width, prodigious muscular strength and the ability to put every ounce of his weight and sinew on every pitch," said Chicago outfielder Jimmy Ryan.[7] Rusie's fastball even inspired a book that bore the title: *Secrets of Amos Rusie, the World's Greatest Pitcher, How He Obtained His Incredible Speed on Balls*. As is often the case with young power pitchers, he lacked control, setting the major league record of 289 walks in his second season of 1890. In the same year, he led the league with 341 strikeouts.

When Rusie entered the majors in 1889, pitchers delivered the ball 55 feet from home plate, from a 4 foot × 5½ foot box. When the distance increased to 60 feet, 6 inches in 1893, Rusie's season strikeout total dropped from 288 to 208.

Rusie threw fastballs and curveballs. It is not known whether he threw

12. Endurance, Durability, and Longevity

all his pitches at maximal effort, but with the most crowd-pleasing fastball of his era, he probably threw most of them at max-effort. A faithful patron of New York saloons, he was most surely lacking in aerobic fitness, and he was known to have hated spring training. From the perspective of a century later, he was a pitcher of contradiction — having exceptional endurance on the mound and the power of a closer. He pitched 392 complete games in his 10-season career, going the distance in 92 percent of his starts. At age 21, he reached a high of 59 complete games, 95 percent of his starts, in the 1892 season while pitching 541 innings.

There are no records of pitch counts for Rusie's games, but he may have thrown as many pitches to achieve complete games as Nolan Ryan did 80 years later. Why? Because many of the batters he faced either walked or struck out and foul balls did not yet count as strikes. As he once observed, "It took a lot of pitchin' to strike a man out in those days."[8] In 10 seasons, he issued 1,707 walks and struck out 1,950 batters. By comparison, Nolan Ryan, who led the American League in walks eight times, handed out 1,468 free passes in the 10 seasons between 1972 and 1981. Ryan led the league in strikeouts seven times in that period, with a 10-year total of 2,756.

Amos Rusie, who pitched for the New York Giants in the 1890s, had the best fastball of his era, and he led the National League in strikeouts and walks five times apiece. He pitched complete games in 92 percent of his starts (National Baseball Hall of Fame Library, Cooperstown, New York).

Though his endurance and durability were exceptional compared to today's pitchers, Rusie was unexceptional relative to pitchers of the 1890s, or those who pitched in the Deadball Era (1900–1919). Babe Ruth, who at 6-foot-2 and 215 pounds was bigger than Rusie — and no fan of spring training either — completed 90 percent of his starts in his last three seasons with the Boston Red Sox, 1917 through 1919. At age 22, he completed 35 of his 38 starts while pitching 326 one-third innings in 1917 with a 2.01 ERA. Smokey Joe Wood, the fireballer who said he threw so hard he thought his arm would fly right off his body, completed 76 percent of his starts between 1908 and 1915. Christy Mathewson completed 79 percent of his starts with 435 complete games in 17 seasons with the New York Giants, beginning in 1900. He was known for applying the minimum effort necessary to get batters out, a common approach among pitchers of that period. He eased up on weaker hitters, pitching just hard enough to win.[9] Mathewson led the league in hit batsmen in his first three seasons, but once he solved his control problems led the league seven times in fewest walks, averaging less than one walk per nine innings in five of them and at one point going 68 consecutive innings without issuing a walk.

Pedro Martinez's Endurance and Durability

A question of durability followed Pedro Martinez into professional baseball and dogged him through most of his outstanding major-league career. The question arose, however, from his physique rather than any demonstrated inability to sustain his power. As a teenager, he was built more like a marathon runner than a power pitcher. He stood 5-feet-8 and weighed 135 pounds when he signed a contract with the Los Angeles Dodgers at age 16. He enjoyed running for fitness, but he was so thin when he entered professional baseball that his manager threatened to fine him if he caught him running. When he made his major-league debut in 1992 at age 20, he weighed about 150 pounds. His slight frame made scouts skeptical even after he won his first Cy Young Award in 1997. "There is a question whether Martinez is durable enough at 170 pounds to continue to last through major league seasons," read one scouting report."[10] His unexpected trade to the Montreal Expos in 1993 was said to have occurred because Dodger manager Tommy Lasorda doubted Martinez had the strength to endure as a starting pitcher.

12. Endurance, Durability, and Longevity

Though his light frame made scouts and managers worry that he would lack durability, Pedro Martinez pitched for 18 major league seasons, won three Cy Young Awards, and led the league with 13 complete games in the 1997 season (National Baseball Hall of Fame Library, Cooperstown, New York).

The Science of the Fastball

Martinez proved himself quite durable, however, throughout a major-league career of 18 seasons. He was voted an All-Star eight times and won the Cy Young Award three times. In the year he won his first Cy Young Award, he led the National League in strikeouts per nine innings (11.37), ERA (1.90), and complete games (13), and he was second in strikeouts with 305. In his career with the Dodgers, Expos, Red Sox, Mets, and Phillies, he accumulated 219 wins with a 2.93 ERA and 3,154 strikeouts in 2,827 one-third innings (10 strikeouts per nine innings). He exhibited the level of performance, durability, and longevity that virtually guarantees election to the Hall of Fame.

Compared to other pitchers of his era, Martinez had exceptional endurance. Compared to pitchers of the 1890s, however, he had poor endurance. And he was no match for Amos Rusie. If a seven-inning outing in the year 2000 is equivalent of the nine-inning complete game in 1900, Martinez averaged 63 percent "completes" of seven or more innings from 1994 to 2005. This ranged from 39 percent to 86 percent per season with the high mark coming in the year 2000. If instead, endurance is measured by games of 110 pitches or more, he drops to 42 percent of his starts. His outings in which he threw at least 110 pitches ranged from 16 percent to 59 percent per season during his career.

By either measure, Martinez falls far short of the 92 percent complete-game percentage Rusie achieved in his career. He also falls short on durability. Rusie averaged 378 innings per season, and Martinez, 160. Only in longevity was Martinez superior. He pitched 18 seasons to Rusie's 10. He avoided serious injury, going on the disabled list only at mid-season 2001 with a slight tear in his rotator cuff. Rusie's early exit from the major leagues was due to a shoulder injury he suffered at age 27. He remained out of baseball for two years, hoping the injury would heal. When he attempted a comeback with Cincinnati in 1901, however, he pitched poorly, giving up 21 earned runs in his first 22 innings. After pitching in only three games, Rusie quit baseball at age 30.

Compared to Pedro Martinez's training in the 1990s, Rusie's training in the 1890s can be described as minimal. Rusie achieved his endurance simply by allowing his muscles to repair and reload, to restore glycogen by doing what many professional pitchers of his era were known to do between games — rest, socialize, enjoy life, take in the ambience of saloons. He did not complicate and detract from the repair-and-reloading process by lifting weights, throwing long toss or bullpens, or doing pull-ups. The

12. Endurance, Durability, and Longevity

superior endurance and durability that resulted from his lifestyle and limited training are best explained by sportswriters' habit of writing that such a pitcher has an "electric arm." Glycogen storage within the fast-twitch fibers is much like a rechargeable battery. By the time Rusie planted his stride foot to deliver the first pitch of a game, he had fully recharged his arm with enough energy to fire perhaps 10 dozen powerful pitches. He probably performed no training exertions between starts that would cause a partial discharge of this energy.

Martinez represents more rigorous pitcher training. Though modern training varies widely among pitchers and teams, the four rest days between starts may include one or two bullpen sessions at 60 to 75 percent effort, one or two long-toss sessions, weight training for the upper and lower body, and running. If these exercises involve the forceful activation of fast-glycolytic fibers of pitching's kinetic chain, they subtract glycogen in varying amounts from what would be available the next time the pitcher goes to the mound.

Pitch Counts

Most major-league organizations employ the pitch count to manage the workload of each pitcher within pre-determined limits during a game.[11] A pitch limit is a practical approach to protect against the effects of over-pitching, but it remains controversial. Critics charge that the typical limit of 100 pitches is too conservative. They also point out that a pitch limit is ineffective in determining when fatigue or muscle damage will place the pitcher at risk, since physiologic signs of over-pitching are usually delayed by at least a day.

Yet another problem with a pitch limit is the period over which pitches are counted. Conventionally, this period is the time spent on the mound. Relative to the physiology of the fast-glycolytic muscle fibers, however, the pitch count period should be longer, so as to include the period in which muscle fatigue and muscle damage are resolved. Consequently, it should extend to the recovery period for both muscle fatigue and muscle damage and include the workouts done during this period. How much time does it take the fast-glycolytic muscle fibers to repair and fully restore glycogen? It ranges from two days to approximately seven days, and it is longer and more variable than it was in the early 1900s

The Science of the Fastball

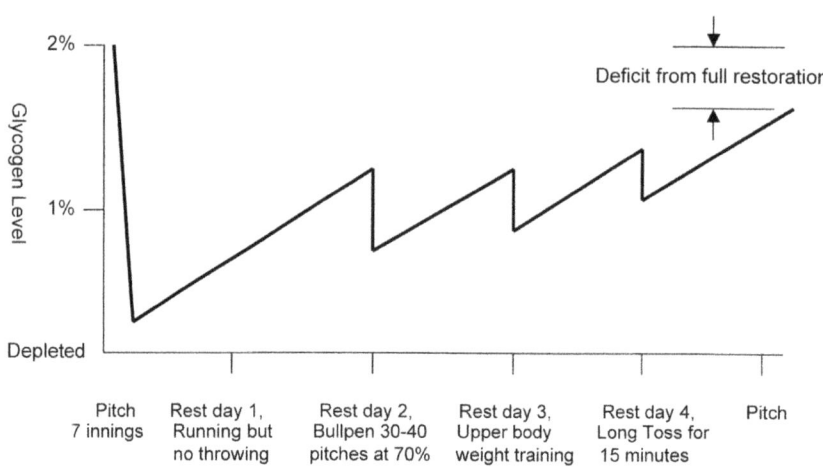

Figure 8: This qualitative graph shows how glycogen levels of forearm flexor muscles might vary between starts when the pitcher works out on three of the rest days. Because slight inflammation is assumed, the slope of the restoration lines is one that would require five days for complete restoration.

because pitchers generally apply more power per pitch in response to greater power at the plate.

Figure 8 is a graph representing the recovery — the repair and restoration — of the pitcher's forearm flexor muscles as they would likely be affected by workouts involving the fast-glycolytic fibers of these muscles between starts. It is qualitatively similar to the graph derived from actual glycogen data from the vastus lateralis muscles of runners' legs presented in *Figure 7* earlier in this chapter.

With the estimated effects of a bullpen session, weight-training, and long toss, the pitcher represented by the sawtooth plot *of Figure 8* does not fully restore the glycogen to his forearm flexor muscles before he returns to the mound. He enters his next outing with a deficit, meaning he is less likely to remain effective for seven innings or for the same number of pitches in his next performance.

This deficit can be carried forward if the pitcher proceeds with the same routine, the same number of pitches per outing and the same training regimen. The deficit can accumulate to produce a poor performance after several outings. This cumulative effect may produce inconsistency or shorter periods of effectiveness with each outing; that is, a week-to-week

12. Endurance, Durability, and Longevity

decline, building a glycogen or muscle-repair deficit in small increments that eventually becomes large enough to produce a bad outing, an extended slump, or the familiar mid- to late-season swoon. With a diminishing and unknown level of intramuscular stored energy, the pitcher may enter a game with enough glycogen to get through five innings, for example, before his forearm flexors begin to produce less force and contraction speed. In the extreme, the cumulative deficit may allow him only to get through the warm-up, producing a dreadfully short outing in which he can't pitch himself out of the first inning. The effect of a cumulative deficit is well illustrated by Bob Feller's pitching slump of 1938, which is described in the next chapter. The deficit can be increased by an exceptionally long outing, such as a complete game no-hitter. Such rare gems are often followed by poor performances, indicative of the link between muscle damage and glycogen restoration.

As muscle damage increases, the slope of recovery decreases, because some but not all fibers of the pitching muscles may sustain greater damage and consequently develop inflammation, which further delays glycogen restoration. This effect on a varying portion of the fibers occurs because of uneven distribution of glycogen to intramuscular storage and uneven strain distribution among muscle fibers. As the number of muscle fibers with inflammation grows larger, the inflammation may reach the threshold for delayed-onset muscle soreness, forcing the pitcher to miss a start or resort to the undesirable alternative of taking NSAIDs.

The slope of the recovery line, rising from left to right, is not as steep as it would be after a shorter outing. A reliever pitching two innings, for example, would have a steeper recovery line. He would recover at a faster rate because he would be less likely to experience significant inflammation after two innings of work. Consequently, the restoration of glycogen would likely be closer to 48 hours (with minimal workouts between appearances). A faster rate of recovery, a steeper slope on the graph, would result from less exertion on each pitch, and/or fewer pitches, as would have been the case in the early 1900s. When pitchers were able to ease off against poor hitters as Christy Mathewson did, the recovery slope would have been steeper than that shown in the figure above. A century after Mathewson, major-league teams are less likely to carry weak hitters, except of course the pitchers of the National League, so there are fewer opportunities for a pitcher to dial down the power level.

How significant are workouts between starts in slowing the restoration of glycogen? The effect can be estimated based on two criteria: first, if the exercise activates the fast-glycolytic fibers with many repetitions, particularly in the muscles near the end of the kinetic chain; secondly, if the exercise involves training with large resistance or heavy weights. Significant glycogen consumption occurs each time the fast-glycolytic muscle fibers used in pitching are forcefully activated, and this is most important in the muscles of the rotator cuff and the forearm flexors, which are the most highly active in pitching.

- Weight-lifting. Weight-lifting has been shown to preferentially deplete glycogen from fast-glycolytic muscle fibers, rapidly consuming stored energy from them.[12] Glycogen consumption in weight-lifting varies with the amount of weight lifted, the distance it is lifted in each repetition, and the number of times it is lifted. The product of these three variables is the amount of work performed, which equates to the amount of energy consumed. If heavy weights are used, ones close to the maximum single-weight rep, the cost in terms of glycogen is high. Few repetitions with light weights have a smaller effect on glycogen (but also a smaller benefit). As noted in Chapter 9, three sets of 10 repetitions may cause a 25 percent reduction in muscle glycogen. The most serious effect occurs in exercises of the forearm flexors. If the double play is a pitcher's best friend, the wrist curl is his most ambivalent friend—his worst friend during the season and his best friend in the off-season. The wrist curl is perhaps the simplest resistance exercise to perform and the easiest to sustain from a rehab routine. The forearm flexor muscles are also subject to the effect of multiple exercises. They are involved in exercises other than wrist curls because they are activated in gripping and holding the barbell or dumbbell. Weight-lifting has a similar effect on the rotator cuff in that multiple exercises work the rotator cuff and can cause the pitcher to unknowingly over-work this very important group of muscles.
- Long toss. True long toss involves near-maximal effort, so each throw can be considered equivalent to a pitch. Limiting the distance thrown is an effective way of limiting the amount of energy consumed. With a limit of 120 feet, for example, substantially less energy is consumed per throw than one of 300 feet.
- Pitching bullpen sessions or batting practice. Both are typically done at 60 to 75 percent, a subjective measure of effort; consequently, they require less power and consume less glycogen than game-speed

pitches. At this effort, each pitch might require about one-third less energy than pitches at maximum speed.
- Warm-up pitches. The 25 to 30 warm-up pitches thrown prior to going to the mound are, in effect, already included in the pitch count. They are essential and typically most are thrown at near max-effort.
- Light resistance exercises with bands or dumbbells. Elastic bands usually involve less resistance than weight lifting, but the tendency is to perform more repetitions. Consequently, the exercises can involve substantial work and a energy expenditure by the targeted muscles if many repetitions are performed.
- Calisthenics. The pull-up is an exercise that can have a substantial effect on glycogen levels of the rotator cuff muscles because of the high resistance in lifting the weight of the body. Pull-ups or chin-ups can be beneficial in the off-season but detrimental during the season.
- Running. Moderate distance running does not activate the fast glycolytic fibers so there is no effect; however, running sprints on the field or uphill does forcefully activate the fast glycolytic fibers of the legs, which can lead to fatigue of the leg muscles used in pitching or in sprinting to cover first base during a game.

Longevity: Sustaining the Ability to Recover

A pitcher's endurance and durability are determined by his recovery ability, for which the main processes are the restoration of glycogen and repair of muscle fibers. A pitcher's longevity is determined by how well he sustains this recovery ability over the long term despite the effects of aging, illness, and the wear-and-tear on muscle, connective tissue, and nerve tissue. Aging produces many changes. Connective tissue loses its elasticity. Muscle tissue loses mass. Organs lose some of their reserve capacity. Cell membranes become less permeable, slowing the rates at which tissues receive oxygen and nutrients and remove carbon dioxide and wastes. No single process explains all of the changes; there are many factors, including heredity, environment, diet, exercise, illnesses, wear-and-tear, and others. The rate of aging varies from person to person, but studies indicate that aerobic exercise can forestall many of them and that strength training can

The Science of the Fastball

halt the loss of muscle mass. Strength training and aerobic endurance training thus provide insurance against a rapid decline. The focus of recovery is on the muscles of the kinetic chain of pitching, which not only supply the power of the fastball, but also protect the elbow and shoulder joints, the points of injury that typically work against longevity.

Two pitchers of exceptional longevity were Nolan Ryan and Satchel Paige. Ryan pitched 27 seasons in the major leagues, more than any other pitcher in the history of the game. He started 773 games, more starts than anyone except Cy Young. He pitched with little apparent change in his power until his elbow ligament failed him at age 46. Paige pitched 24 seasons in professional baseball, including five major-league seasons from age 42 to 46 but not including his three-inning start for the Kansas City Athletics at age 59. He entered the major leagues in 1948 after 22 years as the brightest and most colorful star of the Negro Leagues. In his third start for the Cleveland Indians, he pitched a 3-hit shutout over the White Sox before a record night-game crowd of 78,382. He was elected to the Baseball Hall of Fame in 1971.

Ryan and Paige may have been the two fastest pitchers of all time. The velocity of Ryan's fastball was of course measured scientifically, though not precisely, in 1974. No velocity measurements were ever made on Paige's fastball but many of those who saw him pitch believe he was among the fastest ever. In a 2010 *Sports Illustrated* article, Joe Posnanski ranked Paige first on his list of the 32 fastest pitchers in the baseball history. He placed Nolan Ryan second, Walter Johnson third, and Bob Feller fourth. Posnanski supports his rankings with assessments by Hall of Famers who played with or against them": Joe DiMaggio would say that Paige was the best he ever faced. Bob Feller would say that Paige was the best he ever saw. Hack Wilson would say that the ball looked like a marble when it crossed the plate. Dizzy Dean would say that Paige's fastball made his own look like a changeup."[13]

Ryan and Paige had little common ground with regard to training methods. Their approach to training presents an even sharper contrast than do Amos Rusie and Pedro Martinez. Ryan's highly disciplined approach, which included both strength and endurance training for 22 years, presents the most convincing argument that a combination of aerobic exercise and strength training is the key to longevity for a pitcher. Paige's undisciplined approach presents the most convincing argument that genetics is important to a pitcher's longevity.

12. Endurance, Durability, and Longevity

Thought to be among the fastest pitchers of all time, Satchel Paige set the standard for longevity. He entered the major leagues at age 42 after 22 seasons in the Negro Leagues. He made a three-inning appearance at age 59 with the Kansas City Athletics (National Baseball Hall of Fame Library, Cooperstown, New York).

"Thanks may be due to some genetics that have allowed me to age more slowly than most," Ryan commented in his 1992 autobiography. "But there's no secret to what it takes to stay in shape at this age. And that's hours and hours of workouts."

"Things have changed for me as I have gotten older," Ryan revealed in his mid–40s. "I've had to vary my workouts to make up for longer recovery times. I feel many effects of age. My back bothers me at times. I get stiffer quicker. I can run only so much. But I still put myself through the paces of a long, hard workout nearly every day, because it's worth it to me…. I can't run three days in a row like I used to because I get too sore or too stiff, but I still have to run two or three times a week. During the off-season I get a lot of roadwork in, just logging the miles. During the season I do sprint work." Ryan also continued the weight workouts he began in Anaheim in 1972. "There's no doubt in my mind that if it hadn't been for that weight room, I would have been out of the game many years ago."[14]

Building aerobic endurance, whether by running, riding a stationary bike, or any other aerobic exercise, unquestionably benefits a pitcher's longevity, endurance and durability. Aerobic exercise improves and sustains cardiovascular efficiency, maintaining the supply system vital to muscles, organs, and glands, and keeping the recovery process of repairing muscles and restoring glycogen functioning efficiently. Many scientific studies have demonstrated the connection between aerobic fitness and health and its importance in slowing the effects of aging.

"Avoid running at all times," was one of Paige's six rules for healthy living. He too showed remarkable endurance, durability, and longevity though he never adhered to training regimens or curfews throughout his long professional career, which began in 1926 with the Chattanooga White Sox of the Negro Leagues.

A notebook that Paige carried for recording the details of every game shows he pitched in more than 2,500 games. "The numbers were dizzying, but each required an asterisk explaining that Satchel kept records the way he set them: with flair, grace, and hoopla," wrote biographer Larry Tye. "The numbers changed as he added to his accomplishments and as yet another reporter wanted to peek at his books…. His tally of no-hitters was as low as 20, as high as a hundred…. Just when any serious statistician might be tempted to dismiss it all as a ruse, closer scrutiny suggests that much of it was true…. [He] played as a semipro and professional, in the

12. Endurance, Durability, and Longevity

Negro Leagues, on barnstorming tours, in Latin America and Canada as well as the United States, and in the major and minor leagues. He played spring and summer, fall and winter. He often threw just three or four innings a game, but he did it every day or two for 41 years."[15]

Paige's durability may have been unmatched, but he discovered that he did have limitations at age 32. One day in the late summer of 1938 while pitching in the Mexican League, he had difficulty loosening up his arm. Despite the stiffness, he continued to pitch, lying to his manager and claiming that his arm was okay. In what has been described as one of his best performances ever, he pitched seven shut-out innings against eventual champion Club Azules despite excruciating pain. When he walked off the mound, he was unable to pitch again for seven months. "Devastated by the betrayal of his near-ecclesiastical throwing arm, when doctors in Mexico City told him he would likely never be able to pitch again, they might as well have told him he was going to be destroyed like a broken-down horse," wrote biographer Mark Ribowsky.[16]

There was no therapy beyond rest for Paige's injury, which was assumed to be career-ending and was never accurately diagnosed. But his remarkable power of recovery that had sustained him for 12 years of pitching volume that would disable ordinary pitchers, brought him back to the mound after seven months. The revelation that he could throw again, the throw-down-the-crutches-and-walk moment came in pre-game warm-up before a Kansas City Monarchs game. When an errant throw to first base came his way, Paige picked up the ball and threw it back to the pitcher.

"Just about every player on the field seemed to see it and stop stockstill," wrote Richard Donovan in a 1953 *Collier's* magazine article. "Walking thoughtfully toward the dugout, Paige picked up a glove and called for the ball. Without a word, the Monarchs' catcher left the plate and stationed himself about pitching distance from Paige. Then Paige began to throw, easily at first, then harder and harder. Nobody moved, the stands were silent, the game waiting. Then, abruptly, he stopped, and gazed around at all the eyes upon him. 'Well,' he said. 'I'm back.'"[17]

"After my arm first came back, I didn't know for sure I could blaze away until I got back into some games and really had to," recounted Paige in a 1962 autobiography. "I could. That hummer of mine just sang a sweet song going across the plate. It was the finest music I'd ever heard."[18]

Nine years later he would enter the major leagues as a rookie with Cleveland. With the Indians in a pennant race and in need of more pitch-

The Science of the Fastball

ing, owner Bill Veeck brought in Paige to try out with his team. On his 42nd birthday, Paige signed his first major-league contract, becoming the first Negro League pitcher in the American League.

In that summer of '48, he compiled to a 6–1 record with a 2.48 ERA and two shutouts. He concluded the season with two-thirds of an inning in relief in the fifth game of the World Series. It was a glorious moment, with Paige entering the game as the huge crowd chanted his name. But it held disappointment for him as well; it was his only appearance of the series, in which he had hoped to be used as a starter. Entering with one out in the seventh inning, he faced only two batters with the Indians trailing 11–5 after starter Bob Feller and two other relievers had given up six runs in the seventh inning to relinquish the lead.

Paige did not pitch as well in the 1949 season, due in part to continuing stomach problems, gallstones, and badly infected teeth. The Indians let him go, and Veeck signed him in 1951 to play for the St. Louis Browns, where his immediate impact was to help double the attendance. With the Browns in August 1952, he became, at age 46, the oldest major leaguer to pitch a complete game — a 12-inning, 1–0 victory over Detroit in which he struck out nine. In 138 innings that season, he struck out 91 batters. He was, however, used mainly as a reliever, and he led the league in relief victories and relief innings pitched. He made the All-Star team in 1952 and 1953 with the Browns.

Paige pitched a total of just 317 innings in his last three major league seasons. Ryan pitched 391 in his last three. Though Paige pitched in the majors to age 47, and Ryan to 46½, they arrived at the terminal point of their careers in different ways. Paige was a pitcher with fine control, skill, and deception, but his fastball had slowed substantially. Ryan remained a power pitcher, still able to register low- to mid–90s on the radar gun.

Ryan saw his power diminishing as he began the 1993 season. Just before the season, he announced that it would be his last, and indeed it was. He went 5–5 with a 4.88 ERA in 13 starts and struck out 46 in 66 innings, making it only the second season of his career in which his strikeout rate fell below 0.9 per inning. Though his power, and his ability to recover between starts were waning, the season would not end without a final demonstration of his strength, in a unique way. In a night game on August 4 against the Chicago White Sox before 32,312 fans in Arlington, he hit Robin Ventura with a pitch in the third inning. Ventura charged the mound. Ryan grabbed the 26-year-old third baseman, twisted him

12. Endurance, Durability, and Longevity

into a headlock, and pummeled him with his fist until catcher Iván Rodríguez intervened. Ryan later described his response to Ventura's charge as the same maneuver he applied in branding cattle on his Texas ranch. Video of the incident was shown nationally and became as well known to baseball fans as any of his seven no-hitters. He earned the victory that night, 5–2, giving up three hits and one earned run, and striking out five in seven innings.

Seven weeks later, Ryan's right arm suffered a catastrophic power loss. In Seattle on September 22, the anterior band of his ulnar collateral ligament tore in the first inning, terminating his career two starts short of his scheduled finale. In this, his last outing, he allowed four walks, a grand slam, and a single in the first inning without recording an out. "I heard the ligament pop like a rubber band," he said. "There's no way I'll ever be able to throw again. My body is telling me it's time to move on and do something else."[19]

13

Differential Power Loss
Outliers, Slumps, and Downward Trends

"I've had a lot of bad games where I just didn't have it and got shelled early."—Nolan Ryan, in his 1992 autobiography

Much can be learned about pitching power by examining the loss of power. All pitchers occasionally get shelled, a seemingly random misfortune having no cure or prevention — baseball's equivalent of the common cold. A bad game, not having one's best stuff, occurs more frequently for some pitchers than others and more often in the latter half of the season. At its cruelest, a shelling unfolds as a 10-run first inning that becomes a career setback for a rookie adjusting to a heavier workload. It also strikes great pitchers randomly when the stakes are highest. Take Mordecai (Three-Finger) Brown, for example. In game six of the 1906 World Series, the Chicago Cubs ace failed to make it out of the second inning. Brown, whose career ERA is third best among all Hall of Fame pitchers, gave up seven runs on eight hits in less than two innings. Smokey Joe Wood suffered through a dismal outing in the seventh game of the 1912 World Series. The 23-year-old Boston Red Sox fireballer, a 34-game winner that season, gave up six runs in a 13-pitch first inning. In the fifth game of the 1948 World Series, Bob Feller gave up seven earned runs in six innings, including three home runs. Wood's shelling was blamed on an inadequate warm-up. Brown's was attributed to pitching on short rest. Feller called it "just one of those days when a pitcher just doesn't have his good stuff."[1] Getting shelled is typically blamed on a variety of difficulties — poor mechanics, control problems of unknown origin, mistakes on critical pitches, or mental lapses. There is a substantial mental component in pitching, and the default culprit for bad games is often the pitcher's mind. But many if not most bad games relate to power loss, specifically a differential power loss in muscles of the kinetic chain caused by two recovery processes being incom-

13. Differential Power Loss

When he was with the Houston Astros, Nolan Ryan pitched the fifth of his seven no-hitters at age 34. He demonstrated his exceptional recovery ability by pitching a complete-game victory five days later (National Baseball Hall of Fame Library, Cooperstown, New York).

plete — the restoration of glycogen and the repair of routine damage to muscle fibers.

Even Nolan Ryan sometimes lost power and by his own assessment pitched badly. When the 44-year-old Ryan arrived at Arlington Stadium on May 1, 1991, to make his fifth start of the season for the Texas Rangers, he felt very much like any middle-aged laborer might feel at the end of a hard week. Five days earlier, he had absorbed a 5–2 loss in Cleveland in a 133-pitch outing. After four rest days, he awakened on game day with stiff back muscles, the same soreness that had put him on the disabled list previously. "I feel old today," he said as he was warming up to face the Toronto Blue Jays. "My back hurts, my finger hurts, my ankle hurts. Everything hurts."[2]

Ryan opened the game by striking out the leadoff man. In the second inning he struck out all three batters swinging with curveballs. Then, before a Wednesday night crowd of 33,000, he proceeded to pitch a no-hitter with 16 strikeouts, 13 of them on swinging strikes. He induced a total of 29 swings and misses, 24 percent of his 122 pitches. His curveball was working well, and he described his fastball as "really hopping." His velocity peaked at 96 mph in the fourth inning and averaged 93 mph for all nine innings. His last pitch was a 93-mph fastball to strike out Roberto Alomar swinging. It was his seventh career no-hitter, a major league record, and perhaps the most dominating of all his no-hitters.

Ryan's soreness had no apparent effect on his performance. The pain in the finger was apparently below a threshold that would have hindered power transmission. The pain in the back muscles, antagonists of trunk flexion, would have adversely affected his mechanics if not controlled with pain medicine. That his curveball was working well and his fastball was hopping indicate that the flexor muscles of his forearm were at or near full power throughout the game.

No-hitter number seven demonstrated Ryan's remarkable durability and resilience. Juxtaposed with his following start, it also illustrates the vagaries of recovery. On the mound seven days later against the same team, he experienced a much different outcome. As he did on May 1, he opened the game with a strikeout, and in the second inning he struck out the side. In the third inning, however, the proceedings turned against him as he gave up three walks, a triple, and a double. He left the mound in the sixth, after allowing five walks and three earned runs, while throwing only 54 percent strikes, compared to 68 percent strikes in the no-hitter. The per-

13. Differential Power Loss

formance swing between May 1 and May 8 shows that even baseball's career strikeout leader was subject to occasional vulnerability, that a roaring fastball is not omnipotent, and that rest and recovery do not always yield predictable results. Everything hurt on May 1. Everything went slightly awry in the third inning a week later.

Poor performance can be classified by duration — short, medium, or long. Respectively, these are outliers, slumps, and downward trends. When Ryan admitted to a lot of bad games, he was referring to outliers, which are defined as performances markedly different from the norm. A pitching outlier can be indicated by the number of base-runners allowed, the total of walks and hits per inning (WHIP), the ratio of strikes to total pitches, or simply the number of walks in an inning. Throughout Ryan's career, he averaged a 1.247 WHIP and 0.52 walks per inning. There is a statistical test for outliers based on the mean and standard deviation of a data set. Neither baseball statisticians nor baseball managers use this test. Managers have their own subjective test of outliers, which works well and traditionally concludes with pointing to the bullpen, walking to the mound, and passing the ball from the starter to the reliever. Statistically, Ryan's May 1 and May 8 games were both outliers, but of course, it is the unfavorable outliers that produce high anxiety among pitchers, their coaches, and managers.

There were other unfavorable outliers in Ryan's career, but only one other came immediately after a no-hitter. That was on June 16, 1990, five days after he threw 130 pitches in no-hitter number six. He lost, 5–0, in a short outing in which he walked three of the first six batters and gave up five walks, four hits, and three earned runs in five innings. Only 57 percent of his 114 pitches were strikes. He was 43 years old, and age was likely a factor in his recovery between starts.

In his start one week after his seventh no-hitter, Ryan's control was off, as evidenced by his 54 percent strike rate and elevated walk rate. He probably had a diminished spin rate after the second inning, taking some of the movement away from his fastball and perhaps the bite out of his curve. He probably had difficulty keeping the ball down in the zone. These effects are indicative of differential fatigue involving the flexor muscles of the forearm. As noted in Chapter 9, each muscle in the kinetic chain of pitching fatigues at a different rate. The most active, most highly stressed muscles are likely to fatigue most rapidly.

When the muscles that power the hand and fingers fatigue, the result is diminished speed in the hand and finger movements. Consequently, these muscles do not respond at normal speed when the motor neurons fire. If the subscapularis muscle of the shoulder remains at full power, the hand and/or fingers lag behind, disrupting the critical timing of wrist flexion and finger flexion relative to forward arm rotation. Differential fatigue caused by depletion of glycogen is insidious because it produces no sensation of pain in the pitcher's arm. There is no warning signal of tenderness, no perceptible stiffness. The vulnerability of any pitcher lies in making mistakes, and fatigued flexors make mistakes more likely:

- **Release-point error.** Fatigue of the forearm flexors increases the potential for errors in locating the pitch. Differential fatigue involving the slender, segmented finger flexors — the flexor digitorum superficialis and flexor digitorum profundus — can reduce the speed of finger flexion, producing an earlier-than-normal release relative to forward arm rotation. With a high arm slot, this may result in the pitcher being unable to keep the ball down with the normal timing of release he has learned through thousands of repetitions. Or he may overcompensate for this error, putting a pitch in the dirt. With a lower arm slot, he will miss the strike zone laterally, perhaps hitting the batter. In outlier performances the pitcher usually has a low percentage of strikes, less than 55 percent, for example. Finger flexion speed also affects spin rate and linear velocity; thus, fatigue of the finger flexors can cause a reduction in movement and velocity.
- **Reduced movement and velocity.** If release-point error is the first indication of forearm flexor fatigue, diminished movement (spin rate) is likely to be the second. Deficient movement compounds the effect of diminished control. The pitcher falls behind in the count and lacks control to keep pitches off the middle of the plate, making them more easily hittable because of less-than-normal movement. All the flexor muscles of the forearm flex the hand at the wrist, a movement that contributes substantially to fastball velocity in pitchers who have large wrist-extension angle and high wrist-flexion speed. Fatigue results in both a loss of force and a slowing of the speed of contraction, so the differential fatigue of the flexors disrupts the precise timing between wrist flexion and forward arm rotation. As discussed in Chapter 6, this causes the hand to lag behind the

arm — probably on the order of one-thousandth of a second — which yields a lower spin rate, less movement, and less linear velocity. A diminished spin rate can produce a difference in bat contact that can result, for example, in a home-run ball instead of a pop-up.
- **Hanging curveball or slider.** Besides flexing the hand at the wrist, the flexor carpi ulnaris, with its tendon insertion point on the side opposite the thumb, adducts the hand toward the pinkie finger. This provides the forward spin to the ball around a near-horizontal axis to produce a curveball. Differential fatigue involving this muscle can produce a reduced spin rate on the breaking pitch, causing it to hang and be easily hittable. At times when the pitcher gives up on his curveball, finding that it isn't working reliably, the cause is likely fatigue of this muscle, which is relatively small, typically weighing less than an ounce.

Why would the effects of differential fatigue appear at times in the first inning but at other times in later innings? As noted in the previous chapter, glycogen is stored within the fast-glycolytic fibers, and its energy storage characteristics make it similar to a rechargeable battery. The energy remaining in a battery can be estimated with an energy balance equation, calculating for example how long it takes a car battery to lose its charge if the headlights are left on without the engine running. An energy balance also applies to pitching, but there are many variables that determine how much charge is available in the arm and shoulder muscles when a pitcher enters a game. These variables include the number of pitches thrown, the energy expended on each pitch, the threshold level of fatigue, the activity of each muscle in pitching, and the energy expended on other exertions involving the same fast-glycolytic fibers during the cycle of glycogen depletion and restoration.

In 22 seasons from 1972 through 1993, about 12 percent of Nolan Ryan's starts could be described as outliers, performances he might have had in mind when he said he pitched a lot of bad games. These were short outings in which he lasted four innings or less with a WHIP greater than 2 and an exceptional number of walks.

Sandy Koufax had a similar percentage of outliers, about 12 percent of his starts from 1961 through 1965. Bob Feller's rate was about the same in his first seven seasons but doubled in the five seasons of 1948 through 1952, probably because he continued to pitch on a four-day cycle with a workload of 210 to 280 innings per season as his ability to recover from start to start diminished.

Like Feller, Ryan had remarkable recovery ability when in his twenties. This was apparent in Ryan's three outstanding seasons of 1972 through '74 in which he pitched a total of 942 two-thirds innings. On June 14, 1974, when he was 27 years old, he threw 235 pitches in a 13-inning game in which he struck out 19. Four days later, he pitched six shutout innings, and four days after that, a complete-game with 10 strikeouts. Five days later, he pitched a complete game one-hitter — one of six one-hitters in his career. In that 1974 season, in which he struck out 9.9 batters per nine innings, he pitched on three rest days (four-man rotation) 23 times and on four rest days 14 times.

Yet, he was not immune from fatigue. Thirteen days after his one-hitter, the heavy load caught up with him. In a game against the Baltimore Orioles, he opened the third inning by giving up a home run, single, single, and home run to the first four batters before ending his night with fly-outs and a groundout. His line: eight hits, six earned runs, two walks, and four strikeouts in three innings. He quickly returned to his normal, dominating performances, however, finishing the season with 22 victories, 22 complete games, and 367 strikeouts in 332 two-thirds innings. A common characteristic in his outliers for which pitch-count data are available (1988–1993) was a lower percentage of strikes, ranging from about 49 to 57 percent, indicative of control problems resulting from fatigue of the forearm flexor muscles.

Ryan averaged 215 innings per season in his twenties and 218 per season in his thirties. After turning forty, he pitched 211, 220, 239, and 204 innings, respectively, before dropping to 173 at age 44. He averaged 10.2 strikeouts per nine innings over a span of seven seasons in his forties. Aside from his high level of aerobic fitness, there was another important factor that apparently helped him sustain his high level of performance into his forties: he had one extra rest day between starts. In those final seven seasons, he pitched with four or five rest days on 157 occasions and with three rest days only 11 times.

The benefit of an additional rest day can also be seen in the statistics of younger pitchers. In his first five major league seasons, Tim Lincecum, San Francisco's Cy Young Award winner, allowed 20 percent more base runners when pitching after four rest days than he did in pitching after five rest days. That is, his average WHIP through five seasons was 1.262

with four rest days and 1.056 with five. His ERA was 36 percent lower, 2.61 versus 3.56, with the extra day of rest. Other pitchers show no significant difference, however, probably because of individual differences in the intensity of the training between starts, the level of exertion on pitches, and variability in recovery ability. Koufax, who pitched on a four-day cycle, was not significantly different on three rest days (0.968 WHIP) versus four rest days (0.952 WHIP) from 1961 through 1965.

Bob Feller's Slump of 1938

In late June 1938, just two years after his first major-league fastball roared over the plate, Bob Feller was named to the American League All-Star team with a 9–2 record. At 19, he was the youngest player ever selected. Just one week later, however, Feller pitched poorly, giving up eight walks and 10 hits in eight innings against Detroit. Of his six starts in the month of July, three were clearly outliers in which he yielded a total of 24 walks and 28 hits in 25 two-thirds innings.

Feller describes this period of inexplicable decline in his book, *Now Pitching Bob Feller*. At one point, Feller's manager, Ossie Vitt, admonished him about his lack of control: "I've seen lots of pitchers with as much stuff as you've got and more, and they never amounted to a damn because they didn't know where the ball was going when they turned it loose." Near the end of July, Feller expressed discouragement about his slump in a casual remark to reporter Ed McAuley of the *Cleveland News*, saying, "maybe I've lost my fastball." On the following day, July 23, 1938, the *Cleveland News* and the *Cleveland Plain Dealer* proclaimed in headlines: "'Fastball is gone,' Feller says," and "My Old Fastball is Gone and My Control is Not Good Enough to Work the Corners — Feller."

The Heater from Van Meter had indeed cooled off, but the worst was yet to come. The power loss worsened in August, as his ERA for the month soared to 8.71. He walked 11 in seven innings on August 5; gave up seven walks, seven hits, and seven earned runs on August 18; and reached the nadir of his season on August 26 when he allowed 15 hits, 15 earned runs, and nine walks in seven innings against the Yankees. He was pitching on empty. His outliers had coalesced into a slump, but he was still taking the mound to pitch a complete game every fourth or fifth day. There was apparently no soreness, so there was no reason for an extended rest. Skipping two starts would likely have ended his slump, as there was probably a glycogen deficit in the flexor muscles of his forearm, the cumulative result of partial restoration over the previous two months. This apparently was a deficit that did not reach the point of DOMS.

His fastball hadn't actually vanished, however, as the newspapers had proclaimed. It was temporarily without power. The power finally began to return on September 23 against Detroit when he struck out 10 in nine innings and gave up just one walk. Four days later, he won again with 10 strikeouts. He then presented a grand finale, heralding the return of his prodigious power to a home crowd of 27,000 against the Detroit Tigers on the last day of the season when he struck out 18 batters. "It was one of those days when everything feels perfect — your arm, your coordination, your concentration, everything," he said in his baseball memoir, *Now Pitching, Bob Feller*. He struck out Hank Greenberg twice that day, and denied the big first baseman, who had hit 58 homers that season, a shot at Babe Ruth's record of 60.

Feller's slump — which took him from a 9–2 record in the first half of the season to an 8–9 record in the second half — had finally ended. Whether a result of glycogen depletion, incomplete repair of muscle-fiber damage, or both, a slump develops and sustains itself because of inadequate recovery. For Feller, it was likely brought on by the overuse of his formidable fastball, throwing too many max-effort pitches. Once into a pernicious cycle, as he apparently was, it takes longer than the normal four-days' rest to emerge from it. Perhaps one to two skipped starts in the rotation, or 15 days on the disabled list is the quickest way out. Feller never missed a start during his slump, however, so he inched his way out of it. His emergence from the slump came as he pitched six games totaling 49 innings in September. In that month, he took as much as seven days between starts, instead of the usual four to five. The full restoration and recovery Feller so desperately needed finally came as the season ended.

Walter Johnson's Slump and Downward Trend

Walter Johnson, considered by many to be the greatest pitcher of all time, was in his prime from 1910 through 1919. In that 10-year period, he won 265 games and led the American League in strikeouts nine times. After 15 years of delivering baseball's most intimidating fastball, however,

13. Differential Power Loss

he was beginning to sense a loss of power as the decade ended. "I can no longer depend on my speed as I once could," he told *Baseball Magazine* in 1919, when he was 31. "Some days I believe I am as fast as I ever was. But there are other days ... when I can no longer burn the ball across the platter as I could when my arm was a little younger."[3]

Johnson's unique sidearm delivery minimized eccentric loading of the forearm flexor muscles to provide him an advantage in durability, but it did not protect him from shoulder injury. In March 1920, after two weeks of pre-season games, Johnson awoke one morning with soreness so severe that he could not raise his right arm to put on his necktie. He rested the arm for 10 days, then pitched well in two pre-season games. In the season opener, however, he produced an outlier, giving up five runs in two innings before being taken out of the game. After another 10 days of rest, he pitched a shutout victory over the Red Sox to establish a pattern of inconsistency that lasted for the season. His performance reached a peak six weeks later, when on July 1 he pitched the second no-hitter of his career against the Red Sox, striking out 10 with a fastball that had surprising velocity and a curveball that was sharply breaking. His arm soreness immediately returned, accompanied by groin soreness, forcing him to miss his next scheduled start. After another 10 days' rest, he pitched again but took a 4–0 loss, in which he gave up 10 hits in seven innings. After that, he could no longer throw even lightly in practice. The arm pain persisted, terminating his season on the mound. He won only eight games in 1920, a career low.

Johnson's outliers of 1920 turned into a slump, a performance downturn of longer duration. Though his slump seemed to begin with muscle soreness, it likely began before the soreness appeared, with glycogen depletion. It was to Johnson's benefit that the radar gun had not yet been invented when his velocity began to wane about 1920. Consequently, he did not chase his normal velocity and worsen the cycle. Had he seen a measurable loss of speed, he might have perceived that at 32 he had reached the age of inevitable decline. He did not, however. He made a slow but steady comeback from injury after that season, pitching six more years and winning 15 to 23 games each season, except for his last season at age 39.

In the 12 major league seasons before his injury, Johnson pitched an average of 13 innings per week, which included up to 42 starts and three to 10 relief appearances in a season. This was far more than Feller (11 innings per week in his 11 heaviest seasons) and Ryan (7.7 innings per week) pitched in their careers. Johnson was a max-effort pitcher until his fourth major-league season, when he learned to apply his most powerful fastballs sparingly, relying more on craftiness to induce ground-ball and fly-ball outs.

Coming four years after his slump ended, Johnson's 1924 season was an outstanding one in which he captured his third triple crown of pitching, earned the American League MVP honors, and led the Senators to the World Series. Two years later, at age 38, he pitched what some consider his masterpiece in front of an opening day crowd of 25,000 in Washington — a 15-inning shutout against Philadelphia, giving up only six hits and three walks, while striking out nine. Predictably, his next start, seven days after his 15-inning marathon, was a short outing in which he gave up eight hits and two walks in just three innings.

Though he won 15 games in 1926, the following season was one of decline, hastened perhaps by an injury in spring training. A line drive off the bat of teammate Joe Judge smashed into his left ankle, fracturing his fibula. He didn't make his first start of the 1927 season until Memorial Day, but when he did, he shut out the Red Sox in a complete-game three-hitter. It seemed that he had come back yet again from injury, but he had done so without his characteristic power. He struck out only one batter in the game. "Deprived of his famed speed ball by father time or one of his descendants, Johnson again resorted to curves, which were slammed back at him," wrote Shirley Povich in the *Washington Post* after a loss to St. Louis nine days later on June 9, 1927.

He started 15 games in his final season, winning five and losing six, and his ERA for the season rose to 5.10. His last complete game as a pitcher was a 7–3 loss on August 22, 1927, in which he gave up six runs in 3 one-third innings. A game against the Yankees on September 30 marked the end of his magnificent 21-season career. One month shy of his 40th birthday, he appeared as a pinch hitter, and in his last at-bat hit a fly ball into the glove of a Yankee right fielder named Babe Ruth.

Feller's Downward Trend

Fourteen years after he emerged from his slump in dramatic fashion, Bob Feller revealed his remaining goals in baseball to the sportswriters of Cleveland. As the 1952 season approached, he told reporters that he hoped to reach the 300-win milestone before retiring, to pitch his fourth no-hitter, and to help the Indians reach the World Series again. He was 33 then, so all three goals seemed within reach. He had pitched well the previous season, winning 22 games to bring his career victory total to 230 and finishing fifth in league MVP voting.

Though his velocity appeared to have diminished in the 1952 spring training, he began the 1952 season well, pitching an eight-inning one-hitter against the St. Louis Browns on April 23. He gave up the lone hit, a triple, to the first batter he faced, and the only run he surrendered came when the next batter reached base on an error. Six days later against the Philadelphia Athletics, however, he gave up 18 hits, five walks, and seven earned runs, while facing 50 batters. Four days after that, on May 3, he pitched 5 one-third innings and allowed 5 earned runs. On May 8, he allowed 12 singles in another short outing of 5 two-thirds innings.

His next four starts were no better, with lots of hits and walks and few strikeouts. On June 8, before a Sunday afternoon crowd of 21,949 in Philadelphia, Feller arrived at a career low point, a pitcher's nightmare. Ten days after his previous start, he found himself powerless to complete the first inning, giving up seven walks and five earned runs in just two-thirds of an inning. He forced in three runs with bases-loaded walks. There, 16 years after his marvelous debut, after pitching almost 4,000 innings, after leading the American League in innings pitched for five seasons, the power of his incomparable fastball had indeed vanished. He made 30 starts during the 1952 season and won only 9 games. He acknowledged that his fastball had lost its zip and he told the press that he was working on a knuckleball.

Feller won 10 games in 1953 and 13 in 1954. In 1955, he made 11 starts and finished at 4–4. In 1956, his final season, he made 19 appearances and was 0–4 in four starts. He played the last game of his 18-season career at age 37 on September 30, 1956. He pitched a complete game, the 279th of his career, giving up 14 hits and eight earned runs in an 8–4 loss to Detroit. He struck out no one.

The best season of Feller's career came in 1946, the first full season after an absence of almost four years while serving in the Navy during World War II. In his last five seasons, 1952 to 1956 (age 33 to 37), there was a distinct downward trend in his pitching. His performances, however, had begun a gradual decline as early as the 1948 season, when he was 29 years old. This was apparent in a rising WHIP, a falling strikeout rate, and an increasing number of outlier performances. His pitching, in short, became inconsistent. "When you approach the end of your career as an athlete, inconsistency becomes your enemy," said Feller. "On certain days, you can perform well enough to win ... but the problem is being able to do it on a consistent basis."[4]

Inconsistency is the performance indicator of what physiologists refer to as overtraining, the condition in which the volume and intensity of training and/or competition exceeds the athlete's capacity to recover, a capacity that diminishes with age. Feller's decline, the onset of inconsistency, came at a younger age than it did for Johnson or Ryan, much sooner after his career peak in workload. Feller reached a peak of 371 innings at age 27. Johnson pitched 371 at age 26, and Ryan, 332 at age 27.

Why did Feller's decline come much earlier than those of Johnson and Ryan? Did he not maintain good aerobic fitness? Did he not re-strengthen his pitching muscles in the off-season? Did he not adequately recover in the off-season from the cumulative effects of pitching 300-plus innings? Did he simply deliver too many max-effort fastballs for too long?

Feller exercised year-round to stay fit throughout his career. "I stepped up my conditioning program with more of everything — calisthenics, lifting, and running," he said about his preparations for the 1953 season. "It's critical for pitchers to get in as much running as they can, all year long. They should run in the off-season, and during the season they should run sprints in the outfield during batting practice."[5] One of the six rules in Feller's recipe for a good life in baseball was to exercise all year round.[6]

Though he performed weight lifting, it is unlikely that he significantly re-strengthened his arm and shoulder muscles in the off-season. His weight-lifting regimen was limited to light weights, which, as noted in Chapter 10, does little to increase muscle mass and cross-section area as is necessary to increase muscle strength. "I've always used weights, and have always done physical exercise. You need long, lean muscles. Therefore, you shouldn't use heavy weights."[7]

Feller's decline may have been hastened by post-season pitching that delayed or prevented his full recovery from the cumulative effects of pitching 300 or more innings in the major-league season. When he was aboard the *USS Alabama* during World War II, Feller conceived an idea for an expanded and improved barnstorming tour. After the war, he received permission from the commissioner of baseball to increase the tour length from 10 to 30 days and Feller made the arrangements to take baseball's stars to the heartland after the World Series in 1946 and '47. He recruited

13. Differential Power Loss

a team of major-league stars and hired Satchel Paige to assemble and pitch for a team of Negro League stars. The two teams traveled in two DC-3 passenger planes belonging to Flying Tiger Airlines, playing before crowds totaling 250,000 in a packed schedule of daily games. Feller's All-Stars played Paige's All-Stars in as many as 35 games during the month-long tour. The players were paid $3,500 a piece for the month, and Feller earned as much as $80,000 as the promoter, $30,000 more than his annual base salary with the Indians. There was thus plenty of financial incentive for him to display his formidable fastball to the fans, and he pitched in about 30 of the 35 games, working two to five innings in each game. In 1946, he consequently added about 100 innings to his season total of 371 innings. Did he dig himself into a hole of muscle micro-trauma with the additional innings?

His 371 innings in the regular season were more than any pitcher since the dead ball era. If he added 100 innings in the tour, his total would have been the highest since Amos Rusie pitched 482 innings in 1893. Rusie, a hard-thrower like Feller, lasted nine years in professional baseball. Feller may have pitched all the innings at maximal effort. He was still throwing high heat in his late twenties, as attested by his description of a game in which he poised to set a new major-league strikeout record in June 1947: "I missed the '47 all star game because of an injury to my back. I hurt it in my last start before the game after striking out 10 of the first 12 batters against the Philadelphia A's," he explained. "I was going for 20 [strikeouts] that night, but was throwing so hard by the fourth inning, that my left foot slipped and I tore some muscle in my back." He went three more innings and exited with 12 strikeouts. Despite the injury, he never missed a start the remainder of the 1947 season, accumulating 299 innings, pitching 20 complete games, and finishing with a 20–11 record.

What were probably cumulative effects became fully apparent in Feller's 1952 season when he reached career highs in his ERA, 4.74, and WHIP, 1.576. The structural and functional effects could have resulted in diminished strength in his arm and shoulder muscles, instability of the elbow or shoulder joint, or loss of elasticity. The anterior band of the ulnar collateral ligament of his right arm could have become more compliant as collagen fibrils permanently stretched, resulting in diminished velocity. Feller's pitches in the 1952 season were more easily hittable, indicating not just a loss of velocity but also a loss of his exceptional hand speed, which had long produced a fastball with a high spin rate and movement. With a compliant elbow ligament comes the loss of elastic-strain energy-storage-and-return capability, which means that less energy can be transferred from the trunk to the arm and shoulder. Even without the severe stresses of pitching, the elasticity of ligaments and tendons diminishes with age.[8] There can also be a loss of muscle-fiber elasticity with age, particularly with fast-glycolytic fibers, as a result of repetitive stresses.[9] The loss of muscle fiber elasticity can reduce both arm speed and hand speed. Aging may also affect muscle function through changes to the nervous system. Experiments in which old muscle is transplanted into young animals indicate that the nervous system may play an important role in loss of muscle function with age.[10]

Is a pitcher's downward trend reversible? For one who maintains good health and a high level of fitness, it appears possible to turn a downward trend into a mere slump. Muscles retain their plasticity throughout life in a fit, healthy person. Muscles can be strengthened with judicious, progressive-overload weight lifting. They simply take more time to repair and regenerate themselves. Ligaments can be surgically replaced. Starters can become relievers. And the control, skill, deception, and mental agility developed during the high-power phase of a pitching career can take over to sustain a pitcher far longer than a roaring fastball can.

14

The Fourth Prodigy?

"He has the potential to pitch a no-hitter every time out."—Orioles manager Earl Weaver, 1975

On May 6, 1998, a 20-year-old rookie named Kerry Wood made his fifth major league start for the Chicago Cubs. His performance on that overcast day before 15,758 fans at Wrigley Field surpassed what 17-year-old Bob Feller did in his fifth major league start 62 years earlier. Wood struck out 20 batters—12 of them on swinging strikes—in nine innings against the Houston Astros.[1] He faced 29 batters, just two more than the minimum, giving up only one hit and no walks. He threw 122 pitches, 84 of them for strikes in one of the most dominating pitching performances in baseball history.

The 6-foot-5, 210-pound Texan presented fastballs that reached 100 mph and punctuated them with sharply breaking curveballs to join Feller as only the second pitcher to achieve strikeouts equal to his age in a major-league game (Feller struck out 17 at age 17). Wood seemed to fit the mold of the three fastball prodigies who preceded him, exhibiting phenomenal velocity and precocious strikeout ability. Just as Feller and Ryan had been rookies, Wood was a bit wild, a tendency he had demonstrated one year earlier by leading all minor-league pitchers in walks with 131. The fourth fastball prodigy had arrived, almost on schedule, three decades after the third. Or so it appeared.

Wood went 13-6 in the 1998 season, striking out 233 batters and earning National League Rookie-of-the-Year honors. In the last month of the season, however, he developed elbow pain. In his first spring training start the following year, he tore the anterior band of his ulnar collateral ligament and underwent Tommy John surgery. It was the first of many injuries that would derail what seemed destined to be a Hall-of-Fame career. He was placed on the disabled list 14 times in his first 13 major-league seasons. A 2007 *New York Times* article implied that the seeds of

Wood's elbow injury had been sown in high school four years earlier. In one playoff doubleheader during his senior year, he threw a total of 175 pitches. His high-school coach insisted that he was protective of his highly valued pitcher, but forearm fatigue may have left his elbow ligament temporarily unprotected during the doubleheader, initiating a slow, progressive failure of its anterior band or perhaps worsening an injury progression that had already begun.[2] When he was at full power, Wood was phenomenal. In 2003 — during an All-Star season of 14 wins and 266 strikeouts — he averaged 11.3 strikeouts per nine innings and threw 1,138 pitches at 95 mph or faster.[3] He eventually became an outstanding relief pitcher, and as of 2011 had pitched 13 seasons and 1,350 innings in the major leagues, striking out 10.3 batters per nine innings.

The 30-year pattern aside, the fourth prodigy could have been Randy Johnson, who came up with the Montreal Expos in 1988. With a fastball velocity measured by radar as high as 102 mph, he became a five-time Cy Young Award winner and a 10-time All-Star. The 6-foot-10 left-hander led the league in strikeouts nine times and pitched a perfect game in 2004. Drafted in 1985 at age 22 out of the University of Southern California, he spent three seasons in the minors and came up just after his 25th birthday. He too had a very high walk rate in the minor leagues, and he led the American League in walks three times and in hit-batsmen twice. But he improved his control and went on to accrue Hall-of-Fame numbers with 303 career wins, 372 strikeouts in a season and 4,875 in his career to rank second behind Nolan Ryan. For his career, he averaged 10.67 strikeouts per nine-inning game. Pitching for the Arizona Diamondbacks against Cincinnati on May 8, 2001, he struck out 20 batters, 19 of them on swinging third strikes. In another 2001 game, he struck out the side on nine pitches. He retired at age 45 after a 22-season major-league career with eight different teams. Two of those seasons were shortened by injury, but not to the arm or shoulder. He was sidelined for much of 1996 with a back injury and spent most of the 2003 season on the disabled list with a knee injury.

Also outside the 30-year cycle was Sandy Koufax, the first pitcher to average fewer than seven hits allowed per nine innings in his career (6.79 hits) and to strike out more than nine batters (9.28 strikeouts) per nine innings in his career. He came into the majors at age 19 in 1955 with the Brooklyn Dodgers, bypassing the minor leagues, but he spent most of his first five seasons in the bullpen. In a night game in June 1959, he struck

14. The Fourth Prodigy?

out 16 batters, a record for a night game, and two months later struck out 18, but in 1960 he asked to be traded because he wasn't getting enough playing time. He once led the National League in wild pitches, and early in his career walked almost as many as he struck out. On two occasions, he struck out three batters in an inning with just nine pitches. His final five seasons were among the best by any pitcher in baseball history, despite chronic elbow pain that eventually forced him to retire at age 30. Though his career was relatively short, he was a first-ballot selection for the Hall of Fame in 1972.

Another candidate for the fourth prodigy would be Roger Clemens, who on April 29, 1986, became the first pitcher in major-league history to strike out 20 batters in nine innings (12 on swinging third strikes) against Seattle at Boston's Fenway Park. He matched this performance a decade later against Detroit with 14 of his 20 strikeouts coming on swinging strikes. Clemens was the consummate power pitcher who sustained his power to a Nolan Ryan — like extent through 24 major-league seasons, winning 354 games before retiring in 2007 at age 45. With 4,672 career strikeouts in 4,916 innings, seven Cy Young Awards, and 11 All-Star appearances, he had Hall-of-Fame certainty until allegations of his steroid use were made in 2008. His fastball registered 100 mph on several occasions. But Clemens, a devotee of strength training, never had a deficiency of control, maintaining a high strikeout-to-walk ratio even in his only minor-league season and his early years in the majors.

Then there was Stephen Strasburg, who debuted at 21 with the Washington Nationals on June 8, 2010, capturing the nation's attention as young Bob Feller had 74 years earlier. Strasburg filled stadiums with record crowds, even in his perfunctory two-month stint in the minor leagues. His first trip to the mound in D.C. was what Walter Johnson's might have been like had Johnson arrived a century later in the era of media hype. Strasburg's first performance in the nation's capital was even better than the Big Train's, as he struck out 14 in seven innings against Pittsburgh with a mix of roaring fastballs, hard-biting curveballs, and 90-mph changeups. PITCH f/x technology, infinitely better than the bullet-timing machine into which Johnson once pitched, was on hand for Strasburg's debut to record his power immediately and precisely. One-third of his pitches were in the 98 to 100 mph range, with two hitting 100 mph. Strasburg struck out batters at almost the same rate in the majors as he had in college ball, with 92 strikeouts in 68 innings in two months of his rookie season. As

Johnson had in 1907, Strasburg seemed to throw every fastball at max effort. Unlike Johnson, however, Strasburg ended his rookie season earlier than scheduled, suffering a torn ulnar collateral ligament on August 27, 2010. Perhaps the most protected pitcher ever, Strasburg was kept on a strict 100-pitch limit with four to five rest days between starts. That he suffered a torn anterior band makes it seem certain that the damage to it was initiated before he signed his $15-million professional contract. This time there was no 175-pitch outing in high school to point a finger at, which shows the insidious nature of this type of injury. Strasburg underwent Tommy John surgery, a transfer of the gracilis tendon from his left leg to his right elbow, in September 2010, and he returned to the mound 12 months later with the biological springs in his arm apparently renewed to their original elastic stiffness.

There have been other fastball phenoms, too many to name. Many have doubtless come along with the same rare combination of genetic gifts as Johnson, Feller, and Ryan—a level of natural power that may not be as rare as the 30-year cycle would imply. Many have likely come and gone too quickly, unable to preserve their high-performance muscle fibers and stiffly elastic ligaments and tendons against the demands of max-effort pitching and the heavy workload of professional baseball.

Professional baseball casts an ever-wider net and indeed finds greater numbers of adolescents with high-velocity arms, adhering to Alva Bradley's observation that a kid pitcher has to have a fastball to succeed in the big leagues. More precisely, a kid pitcher has to have a fastball that roars or at least hisses to be taken in the net of scouting and be rewarded with a trial in the minor leagues. It is curious that professional baseball places a high dollar value on velocity but does not consistently develop it. Fastball velocity decreases more often than it increases in the minor leagues, the training ground Bradley envisioned for teaching the curveball and other skills of pitching. Learning to throw a reliable and deceptive off-speed pitch to complement the fastball is indeed an important part of pitcher development, of producing the metamorphosis from thrower to pitcher. But just as a fastball consistently above 90 mph is a ticket into the minor leagues, one that becomes consistently less than 90 mph is a ticket out, a simple basis for culling the vast herd of prospects. The development of a professional pitcher has evolved into a race between two opposing rates of change—diminishing speed and rising skill—giving each hopeful a limited time in which to improve. The stadium pitch-speed display thus takes on

14. The Fourth Prodigy?

a role of a digital timekeeper, working on both ends of the career cycle — dispatching young pitchers to other careers if skill and control improve too slowly, and sending others to retirement or independent leagues when speed diminishes too quickly. As Bob Feller learned at age 19, speed can be capricious in its coming and going. Cleveland newspapers declared his fastball gone just two years after he debuted and two months before he set the major-league single-game strikeout record. Stephen Strasburg too learned about the fickle nature of pitching power.

Comparing Strasburg's rookie performances to those of Feller, Johnson, or Ryan is like comparing the Olympic 100-meter dash victory of Jesse Owens in 1936 to that of Usain Bolt in 2008. Though the stopwatch is a near-perfect umpire, differentiating between sprinters of prodigious talent is best done in adjacent lanes of the same track. Like Olympic sprinters, the fastball prodigies were each blessed with a generous portion of fast-glycolytic fibers — those that produce the most powerful bursts of energy — in the arm and shoulder muscles. Like sprinters, they also benefited from power amplification through elastic-strain energy storage and return. In combination with exceptional muscle speed, the biological springs in the tendons, ligaments, and muscles of their arm and shoulder enabled them to pitch near resonance with great speed and energy efficiency. The effect of elasticity is to store the kinetic energy of the trunk briefly and transfer it to the ball with amplified power during arm acceleration. The burst of energy produced by elastic recoil, damped less than normally by the muscles on the back of the rotator cuff, may have been the reason for the control difficulties high-velocity pitchers like Steve Dalkowski experienced early in their careers. In these prodigies, the natural arm speed remained high until the loss of elasticity and power with age and innings pitched resulted in a lower natural frequency of the arm.

The important products of the high-performance muscle fibers and power-amplifying collagen fibrils are exceptional arm speed and hand speed. Hand speed, perhaps the most underappreciated attribute of a pitcher, is produced by the most important muscles of the pitcher's power train — the wrist- and finger-flexors of the forearm. These lightweights are essential for control, late acceleration, and high spin rates that produce a late hop of the fastball and a sharp break of the curveball–important traits in producing swinging strikes and record strikeout numbers. The flexor muscles of the forearm also have the critical role of sharing the load with the anterior band of the ulnar collateral ligament, the piece of sinew that

The Science of the Fastball

is the pitcher's most valuable biological spring. There are other superlatives to describe the forearm flexors' role in pitching: most heavily worked, most abused by max-effort pitching, most susceptible to the damage of eccentric contractions, most susceptible to fatigue, and weakest among the links of the kinetic chain of pitching. The forearm flexors are the only muscle group that, when fatigued, can adversely affect all three attributes of the fastball: control, movement, and velocity. In a glycogen-depleted state, they are most likely to cause performance outliers as a result of differential fatigue.

Properly developed, protected, and maintained, the fast-glycolytic fibers and the elastic fibrils of the elbow's anterior band are genetic gifts that can bless a young man with a hyper-velocity fastball. These are not unlike the finely tuned engine and transmission of a racing car. Consequently, the old automobile-safety adage applies, slightly altered: the speed that thrills is the speed that kills speed — if it is applied too often without the proper maintenance downtime. The fast-glycolytic fibers, also known as fast-fatigable fibers, do have special maintenance requirements. Sustaining power means forestalling fatigue, which in turn means managing the supply of glycogen granules stored within the muscle fibers during the season, both on and off the mound. It also means optimizing pitching mechanics to derive maximum power from the largest muscles of the kinetic chain, power transmitted from the trunk and amplified by the biological springs of the arm and shoulder. Doing so reduces the power needed from the muscles of the arm and shoulder.

Baltimore Orioles manager Earl Weaver once said of Nolan Ryan: "He has the potential to pitch a no-hitter every time out."[4] Remarkably, Ryan retained that potential well into his forties, sustaining his phenomenal power with two decades of regular weight training and fitness training. His training helped produce a cultural shift in pitching toward strength training. Strength training is an effective means of improving velocity, particularly if it is done patiently by applying the principle of progressive overload. Its maximum benefit is unlikely to be realized, however, if it is performed during the season, squeezed into the recovery period between pitching starts. Its effects are not independent of pitching. Each causes eccentric-contraction-induced fiber damage and depletes glycogen. Overlapping these effects can tip the scale from benign muscle damage, the stimulus for muscle growth, to excessive muscle damage, the reason for strength loss and the essence of overtraining.

14. The Fourth Prodigy?

The shift toward strength training has ill-defined boundaries: how much is enough, and most critically, how much is too much during the season? The baseball community may have viewed Ryan's success as the result of a train-hard-throw-hard approach to pitching, which is neither accurate nor as simple as its four-syllable description implies. The culture of sports in America exalts hard work, implying that a pitcher who works hard will improve, and a pitcher who works harder will improve more. It may seem counter-productive to train very lightly between starts, as pitchers like Amos Rusie did 100 years earlier. The issue, however, is not whether to work hard, but when to work hard — in-season or off-season — and when and how to rest. The parameters of training hard in-season have never been well defined since the introduction of strength training; consequently, the train-hard-throw-hard approach has not consistently brought success to pitchers who have less recovery ability than Nolan Ryan had. The yield has too often been erratic performance, short outings, late-season swoons, elevated injury rates, short careers, and costly turnover in pitching staffs.

Baseball history shows that a pitcher's decline in power typically begins in his mid to late 20s. For some of the more powerful pitchers, it begins earlier, probably as a result of energy mismanagement — expending energy on the mound too frequently without giving the remarkable muscle repair and restoration processes time for full recovery. Opportunities for abuse of muscle and connective tissue abound: long seasons, emphasis on velocity, expectations of pitching complete games, working hard between outings, and pitching in fall or winter leagues. The combined effects of these is why pitching careers of enduring dominance have never been common.

Three weeks before he threw the final pitch of his career, Walter Johnson was presented with a diamond-studded American League Distinguished Service Medal on his 20th anniversary with the Senators. Standing before 20,000 fans in Griffith Stadium, Johnson was almost speechless, overcome with emotion over receiving gifts and adulation from his many fans. Though he was as beloved as any baseball player, he could not find the same eloquence Lou Gehrig would find in 1939 when he stood before tens of thousands of fans in Yankee Stadium and declared himself "the luckiest man on the face of the earth."

The end of a pitching career is seldom an occasion of grand ceremony like that of Walter Johnson. No, the end usually comes in a decline and disappearance noted only by a line of agate type under Baseball Transactions. "That was it. Just a few lines in the paper and I was out of the majors, out after only two years — two years it'd taken me 22 years to get to," was how Satchel Paige described his termination by the Cleveland Indians after the 1949 season.

For a pitcher, a grand ceremony should be presented as a coming-of-age celebration, a sort of bar mitzvah upon reaching 27, the age at which velocity typically starts to wane. At such a ceremony, the gifted young fireballer would stand on a brilliant green diamond before thousands of fans, his cap in his hand and his teammates behind him, and he would lean over a microphone to thank his many supporters. He would declare himself to be the luckiest man on the face of the earth, because his genetics endowed him with an exceptional number of fast-glycolytic muscle fibers in his arm and shoulder, a strong, stiffly elastic ulnar collateral elbow lig-

Walter Johnson was given a grand ceremony as he neared retirement. Twenty-thousand fans turned out to honor him on his twentieth anniversary with Washington (Library of Congress, LC-DIG-npcc-16919).

14. The Fourth Prodigy?

ament, superb coordination, and the hand speed to spin his four-seamer at 3,000 rpm for late hop. With the zeal of an Oscar recipient, he would recognize his coaches in amateur baseball who never let him exceed his pitch limit or remain on the mound with signs of fatigue. He would thank his dad for the backyard practice sessions as a teen that helped him establish near-perfect mechanics early on and later to program the motor skills to throw deceptive off-speed pitches. He would express gratitude to his college strength coach for the off-season weight-lifting workouts that strengthened his subscapularis and forearm flexors along with every muscle group, and for admonishing him to avoid strength training during the season. He would credit the lessons he learned from great pitchers before him who pitched at unexceptional velocity but excelled by applying great skill and deception. And he would praise his pitching coach for giving him the confidence not to pitch at max effort, even as thousands of fans critique his work in real time through the technology of PITCH f/x.

These are a pitcher's reasons for a grand celebration.

Glossary of Technical Terms Related to Pitching Power

Aerobic   Requiring oxygen. Aerobic exercise uses oxygen supplied by the blood to produce the energy-transfer molecule ATP, which the muscle needs to contract. This aerobic energy conversion process involves complete oxidation of glucose or fatty acids.

Agonist   The muscle that is the prime mover, the main source of power for a given movement. Some movements involve one prime mover, while others involve more than one. The two prime movers involved in a push-up, for example, are the triceps and the pectoralis major.

Anabolic steroid   Any one of many synthetic forms of testosterone that have anabolic properties (promoting growth of muscle and bone) but relatively weak androgenic properties. Anabolic steroids mimic the effects of testosterone, increasing protein synthesis in cells to produce tissue growth, especially muscle growth.

Anaerobic   Not requiring oxygen. In anaerobic exercise, muscle fibers process energy by glycolysis, in which enzymes convert glucose to pyruvate, releasing energy to form the ATP necessary for muscle contraction. Oxygen is not necessary for this inefficient process.

Antagonist   A muscle that acts in opposition to the movement of a prime mover. Skeletal muscles work as antagonistic pairs; when a muscle contracts, the opposing muscle must relax. In the extension of the elbow, the biceps muscle is the antagonist of the triceps, which is the prime mover. In elbow flexion, the biceps is the prime mover and the triceps is the antagonist.

Arm acceleration phase   This is the launching phase of a pitch, beginning with the arm fully cocked to a near-horizontal position and ending with the release of the ball. This phase includes three movements: forward arm rotation, elbow extension, and wrist flexion.

ATP   Adenosine triphosphate is the energy-transfer molecule, the carrier and storage unit of energy for cells, including muscle fibers. It transports chemical energy within cells for metabolism and is continuously recycled. There is about 50 grams of ATP in the human body.

Glossary of Technical Terms Related to Pitching Power

Biceps The biceps brachii muscle flexes the arm at the elbow and is the antagonist of the triceps.

Biological springs Elastic tissue in the body that stores energy when it is stretched and releases energy when it recoils, just as a metal coil spring does, except that the coil spring has less damping. Tendons are the main biological springs of the body; they are very effective in storing and returning energy in running, jumping, and throwing. Ligaments, which join bone to bone, have the same structure as tendons except there is no sheath around a ligament. It is a ligament, the anterior band of the ulnar collateral ligament, that is the main biological spring of a pitcher's arm. Strands of titin are the biological springs in muscle fibers.

Coefficient of variance In statistics, this is the standard deviation divided by the mean. It indicates the dispersion or variability of measurements.

Concentric muscle contraction The shortening of a muscle while it is producing tension. This is one of three types of muscle action, the other two being eccentric contraction (lengthening while producing tension), and isometric contraction (neither lengthening nor shortening while producing tension).

Connective tissue Fibrous tissue that makes up a variety of structures in the body, including tendons, ligaments, cartilage, bone, and the connective framework of muscle fibers.

Creatine phosphate Also known as phosphocreatine, this is a powerful but limited source of energy for muscle fibers. It can be mobilized rapidly and anaerobically to produce ATP, providing the first shot of energy when a muscle is called into immediate action. It is recycled relatively slowly when the muscle is resting, however, so glycogen takes over as the primary fuel of the fast-glycolytic fibers.

Damping Damping is a reduction in the amplitude of an oscillation through the dissipation of kinetic energy as heat. The shock absorbers on a car damp the oscillations of the car's springs when driving on a rough road. Two rotator cuff muscles, the infraspinatus and teres minor, damp the recoil of the biological springs in the arm and shoulder during the arm acceleration phase of a pitch.

DOMS Delayed-onset muscle soreness, a condition involving inflammation, pain, and stiffness in muscles as a result of damage caused by eccentric contractions. The soreness usually begins one to two days after the muscle damage occurs.

Drag coefficient A dimensionless number greater than zero that indicates the aerodynamic efficiency of an object such as a baseball in flight. The drag coefficient, determined through wind-tunnel experiments, indicates the resistance or drag of an object as it moves in air or water. A streamlined object that creates very little drag has a drag coefficient close to zero. An object that creates a lot of turbulence as it moves through the air has a higher drag coefficient.

Drag crisis The rapid change in flow pattern and turbulence downstream of a sphere in flight that occurs in a certain velocity range, causing the drag coefficient to change rapidly. The drag crisis is what makes the knuckleball dance.

Glossary of Technical Terms Related to Pitching Power

Eccentric muscle contraction   The lengthening of a muscle while it is producing tension. This is one of three types of muscle action, the other two being concentric contraction (shortening while producing tension), and isometric contraction (neither lengthening nor shortening while producing tension).

Elastic-strain energy storage and return   This is the action of a spring or elastic band in which kinetic energy is rapidly converted to potential energy and back to kinetic energy. In pitching, this is a means of power amplification and time-shifting the transfer of energy from the stride, trunk flexion, and trunk rotation to the arm and shoulder by storing the energy momentarily in the biological springs of muscles, tendons, and ligaments.

Elbow extension   One of the six movements of pitching, elbow extension increases the angle between the forearm and upper arm. The triceps is the prime mover for this movement, which occurs during forward arm rotation to transition the baseball from a rotational path to a linar path.

Electromyography   A means of recording the electrical activity of muscle or nerve that involves inserting needle electrodes or attaching electrodes to the skin. In biomechanical studies, electromyography is often used to determine activation patterns of muscles and the timing and coordination among various muscles. It can also be used to roughly measure the relative strength of muscle contractions.

Enzyme   Any one of the various proteins produced by cells that act as a catalyst to bring about a certain biochemical reaction. Enzymes in the muscle fiber are catalysts to the aerobic and anaerobic metabolisms.

Fast-glycolytic muscle fiber   This is the high-performance muscle fiber that provides explosive power for activities such as sprinting, jumping, and throwing. This type of fiber contracts most rapidly, about five times faster than the slow-oxidative fiber, but it fatigues most rapidly, even though it stores more glycogen in the fiber than the other fiber types. This fiber is served by faster, high-frequency neurons and has enzymes that produce a faster reaction than that of the slow-oxidative fiber. It functions with the anaerobic (without oxygen) energy conversion process of glycolysis. It can produce more force than the other fiber types because it has a larger fiber diameter; it is also grouped in larger motor units. It has few mitochondria, few capillaries, and a low concentration of myoglobin, so it has a very low capacity for the aerobic process. Through endurance training, however, the fast-glyocolytic fiber can remodel itself to add these oxygen-processing components and become a fast-oxidative-glycolytic fiber. With disuse, however, the remodeled fibers convert back to fast-glycolytic fibers.

Fast-oxidative-glycolytic muscle fiber   This is the hybrid fiber, the intermediate model that has speed, strength, and fatigue resistance between that of the slow-oxidative fiber and the fast-glycolytic fiber. This type of fiber is activated by high-frequency nerves and neurons that are faster than those of the slow-oxidative fibers, and it is grouped in large motor units. It applies both the aerobic and anaerobic processes, but at peak exertion, the aerobic process can produce only about one-third of the ATP needed, so glycogen remains the main energy source for strong exertions. Some of these fibers are predominantly oxidative and some are predominantly glycolytic, but all have less speed and power than the fast-glycolytic fiber.

Fibril A muscle fibril is normally referred to as a myofibril, with myo being the prefix for muscle. It is a string of many sarcomeres attached end to end. Many fibrils bundled together in parallel form a muscle fiber. Fibril also refers to the very fine collagen strands that make up tendons and ligaments.

Forearm flexor muscles These muscles on the palm side of the forearm flex the wrist and fingers in the direction of the palm. In pitching, they provide control, spin, and a substantial amount of the linear velocity of the fastball. The two finger flexors are the flexor digitorum superficialis and flexor digitorum profundus. The two wrist flexors are the flexor carpi radialis and flexor carpi ulnaris, the latter providing the power to spin the curveball.

Forward arm rotation Commonly known as shoulder internal rotation, this is the primary movement of the launching or arm acceleration phase, which begins with the arm fully rotated rearward (cocked) and ends with ball release. The subscapularis is the prime mover of forward arm rotation.

Glucose A simple sugar, or carbohydrate, transported in the blood to provide energy to the cells.

Gluteus Muscles of the buttocks. The gluteus minimus and gluteus medius, two of the three gluteus muscles of each buttock, supply the power for pelvis rotation, the initial movement of trunk-and-shoulder rotation by rotating the femurs inward and outward relative to the pelvis.

Glycogen The storage form of glucose, which is stored as tiny granules among the fibrils of a muscle fiber. Fast-glycolytic fibers store more glycogen than slow-oxidative fibers, but they also consume the glycogen much more rapidly because of the inefficiency of the anaerobic reaction.

Glycolysis The breakdown of glucose and glycogen by enzymes in the muscle to produce the energy-transfer molecule ATP and lactic acid. This is the anaerobic metabolism of the fast-twitch muscle fibers.

Hierarchy of activation In any exercise, the slowest, least-powerful muscle motor units (groups of fibers of the same type) are forcefully activated first, and the fastest, most-powerful motor units, last as the intensity of effort increases. If a task requires little power, e.g., weak muscle contraction, only the slow-oxidative fibers are activated. If a stronger contraction is required, the fast-oxidative fibers are activated next to assist the slow-oxidative fibers. As the power requirement increases further, the fast-glycolytic fibers are forcefully activated last.

Hormone A messenger molecule of the body. Many of these chemical substances are produced and secreted by the endocrine system to regulate the functions of certain cells and organs. Hormones are messengers of the endocrine system, which, like the nervous system, is an information signal system of the body. The effects are slower to initiate and more prolonged in their response, lasting hours to weeks. Hormones are transported in the blood and act by binding to specific receptors in the target cells.

Inertia An object's resistance to a change in velocity. An object at rest tends to remain at rest, and an object in motion tends to continue moving at the same velocity and direction unless acted upon by an external force.

Infraspinatus One of two muscles that rotate the upper arm in the rearward direction. An antagonist of the subscapularis, this muscle is prone to injury in pitching because it applies the brakes to the arm once the ball is released and does so with eccentric loading. Located on the rear side of the rotator cuff, the infraspinatus stabilizes the shoulder joint and places drag on the forward arm rotation.

Intramuscular storage of energy Two forms of energy, glycogen and fatty acids, are stored within muscle fibers for immediate use by the fibers. Unlike the energy supplied by the blood for the aerobic metabolism, energy stored intramuscularly can be put to immediate use only by the muscle fiber in which it is stored.

Kinetic chain of pitching This is the series of movements in which energy is transferred from each of many muscles to the ball. This transfer occurs through connective tissue and bone and is coordinated by the brain and its nervous system.

Kinetic energy The energy of motion. A baseball in flight has kinetic energy equal to one-half its mass times its velocity squared. A baseball resting on the ground has no kinetic energy.

Lactic acid A product of incomplete anaerobic metabolism in the muscle fiber. This diffuses out of the muscle fiber and is carried by the blood to the liver, where it is recycled, converted back to glucose to gain the remaining energy from it. It is also recycled (as pyruvate) by oxidation in the mitochondria of muscle fibers.

Ligament Flexible, viscoelastic cord-like connective tissue that attaches bone to bone. A ligament is made of strong fibrous collagen tissue and is similar to tendon except that it does not have a sheath, as some tendons do.

Macrophage A large white blood cell, about twice the size of a neutrophil, which captures and digests foreign particles and microorganisms. It is a versatile cell that also secretes substances that direct the repair, growth, and regeneration of muscle fibers. The word macrophage is Greek for "big eater."

Magnus force The force perpendicular to the direction of motion of a spinning object moving through the air or other fluid. The magnus force on a four-seam fastball with its backspin is upward, producing lift. The force is downward on a curveball because it is delivered with topspin.

Glossary of Technical Terms Related to Pitching Power

Metabolism The chemical processes that occur in cells of the body to sustain life. These processes yield energy or synthesize substances necessary for life.

Mitochondria The microscopic energy-processing plants of a cell. In muscle cells (muscle fibers), the mitochondria process energy and oxygen to produce ATP, the energy-transfer molecule needed for muscle contraction. A single muscle fiber may have thousands of mitochondria, which are about the size of bacteria. Endurance exercise causes an increase in the number of mitochondria over time in the muscle fibers being exercised.

Moment arm The perpendicular distance from the point of rotation. In the launching phase of a pitch, the moment arm is equal to the length of the forearm at the beginning of the forward rotation. The moment arm decreases as elbow extension occurs during forward rotation.

Momentum The impetus of a moving object, calculated as mass times velocity. The momentum developed in the stride toward home plate is transferred to the trunk when the pitcher plants and locks his forward leg.

Motor neuron A nerve cell that forms part of a pathway for electrical impulses to pass from the central nervous system to a muscle to activate a group of fibers in the muscle.

Motor unit A number of muscle fibers controlled by a single motor neuron. The quantity of fibers in a motor unit varies from a few, in the muscles of the eyelids, to thousands in the larger muscles of the body. A motor unit contains only one type of fiber, for example, only fast-glycolytic fibers.

Muscle fatigue The loss in the strength and speed of muscle contractions during sustained, repetitive activity. This temporary loss can occur when there is insufficient supply of energy or oxygen or an increased level of lactic acid in the muscle fiber being exercised.

Muscle fiber A cylindrical cell composed of many fibrils (strings of sarcomeres), which contracts when stimulated by electrical impulses.

Muscle twitch The response of a muscle to a single impulse from the central nervous system via its motor neuron.

Myoglobin A red protein, similar to a red blood cell, that carries and stores oxygen within a muscle fiber. Myoglobin combines with an oxygen molecule once the oxygen is released by a red blood cell (hemoglobin) and transfers it to the mitochondria in the muscle fiber, where it is used to produce energy.

Neutrophil The most abundant type of white blood cell in the body, the neutrophil is essential to the process of enveloping and digesting debris and microorganisms for removal from the blood. When muscle damage occurs, neutrophils travel to the site of damage within minutes; their concentration at the site is an indicator of acute inflammation.

Glossary of Technical Terms Related to Pitching Power

Normal distribution The distribution of random variables that is represented as a symmetrical bell-shaped graph. This is the most common probability distribution in statistics.

NSAID A non-steroidal anti-inflammatory drug such as ibuprofen, naproxen, and aspirin.

Obliques Muscles located on each side of the trunk that twist the trunk, providing the power for the trunk-rotation movement. The obliques are strengthened by rotating the trunk against resistance.

Plasticity The ability of tissue to change and adapt to its functional demands and environment. Muscle plasticity involves repair, regeneration, and remodeling of the muscle fiber.

Potential energy Stored energy. In stretching an elastic band, potential energy is stored in the band. When the stretched band is released, its potential energy is converted to kinetic energy. The energy in a charged battery is potential energy.

Power amplification In pitching, the biological springs of the body (tendons, ligaments, muscle titin) amplify power by increasing the speed of a movement through elastic-strain energy storage and return. When they recoil, the springs release their stored energy more rapidly than the contracting muscles can supply the energy. By releasing the stored energy more rapidly than it is supplied, the power (the rate of supplying energy) is amplified.

Prime mover The muscle that has the principal role in producing a particular movement. The subscapularis is the prime mover for forward arm rotation.

Remodeling The adaptation of a muscle fiber resulting in its having more force generators, mitochondria, myoglobin, and/or capillaries in response to its activity demands.

Resonance The tendency of a system to oscillate with greater amplitude at its natural frequency. Resonance can occur when a system, such as a pendulum or weight on a spring, easily exchanges kinetic energy and potential energy.

Rigor Rigidity. Relative to muscle function, rigor is a state of stiffness in which a muscle fiber can neither contract nor relax. This occurs when there is no energy available to the fiber for producing ATP. Rigor mortis is the condition of stiffness that occurs with death because there is no longer an active process for producing ATP in the muscle fibers.

Rotational velocity Also referred to as angular velocity, this is the speed of rotation around an axis, as measured typically in degrees per second or revolutions per minute.

Rotator cuff The large tendon attaching four muscles that wrap around the shoulder. These muscles are the subscapularis, supraspinatus, infraspinatus, and teres minor, listed in order from the front to the top to the rear of the shoulder. These

Glossary of Technical Terms Related to Pitching Power

muscles converge into one large tendon that attaches to the upper end of humerus (the upper arm) at its head (the ball). In the launching phase of a pitch, the subscapularis accelerates the arm to high rotational velocities, then the infraspinatus and teres minor on the backside decelerate the arm. Both the acceleration and deceleration produce high eccentric loading, and shoulder injuries often result from this loading.

Sarcomere The basic building block of skeletal muscle, the sarcomere is the smallest contracting unit of a muscle fiber, so small (about one micron wide and two microns long) that a dust particle of its size suspended in still air would take hours to settle. A string of many sarcomeres attached end-to-end is a fibril and many fibrils bundled together form a muscle fiber. Inside each sarcomere are protein strands, myosin and actin, which produce contraction by moving over each other in a ratcheting action.

Satellite cell A stem cell that lies dormant on the periphery of muscle fibers. When activated by messenger molecules, satellite cells multiply, travel to the site of muscle damage, and fuse to repair the fiber and return it to normal function. Satellite cells are key in the repair and regeneration of muscle fibers.

Skeletal muscle Muscle connected to bone. Skeletal muscle is comprised of sarcomeres, is arranged in bundles, and contracts in short bursts. It differs from smooth muscle and cardiac muscle, which have different structure and function. Smooth muscle (found in blood vessels, gastrointestinal tract, respiratory tract, etc.) has no sarcomeres, is involuntary, and sustains longer contractions. Cardiac muscle has sarcomeres but its fibers connect at irregular angles.

Slow-oxidative muscle fiber This is the economy fiber that employs the oxidative (aerobic) metabolism and draws most of its energy as glucose or fatty acids from the bloodstream. This fiber has a slower speed of contraction with slower neurons and slower enzyme action than fast-twitch fibers. It is very resistant to fatigue with many mitochondria, myoglobin, and capillaries. This type of fiber requires less excitation to cause a contraction, and generates less force. It is suited for maintaining posture and tasks that involve endurance.

Strain Deformation caused by applying force. In pitching, strain is the stretching of muscle fibers, particularly during a forceful eccentric contraction, or the stretching of ligaments or tendons. If the deformation is within the elastic range, the fiber or fibril returns to its original length when the force is removed. If not, structural damage can occur.

Subscapularis This triangular muscle is the larger of two muscles on the forward side of the rotator cuff. It rotates the upper arm (the humerus) at high speed to deliver the strongest pulse of power produced during a pitch. The subscapularis tendon wraps around the bone, giving the muscle very high leverage. It is subjected to eccentric loading during the cocking phase of the pitch.

Glossary of Technical Terms Related to Pitching Power

Supraspinatus One of the four muscles of the rotator cuff. Relative to the other rotator cuff muscles, this muscle plays a smaller role in the acceleration/deceleration of the arm.

Tendon Flexible, elastic cord-like connective tissue that attaches muscle to bone. Tendons, like ligaments, are made of strong fibrous collagen tissue.

Teres Minor This muscle, an antagonist of the subscapularis, is one of two that rotate the upper arm in the rearward direction. It is prone to injury in pitching because it decelerates the arm once the ball is released. It also stabilizes the shoulder joint, but in doing so places drag on the forward arm rotation.

Testosterone The principal male sex hormone (androgen) that is produced mainly by the testes in response to a hormone secreted by the pituitary gland. It is also produced by the adrenal cortex in both males and females. Its chief function is to stimulate the development of the male reproductive organs and secondary sex characteristic, such as the beard. It also encourages growth of bone and muscle and helps maintain muscle strength.

Titin Also called connectin, this is the elastic component, the biological spring in a muscle fiber that bears the passive load to protect the muscle fiber from structural damage during strain. Titin protein chains travel the length of each sarcomere and allow the muscle fiber to store and release energy.

Triceps (triceps brachii) This muscle extends the arm at the elbow and is the antagonist of the biceps in the elbow extension movement of pitching.

Trunk-and-shoulder rotation The twisting of the torso around a near-vertical axis, beginning with the pelvis and continuing in sequence to the trunk and shoulders. Like trunk flexion, this is also an arm-cocking movement.

Trunk flexion The bending of the pitcher's body at the waist toward home plate. This bending results from a transfer of momentum generated by the stride and by the contraction of the abdominal muscles and hip flexors. This is one of the cocking movements of pitching, in that the energy of the trunk forces the arm to rotate rearward and cock the biological springs of the arm and shoulder.

Turbulent flow For a baseball in flight, this is the airflow around the ball that involves irregular fluctuations with continuous, random changes in magnitude and direction, resulting in swirling as the air passes around the ball.

Twitch speed The velocity at which a single type of muscle fiber shortens when activated without any resistance to its shortening.

Ulnar collateral ligament This ligament attaches the humerus and ulna bones on the side of the elbow toward the body. It has three parts: the anterior band, posterior band, and transverse band. The anterior band is the primary stabilizer of the elbow in the pitching motion, and injury to this band is common among pitchers. This is also referred to as the medial collateral ligament.

Glossary of Technical Terms Related to Pitching Power

WHIP Walks and hits per inning pitched.

Wrist extension The bending of the wrist away from the palm. The extensor muscles of the forearm produce the movement of wrist extension.

Wrist flexion The bending of the wrist toward the palm, a movement produced by contraction of the flexor muscles of the forearm.

Z-disk The disk that defines the ends of each sarcomere. This is the structural part of the muscle fiber that is often damaged in the strain of eccentric contractions.

Chapter Notes

Chapter 1

1. John Sickels, *Bob Feller: Ace of the Greatest Generation* (Washington, DC: Brassey's, 2004).
2. Bob Feller with Burton Rocks, *Bob Feller's Little Black Book of Baseball Wisdom* (Lincolnwood, IL: Contemporary, 2001).
3. Bob Feller with Bill Gilbert, *Now Pitching, Bob Feller* (New York: Harper Perennial, 1991).
4. Nolan Ryan with Jerry Jenkins, *Miracle Man Nolan Ryan: The Autobiography* (Dallas: Word, 1992).
5. *Ty Cobb, My Life in Baseball* (Lincoln: University of Nebraska Press, 1993).
6. Henry W. Thomas, *Walter Johnson, Baseball's Big Train* (Lincoln: University of Nebraska Press, 1995).
7. Feller with Rocks.
8. Anthony Castrovince, "The Beginning of the Feller Legend," August 23, 2006, www.Indians.com.
9. According to Alice Calaprice, author of *The New Quotable Einstein* (Princeton University Press, 2005), this is a paraphrase of a statement in Einstein's 1919 paper "Induction and Deduction."

Chapter 2

1. Test Operations Procedure 4-2-805, Appendix B, "Measurement Technique and Instrumentation," and Appendix F, "Translation of Instrumental Velocity to Muzzle or Striking Velocity" (Aberdeen Proving Ground, MD).
2. Robert K. Adair, *The Physics of Baseball* (New York: Harper Perennial, 1994).
3. L.W. Alaways, "Aerodynamics of a Curve-Ball: The Sikorsky/Lightfoot Lift Data," *The Engineering of Sport* 7 (2008): 429–436.
4. CurveBall Expert Program, National Aeronautics and Space Administration, www.grc.nasa.gov.
5. John Hall, *Los Angeles Times*, September 6, 1974.
6. Tom Lederer, "Remembering the Ryan Express," baseballanalysts.com, September 14, 2006.
7. G. Encina, "Wada Impresses with First Game of Spring," *The Baltimore Sun*, March 19, 2012.
8. "The Fastest Pitcher in Baseball History," *The Baseball Almanac*, www.baseball-almanac.com.

Chapter 3

1. Glenn S. Fleisig, et al., "Kinematic Differences Between Highly Skilled and Less-Skilled Baseball Pitchers," American Sports Medicine Institute (Birmingham, AL).
2. Glenn S. Fleisig, et al., "Kinematic and Kinetic Comparison of Baseball Pitching Among Various Levels of Development," *Journal of Biomechanics* 32 (1999): 1371–1375.
3. Sherry L. Werner, et al., "Relationships Between Ball Velocity and Throwing Mechanics in Collegiate Baseball Pitcher, *Journal of Shoulder Elbow Surgery* 17 (2008): 905–908.

4. Steven W. Barrentine, Tomoyuki Matsuo, Rafael F. Escamilla, Glenn S. Fleisig, and James R. Andrews, "Kinematic Analysis of the Wrist and Forearm During Baseball Pitching," *Journal of Applied Biomechanics* (1998): 14, 24–39.

5. R.E. Vaughn, "Three Dimensional Kinematics of the Baseball Pitch," in J. Terauds and J.N. Barham, eds., *Biomechanics in Sports II* (Del Mar, CA: Research Center for Sports, 1985), 72–78.

Chapter 4

1. S. Holtz, "The Fastest Pitcher in Baseball History," Baseball-Almanac.com, February 2003.

2. Bob Feller with Burton Rocks, *Bob Feller's Little Black Book of Baseball Wisdom* (Lincolnwood, IL: Contemporary, 2001).

3. Jerry Schwartz, "Javelin Thrower Shows Braves His Stuff," *New York Times*, August 8, 1996.

4. Jenifer Langosch, "Indian Hurlers' Inking Opens New Market," MLB.com, November 25, 2008.

5. G.S. Fleisig, R.F. Escamilla, J.R. Andrews, et al., "Kinematic and Kinetic Comparison Between Baseball Pitching and Football Passing," *Journal of Applied Biomechanics* 12 (1996): 207–24.

6. Steven P. Gietschier, "The Longest Throw," www.GreenfieldHistoricalSociety.org.

7. J.G. Preston, "The History of the Record for Baseball's Longest Throw, a Tale That Involves John Hatfield, Honus Wagner, Sheldon Lejeune, Don Grate, Rocky Colavito and Glen Gorbous, Among Others," http://prestonjg.wordpress.com, December 4, 2009.

8. Jerry Crasnick, "Velocity Helps, but Location Is Important Too," ESPN.com, March 26, 2007.

9. "100-mph Club," *Baseball Almanac*, www.baseball-almanac.com.

10. J.A. Rall, "Energetic Aspects of Skeletal Muscle Contraction: Implications of Fiber Types," *Exercise and Sport Sciences Reviews* 13 (1985): 33–73.

11. Brian R. MacIntosh, P.F. Gardiner, and A.J. McComas, *Skeletal Muscle: Form and Function* (Champaign, IL: Human Kinetics, 2006).

12. B.W. Rosser, B.J. Norris, and P.M. Nemeth, "Metabolic Capacity of Individual Muscle Fibers from Different Anatomic Locations," *Journal of Histochemistry and Cytochemistry* 40 (1992): 819–825.

13. Michael D. Mann, "Muscle Contraction," Chapter 14 in *The Nervous System in Action*, http://michaeldmann.net/, 2011.

14. Richard M. Lovering and David W. Russ, "Fiber Type Composition of Cadaveric Human Rotator Cuff Muscles," *Journal of Orthopaedic and Sports Physical Therapy* 38, no. 11 (November 2008): 674–680; R.C. Srinivasn, M.P. Lungren, J.E. Langenderfer, and R.E. Hughes, "Fiber Type Composition and Maximum Shortening Velocity of Muscles Crossing the Human Shoulder," *Clinical Anatomy* 20 (2007): 144–149.

15. L. Larsson and R.L. Moss, "Maximum Velocity of Shortening in Relation to Myosin Isoform Composition in Single Fibres from Human Skeletal Muscles," *Journal of Physiology* 472 (1993): 595–614.

16. D.L. Costill, R. Bowers, G. Branam, and K. Sparks, "Muscle Glycogen Utilization During Prolonged Exercise on Successive Days," *Journal of Applied Physiology* 31 (1971): 834–838.

17. Nick M. DiGiovine, Frank W. Jobe, Marilyn Pink, and Jacquelin Perry, "An Electromyographic Analysis of the Upper Extremity in Pitching," *Journal of Shoulder and Elbow Surgery* (1992): 1, 15–25.

18. J. Friden, R.M. Lovering, and R.L. Lieber, "Fiber Length Variability Within the Flexor Carpi Ulnaris and Flexor Carpi Radialis Muscles: Implications for Surgical Tendon Transfer," *Journal of Hand Surgery*

Chapter Notes

29A (2004): 909–914; Richard L. Lieber, *Skeletal Muscle Structure, Function, and Plasticity* (Baltimore: Lippincott Williams and Wilkins, 2010).

19. S.R. Ward, G.J. Loren, S. Lundberg, and R.L. Lieber, "High Stiffness of Human Digital Flexor Tendons Is Suited for Precise Finger Positional Control," *Journal of Neurophysiology* 96 (2006): 2815–2818.

20. B. Saltin, "Muscle Fibre Recruitment and Metabolism in Prolonged Exhaustive Dynamic Exercise," *Ciba Foundation Symposium* 82 (1981): 41–58.

21. Steven W. Barrentine, Tomoyuki Matsuo, Rafael F. Escamilla, Glenn S. Fleisig, and James R. Andrews, "Kinematic Analysis of the Wrist and Forearm During Baseball Pitching," *Journal of Applied Biomechanics* (1998): 14, 24–39.

22. S. Sakurai, Y. Ikegami, A. Okamoto, K. Yabe, and S. Toyoshima, "A Three-Dimensional Cinematographic Analysis of Upper Limb Movement During Fastball and Curveball Baseball Pitches," *Journal of Applied Biomechanics* (1993): 9, 47–65.

23. R.E. Vaughn, "Three Dimensional Kinematics of the Baseball Pitch," in J. Terauds and J.N. Barham, eds., *Biomechanics in Sports II* (Del Mar, CA: Research Center for Sports, 1985), 72–78.

Chapter 5

1. Peter Handrinos, "Baseball Men: The Phenom," http://cardinalnation.com, October 3, 2005.

2. John Eisenberg, "The Lost Phenom," *The Baltimore Sun*, February 16, 2003.

3. Tim Wendel, *High Heat: The Secret History of the Fastball and the Improbable Search for the Fastest Pitcher of All Time* (Cambridge, MA: Da Capo, 2010).

4. Steve Treder, "Delving into the Dalkowski Depths," *The Hardball Times*, May 29, 2007.

5. Pete McEntegart, "Where Are They Now? Steve Dalkowski," *Sports Illustrated*, June 30, 2003.

6. Robert Graziul, "The Greatest Prospect Never to Make It to the Majors," *Baseball Digest*, December 1990.

7. Ibid.

8. Thomas J. Roberts and Emanuel Azizi, "Flexible Mechanisms: The Diverse Roles of Biological Springs in Vertebrate Movement," *Journal of Experimental Biology* 214 (2011): 353–361.

9. Giovanni A. Cavagna, Norman C. Heglund, and C. Richard Taylor, "Mechanical Work in Terrestrial Locomotion: Two Basic Mechanisms for Minimizing Energy Expenditure," *American Journal of Physiology* 233, no. 5 (1977): R243–R261.

10. R. McNeill. Alexander, "Tendon Elasticity and Muscle Function," *Comparative Biochemistry and Physiology—Part A: Molecular and Integrative Physiology* 133, no. 4 (2002): 1001–1011.

11. R.M. Alexander and H.C. Bennet-Clark, "Storage of Elastic Strain Energy in Muscle and Other Tissues," *Nature* 265 (1977): 114–117.

12. P. Luhtanen and P.V. Komi, "Mechanical Power and Segmental Contribution to Force Impulses in Long-Jump Take-Off," *European Journal of Applied Physiology* 41 (1979): 267–274.

13. Edward Gruver, *Koufax* (Dallas: Taylor, 2000).

14. J. Gandhi, N.S. El Attrache, K.R. Kaufman, and W.J. Hurd, "Voluntary Activation Deficits of the Infraspinatus Present as a Consequence of Pitching-Induced Fatigue," *Journal of Shoulder and Elbow Surgery* (2011): 1–6.

Chapter 6

1. Mark Ribowsky, *Don't Look Back: Satchel Paige in the Shadows of Baseball*, (New York: Da Capo, 1994).

2. Steven W. Barrentine, Tomoyuki Matsuo, Rafael F. Escamilla, Glenn S.

Fleisig, and James R. Andrews, "Kinematic Analysis of the Wrist and Forearm During Baseball Pitching," *Journal of Applied Biomechanics* (1998): 14, 24–39.

3. *Ibid.*

Chapter 7

1. John Walsh, "In Search of the Sinker," *The Hardball Times*, www.hardballtimes.com, June 6, 2007.

2. R.D. Mehta and J.M. Pallis, "Sports Ball Aerodynamics: Effects of Velocity, Spin, and Surface Roughness," *Materials and Science in Sports*, F.H. Froes, ed. (Minerals, Metals, and Materials Society, 2001).

3. C.W. Selin, "An Analysis of the Aerodynamics of Pitched Baseballs," doctoral dissertation, Iowa State University, 1957.

4. M.K. McBeath, "The Rising Fastball: Baseball's Impossible Pitch," *Perception* 19 (1990): 545–552.

Chapter 8

1. Baseball-reference.com.

2. Levon N. Nazarian, John M. McShane, Michael G. Ciccotti, Patrick L. O'Kane, and Marc I. Harwood, "Dynamic US of the Anterior Band of the Ulnar Collateral Ligament of the Elbow in Asymptomatic Major League Baseball Pitchers," *Radiology* 227 (2003): 149–154.

3. Sherry L. Werner, Glenn S. Fleisig, Charles J. Dillman, and James R. Andrews, "Biomechanics of the Elbow During Baseball Pitching," *Journal of Orthopaedic and Sports Physical Therapy* 17, no. 6 (June 1993): 274–278.

4. R.M. Alexander and H.C. Bennet-Clark, "Storage of Elastic Strain Energy in Muscle and Other Tissues," *Nature* 265 (1977): 114–117.

5. P.A. Davidson, M. Pink, J. Perry, and F.W. Jobe, "Functional Anatomy of the Flexor Pronator Muscle Group in Relation to the Medial Collateral Ligament of the Elbow," *American Journal of Sports Medicine* 23, no. 2 (March–April 1995): 245–250.

6. Christopher D. Hamilton, et al., "Dynamic Stability of the Elbow: Electromyographic Analysis of the Flexor Pronator Group and the Extensor Group in Pitchers with Valgus Instability" (Inglewood, CA: Biomechanics Laboratory, Centinela Hospital Medical Center, March 10, 2006).

7. A.C. Vailas, et al., "Physical Activity and Hypophysectomy on the Aerobic Capacity of Ligaments and Tendons," *Journal of Applied Physiology* 44 (1978): 542–546.

8. Nolan Ryan with Jerry Jenkins, *Miracle Man Nolan Ryan: The Autobiography* (Dallas: Word, 1992).

Chapter 9

1. "Events and Discoveries," *Sports Illustrated*. April 23, 1956.

2. Erling Asmussen, "Positive and Negative Muscular Work," *Acta Physiologica Scandinavica* 28 (1952): 364–382.

3. R.L. Lieber and J. Friden, "Muscle Damage is Not a Function of Muscle Force but Active Muscle Strain," *Journal of Applied Physiology* 74, no. 2 (1993): 520–6.

4. Nick M. DiGiovine, Frank W. Jobe, Marilyn Pink, and Jacquelin Perry, "An Electromyographic Analysis of the Upper Extremity in Pitching," *Journal of Shoulder and Elbow Surgery* (1992): 1, 15–25.

5. R.A. Meir, R.P. Weatherby, and M.I. Rolfe, "A Retrospective Analysis of Major and Significant Injuries and their Consequences Reported by Retired Australian Baseball Players," *The Open Sports Medicine Journal* 4 (2010): 119–126.

6. B.R. Eisenberg, "Quantitative Ultrastructure of Mammalian Skeletal Muscle," in L.D. Peachey, R.H. Adrian, and S.R. Geiger, eds., *Skeletal Muscle*, vol. 10

(Baltimore: American Physiological Society, 1983), 73–112.

7. R.L. Lieber and J. Friden. "Mechanisms of Muscle Injury Gleaned from Animal Models," *American Journal of Physical Medicine and Rehabilitation* 81 suppl. (2002): S70–S79.

8. F.X. Pizza, "Neutrophils and Macrophages in Muscle Damage and Repair," in Peter M. Tildus, *Skeletal Muscle Damage and Repair* (Champaign, IL: Human Kinetics, 2008).

9. C.F. Nathan, "Secretory Products of Macrophages," *Journal of Clinical Investigation* 79 (1987): 319–326.

10. Edward Achorn, *Fifty-Nine in '84* (New York: HarperCollins, 2010).

11. Roger Kahn, *The Head Game* (New York: Harcourt, 2000).

12. Jerry Crasnick, "Velocity Helps, but Location Is Important Too," ESPN.com, March 26, 2007.

13. K. Nosaka, "Muscle Soreness and Damage and the Repeated-Bout Effect," in Peter M. Tildus, *Skeletal Muscle Damage and Repair* (Champaign, IL: Human Kinetics, 2008).

14. B.A. Bondesen, S.T. Mills, K.M. Kegley, and G.K. Pavlath, "The COX-2 Pathway Is Essential During Early Stages of Skeletal Muscle Regeneration," *American Journal of Physiology* 287 (2004): C475–C483.

15. D.K. Mishra, J. Friden, M.C. Schmitz, and R.L. Lieber, "Antiinflammatory Medication After Muscle Injury: A Treatment Resulting in Short-Term Improvement but Subsequent Loss of Muscle Function," *Journal of Bone and Joint Surgery* (Am) 77 (1995): 1510–1519.

16. Richard L. Lieber, *Skeletal Muscle Structure, Function, and Plasticity* (Baltimore: Lippincott Williams and Wilkins, 2010).

17. D.L. Costill, *Inside Running: Basics of Sports Physiology* (Indianapolis: Benchmark, 1986).

18. Stephen P. Sayers and Monica J. Hubal, "Histological, Chemical, and Functional Manifestations of Muscle Damage," in Peter M. Tildus, *Skeletal Muscle Damage and Repair* (Champaign, IL: Human Kinetics, 2008); W.M. Sherman, "Recovery from Endurance Exercise," *Medicine and Science in Sports and Exercise*, suppl. 24 (1992): S336–S339.

19. Stirling Carpenter and George Karpati, *Pathology of Skeletal Muscle* (New York: Churchill Livingstone, 1984).

20. Teet Seene, et al., "Overtraining Injuries in Athletic Populations," in Peter M. Tildus, *Skeletal Muscle Damage and Repair* (Champaign, IL: Human Kinetics, 2008).

21. J.A. Rall and R.C. Woledge, "Influence of Temperature on Mechanics and Energetics of Muscle Contraction," Thermal Dependence of Muscle Function Proceedings of the American Physiological Society, 1990: R197–R2003.

Chapter 10

1. Bob Feller with Bill Gilbert, *Now Pitching, Bob Feller* (New York: Harper Perennial, 1991).

2. Bob Feller with Burton Rocks, *Bob Feller's Little Black Book of Baseball Wisdom* (Lincolnwood, IL: Contemporary, 2001).

3. Feller with Gilbert.

4. Nolan Ryan and Tom House with Jim Rosenthal, *Nolan Ryan's Pitcher's Bible: The Ultimate Guide to Power, Precision, and Long-Term Performance* (New York: Simon and Schuster Fireside, 1991).

5. Richard L. Lieber, *Skeletal Muscle Structure, Function, and Plasticity* (Baltimore: Lippincott Williams and Wilkins, 2010).

6. Blake B. Rasmussen, and Stuart M. Phillips, "Contractile and Nutritional Regulation of Human Muscle Growth," *Exercise and Sport Sciences Reviews* 31, no. 3 (July 2003): 127–131.

7. T.J. Hawke and D. J. Garry, "Myogenic Satellite Cells: Physiology to Mo-

lecular Biology," *Journal of Applied Physiology* 91 (2001): 534–551.

8. Rafael F. Escamilla, Kevin P. Speer, Glenn S. Fleisig, Steven W. Barrentine, and James R. Andrews, "Effects of Throwing Overweight and Underweight Baseballs on Throwing Velocity and Accuracy," *Sports Med* 29, no. 4 (April 2000): 259–272.

9. R.L. Lieber and J. Friden, "Muscle Damage Is Not a Function of Muscle Force but Active Muscle Strain," *Journal of Applied Physiology* 74, no. 2 (1993): 520–6.

10. M.S. Clarke and D.L. Feeback, "Mechanical Load Induces Sarcoplasmic Wounding and FGF Release in Differentiated Human Skeletal Muscle Cultures," *Journal of the Federation of American Societies for Experimental Biology* 10, no. 4 (1996): 502–509.

11. Mary F. Barbe and Ann E. Barr, "Workplace and Other Overuse Injuries," in Peter M. Tildus, *Skeletal Muscle Damage and Repair* (Champaign, IL: Human Kinetics, 2008).

12. J.D. MacDougall, S. Ray, D.G. Sale, N. McCartney, P. Lee, and S. Garner, "Muscle Substrate Utilization and Lactate Production During Weightlifting," *Canadian Journal of Applied Physiology* 24 (1999): 209–215.

13. Samir Bannout and Bill Reynolds, *Mr. Olympia's Muscle Mastery: The Complete Guide to Building and Shaping Your Body* (New York: Plume, 1985).

14. Feller with Rocks.

Chapter 11

1. Robert Bahr, *The Virility Factor* (New York: G.P. Putnam's Sons, 1992).

2. I.G. Brodsky, P. Balagopal, and K.S. Nair, "Effects of Testosterone Replacement on Muscle Mass and Muscle Protein Synthesis in Hypogonadal Men: A Clinical Research Center Study," *Journal of Clinical Endocrinology and Metabolism* 81 (1996): 3469–3475; R.J. Urban, et al., "Testosterone Administration to Elderly Men Increases Skeletal Muscle Strength and Protein Synthesis," *American Journal of Physiology* 269 (1995): E820–E826.

3. S. Bhasin, L. Woodhouse, and T.W. Storer, "Hormones and Sport: Proof of the Effect of Testosterone on Skeletal Muscle," *Journal of Endocrinology* 170 (2001): 27–38.

4. Shalender Bhasin, et al. "The Effects of Suprahysiologic Doses of Testosterone on Muscle Size and Strength in Normal Men." *The New England Journal of Medicine* 335 (July 4, 1996): 1–7.

5. Michael Bamberger, "Astro Physics," *Sports Illustrated*, September 20, 1999.

6. Jerry Crasnick, "Velocity Helps, but Location Is Important Too," ESPN.com, March 26, 2007.

7. John Dewan and Bill James, *The 2004 Bill James Handbook* (2003 Statistics), (Chicago: Acta, 2003).

8. Steve Treder, "Examining the Relief of Relieving," *Hardball Times*, www.hardballtimes.com, July 4, 2006.

Chapter 12

1. Baseball Prospectus Team of Experts, *Baseball Between the Numbers: Why Everything You Know About the Game Is Wrong* (New York: Basic, 2007).

2. Joe Sheehan, "Pitcher Workloads," Prospectus Today, BaseballProspectus.com, June 18, 2003.

3. J.A. Potteiger, D.L. Blessing, and G.D. Wilson, "The Physiological Responses to a Single Game of Baseball Pitching," *Journal of Applied Sport Science Research* 6, no. 1 (1992): 11–18.

4. D.L. Costill, R. Bowers, G. Branam, and K. Sparks, "Muscle Glycogen Utilization During Prolonged Exercise on Successive Days," *Journal of Applied Physiology* 31 (1971): 834–838.

5. P.D. Chilibeck, D.G. Syrotuik, and G.J. Bell, "The Effect of Strength Training on Estimates of Mitochondrial Density

and Distribution Throughout Muscle Fibres," *The European Journal of Applied Physiology and Occupational Physiology* 80, no. 6 (November–December 1999): 604–9.

6. Nolan Ryan and Tom House with Jim Rosenthal, *Nolan Ryan's Pitcher's Bible: The Ultimate Guide to Power, Precision, and Long-Term Performance* (New York: Simon and Schuster Fireside, 1991).

7. Ralph Berger, "Amos Rusie," SABR Baseball Biography Project, http://Bioproj.sabr.org.

8. *Ibid.*

9. Harold Seymour, *Baseball: The Golden Age* (New York: Oxford University Press, 1971).

10. John Benson, Larry Bump, and Kevin Wheeler, *Benson's A to Z Baseball Scouting Guide, 2001* (Wilton, CT: Diamond Library, 2000).

11. Alan Schwarz, "Pitchers Go Down for the Count," *Baseball America*, May 12–25, 2003.

12. R.L. Lieber, T.M. Woodburn, and J. Friden, "Muscle Damage Induced by Eccentric Contractions of 25% Strain," *Journal of Applied Physiology* 70, no. 6 (1991): 2498–2507.

13. Joe Posnanski, "Thirty-Two Fast Pitchers," *Sports Illustrated*, September 7, 2010.

14. Nolan Ryan with Jerry Jenkins,. *Miracle Man Nolan Ryan: The Autobiography* (Dallas: Word, 1992).

15. Larry Tye, "Satchel Paige," Society for American Baseball Research, http://sabr.org.

16. Mark Ribowsky, *Don't Look Back: Satchel Paige in the Shadows of Baseball*, (New York: Da Capo, 1994).

17. Richard Donovan, "The Fabulous Satchel Paige," *Collier's*, vol. 131 (May 30, 1953), 65.

18. Leroy (Satchel) Paige and David Lipman, *Maybe I'll Pitch Forever* (Lincoln: University of Nebraska Press, 1993).

19. Talmadge Boston, "Nolan Ryan," SABR Baseball Biography Project, http://Bioproj.sabr.org, September, 1993.

Chapter 13

1. Bob Feller with Bill Gilbert, *Now Pitching, Bob Feller* (New York: Harper Perennial, 1991).

2. Bob Feller with Burton Rocks, *Bob Feller's Little Black Book of Baseball Wisdom* (Lincolnwood, IL: Contemporary, 2001).

3. Henry W. Thomas, *Walter Johnson, Baseball's Big Train* (Lincoln: University of Nebraska Press, 1995).

4. Feller with Gilbert.

5. *Ibid.*

6. Feller with Rocks.

7. *Ibid.*

8. E. Ippolito, P.G. Natali, F. Postacchini, L. Accinni, and C. Demartino, "Morphological, Immunochemical and Biochemical Study of Rabbit Achilles Tendon at Various Ages," *Journal of Bone Joint Surgery* (Am) 62 (1980): 583–592.

9. V. Kovanen and H. Suominen, "Effects of Age and Life-Long Endurance Training on the Passive Mechanical Properties of Rat Skeletal Muscle," *Comprehensive Gerontology* [A] 2 (1998): 18–23.

10. B.M. Carlson and J.A. Faulkner, "Muscle Regeneration in Young and Old Rats: Effects of Motor Nerve Resection with and Without Marcain Treatment," *Journal of Gerontology* 53 (1998): B52–B57.

Chapter 14

1. Baseball-reference.com.

2. Buzz Bissinger, "My Right Arm," *The New York Times Sports Magazine*, June 3, 2007.

3. John Dewan and Bill James, *The 2004 Bill James Handbook* (2003 Statistics), (Chicago: Acta, 2003).

4. "Throwing Smoke," *Time Magazine*, June 2, 1975.

Bibliography

Achorn, Edward. *Fifty-Nine in '84*. New York: HarperCollins, 2010.

Adair, Robert K. *The Physics of Baseball*. New York: HarperCollins, 2002.

Alaways, LeRoy W. "Aerodynamics of a Curve-Ball: The Sikorsky/Lightfoot Lift Data." *The Engineering of Sport 7* (2008): 429–436.

Alexander, R. McNeill. "Tendon Elasticity and Muscle Function." *Comparative Biochemistry and Physiology — Part A: Molecular and Integrative Physiology* 133, no. 4 (2002): 1001–1011.

_____, and H.C. Bennet-Clark. "Storage of Elastic Strain Energy in Muscle and other Tissues." *Nature* 265 (1977): 114–117.

Asmussen, Erling. "Positive and Negative Muscular Work." *Acta Physiologica Scandinavica* 28 (1952): 364–382.

Bahr, Robert. *The Virility Factor*. New York: G.P. Putnam's Sons, 1992.

Bamberger, Michael. "Astro Physics." *Sports Illustrated*, September 20, 1999.

Bannout, Samir, and Bill Reynolds. *Mr. Olympia's Muscle Mastery: The Complete Guide to Building and Shaping Your Body*. New York: Plume, 1985.

Barbe, Mary F., and Ann E. Barr. "Workplace and Other Overuse Injuries." In *Skeletal Muscle Damage and Repair*, edited by Peter M. Tildus. Champaign, IL: Human Kinetics, 2008.

Barrentine, Steven W., Tomoyuki Matsuo, Rafael F. Escamilla, Glenn S. Fleisig, and James R. Andrews, "Kinematic Analysis of the Wrist and Forearm During Baseball Pitching." *Journal of Applied Biomechanics* 14 (1998): 24–39.

Baseball-Reference.com.

Benson, John, Larry Bump, and Kevin Wheeler. *Benson's A to Z Baseball Scouting Guide, 2001*. Wilton, CT: Diamond Library, 2000.

Berger, Ralph. "Amos Rusie. SABR Baseball Biography Project, http://Bioproj.sabr.org.

Bhasin, Shalender, et al. "The Effects of Supraphysioilogic Doses of Testosterone on Muscle Size and Strength in Normal Men." *The New England Journal of Medicine* 335 (1996): 1–7.

_____, Linda Woodhouse, and T.W. Storer. "Hormones and Sport: Proof of the Effect of Testosterone on Skeletal Muscle." *Journal of Endocrinology* 170 (2001): 27–38.

Bissinger, Buzz. "My Right Arm." *The New York Times Sports Magazine*. June 3, 2007.

Bondesen, Brenda A., S.T. Mills, K.M. Kegley, and G.K. Pavlath. "The COX-2 Pathway Is Essential During Early Stages of Skeletal Muscle Regeneration." *American Journal of Physiology* 287 (2004): C475–C483.

Boston, Talmadge. "Nolan Ryan." SABR Baseball Biography Project, http://Bioproj.sabr.org, September 1993.

Brodsky I.G., P. Balagopal, and K.S. Nair. "Effects of Testosterone Replacement on Muscle Mass and Muscle Protein Synthesis in Hypogonadal Men: A Clinical Research Center Study." *Journal of Clinical Endocrinology and Metabolism* 81 (1996): 3469–3475.

Carlson, B.M., and J.A. Faulkner. "Muscle Regeneration in Young and Old Rats: Effects of Motor Nerve Resection with and Without Marcain Treatment." *Journal of Gerontology* 53 (1998): B52–B57.

Carpenter, Stirling, and George Karpati. *Pathology of Skeletal Muscle*. New York: Churchill Livingstone, 1984.

Castrovince, Anthony. "The Beginning of the Feller Legend." www.Indians.com. August 23, 2006.

Cavagna, Giovanni A., Norman C. Heglund, and C. Richard Taylor. "Mechanical Work in Terrestrial Locomotion: Two Basic Mechanisms for Minimizing Energy Expenditure." *American Journal of Physiology* 233, no. 5 (1977): R243–R261.

Chilibeck, P.D., D.G. Syrotuik, and G.J. Bell. "The Effect of Strength Training on Estimates of Mitochondrial Density and Distribution Throughout Muscle Fibres." *The European Journal of Applied Physiology and Occupational Physiology* 80, no. 6 (November–December 1999): 604–9.

Clarke, M.S., and D.L. Feeback. "Mechanical Load Induces Sarcoplasmic Wounding and FGF Release in Differentiated Human Skeletal Muscle Cultures." *Journal of the Federation of American Societies for Experimental Biology* 10, no. 4 (1996): 502–509.

Cobb, Ty. *My Life in Baseball*. Lincoln: University of Nebraska Press, 1993.

Costill, David L. *A Scientific Approach to Distance Running*. Los Altos, CA: Track and Field News, 1981.

———. *Inside Running: Basics of Sports Physiology*. Indianapolis: Benchmark, 1986.

———, Richard Bowers, George Branam, and Kenneth Sparks. "Muscle Glycogen Utilization During Prolonged Exercise on Successive Days." *Journal of Applied Physiology* 31 (1971): 834–838.

Crasnick, Jerry. "Velocity Helps, but Location Is Important Too." ESPN.com, March 26, 2007.

CurveBall Expert Program. National Aeronautics and Space Administration, www.grc.nasa.gov.

Davidson, Philip A., Marilyn Pink, Jacquelin Perry, and Frank W. Jobe. "Functional Anatomy of the Flexor Pronator Muscle Group in Relation to the Medial Collateral Ligament of the Elbow." *American Journal of Sports Medicine* 23, no. 2 (March–April 1995): 245–250.

Dewan, John, and Bill James. *The 2004 Bill James Handbook (2003 Statistics)*. Chicago: Acta, 2003.

DiGiovine, Nick M., Frank W. Jobe, Marilyn Pink, and Jacquelin Perry. "An Electromyographic Analysis of the Upper Extremity in Pitching." *Journal of Shoulder and Elbow Surgery* 1 (1992): 15–25.

Donovan, Richard. "The Fabulous Satchel Paige." *Collier's* vol. 131, May 30, 1953, 65.

Eisenberg, Brenda R. "Quantitative Ultrastructure of Mammalian Skeletal Muscle." In *Skeletal Muscle* 10 (1983): 73–112, edited by L.D. Peachey, R.H. Adrian, and S.R. Geiger. Baltimore, MD: American Physiological Society.

Eisenberg, John. "The Lost Phenom." *The Baltimore Sun*, February 16, 2003.

Escamilla, Rafael F., Kevin P. Speer, Glenn S. Fleisig, Steven W. Barrentine, and James R. Andrews, "Effects of Throwing Overweight and Underweight Baseballs on Throwing Velocity and Accuracy." *Sports Medicine* 29, no. 4 (2000): 259–272.

"Events & Discoveries." *Sports Illustrated*, April 23, 1956.

"The Fastest Pitcher in Baseball History." The Baseball Almanac, www.baseball-almanac.com.

Feller, Bob, with Bill Gilbert. *Now Pitching, Bob Feller*. New York: Harper Perennial, 1991.

Bibliography

———, with Burton Rocks. *Bob Feller's Little Black Book of Baseball Wisdom*. Chicago: Contemporary, 2001.

Fleisig, Glenn S., Rafael F. Escamilla, James R. Andrews, Tomoyuki Matsuo, Yvonne Satterwhite, and Steven W. Barrentine. "Kinematic and Kinetic Comparison Between Baseball Pitching and Football Passing." *Journal of Applied Biomechanics* 12, no. 2 (1996): 207–24.

———, Steven W. Barrentine, Naiquan Zheng, Rafael F. Escamilla, and James R. Andrews. "Kinematic and Kinetic Comparison of Baseball Pitching Among Various Levels of Development." *Journal of Biomechanics* 32 (1999): 1371–1375.

———, Tomoyuki Matsuo, Rafael F. Escamilla, Steven W. Barrentine, and James R. Andrews. "Kinematic Differences Between Highly Skilled and Less-Skilled Baseball Pitchers." American Sports Medicine Institute, Birmingham, AL, 1999.

Friden, Jan, Richard M. Lovering, and Richard L. Lieber. "Fiber Length Variability Within the Flexor Carpi Ulnaris and Flexor Carpi Radialis Muscles: Implications for Surgical Tendon Transfer." *Journal of Hand Surgery* 29A (2004): 909–914.

Gandhi, Jaipal, Neal S. El Attrache, Kenton R. Kaufman, and Wendy J. Hurd. "Voluntary Activation Deficits of the Infraspinatus Present as a Consequence of Pitching-Induced Fatigue." *Journal of Shoulder and Elbow Surgery* (2011): 1–6.

Gietschier, Steven P. "The Longest Throw." www.GreenfieldHistoricalSociety.org.

Graziul, Robert. "The Greatest Prospect Never to Make it to the Majors." *Baseball Digest*, December 1990.

Gruver, Edward. *Koufax*. Dallas: Taylor, 2000.

Hall, John. *Los Angeles Times*, September 6, 1974.

Hamilton, Christopher D., et al. "Dynamic Stability of the Elbow: Electromyographic Analysis of the Flexor Pronator Group and the Extensor Group in Pitchers with Valgus Instability." Inglewood, CA: Biomechanics Laboratory, Centinela Hospital Medical Center, March 2006.

Handrinos, Peter. "Baseball Men: The Phenom." http://cardinalnation.com, October 3, 2005.

Hawke, T.J., and D.J. Garry. "Myogenic Satellite Cells: Physiology to Molecular Biology." *Journal of Applied Physiology* 91 (2001): 534–551.

Holtz, Sean. "The Fastest PItcher in Baseball History." Baseball-Almanac.com, February 2003.

Ippolito, Ernesto, Pier Giorgio Natali, Franco Postacchini, Lidia Accinni, and Cesare Demartino. "Morphological, Immunochemical and Biochemical Study of Rabbit Achilles Tendon at Various Ages." *Journal of Bone Joint Surgery* (Am) 62 (1980): 583–592.

Kahn, Roger. *The Head Game*. New York: Harcourt, 2000.

Kovanen, Vuokko, and Harri Suominen. "Effects of Age and Life-Long Endurance Training on the Passive Mechanical Properties of Rat Skeletal Muscle." *Comprehensive Gerontology* [A] 2 (1988): 18–23.

Langosch, Jenifer. "Indian Hurlers' Inking Opens New Market." MLB.com, November 25, 2008.

Larsson Lars, and R.L. Moss. "Maximum Velocity of Shortening in Relation to Myosin Isoform Composition in Single Fibres from Human Skeletal Muscles." *Journal of Physiology* 472 (1993): 595–614.

Lederer, Tom. "Remembering the Ryan Express." baseballanalysts.com, September 14, 2006.

Lieber, Richard L. *Skeletal Muscle Structure, Function, and Plasticity*. Philadelphia: Lippincott Williams and Wilkins, 2010.

———, and Jan Friden. "Mechanisms of Muscle Injury Gleaned from Animal

Models." *American Journal of Physical Medicine and Rehabilitation* 81 suppl. (2002): S70–S79.

―――, and ―――. "Muscle Damage Is Not a Function of Muscle Force but Active Muscle Strain." *Journal of Applied Physiology* 74, no. 2 (1993): 520–6.

―――, T.M. Woodburn, and Jan Friden. "Muscle Damage Induced by Eccentric Contractions of 25% Strain." *Journal of Applied Physiology* 70, no. 6 (1991): 2498–2507.

Lovering, Richard M., and David W. Russ. "Fiber Type Composition of Cadaveric Human Rotator Cuff Muscles." *Journal of Orthopaedic and Sports Physical Therapy* 38, no. 11 (2008): 674–680.

Luhtanen, Pekka, and Paavo V. Komi. "Mechanical Power and Segmental Contribution to Force Impulses in Long-Jump Take-Off." *European Journal of Applied Physiology* 41 (1979): 267–274.

MacDougall, J.D., S. Ray, D.G. Sale, N. McCartney, P. Lee, and S. Garner. "Muscle Substrate Utilization and Lactate Production During Weightlifting." *Canadian Journal of Applied Physiology* 24 (1999): 209–215.

MacIntosh, Brian R., P.F. Gardiner, and A.J. McComas. *Skeletal Muscle: Form and Function*. Champaign, IL: Human Kinetics, 2006.

Mann, Michael D. "Muscle Contraction." Chapter 14 in *The Nervous System in Action*, www.unmc.edu/physiology/Mann/, 2011.

McBeath, Michael K. "The Rising Fastball: Baseball's Impossible Pitch." *Perception* 19 (1990): 545–552.

McEntegart, Pete. "Where Are They Now? Steve Dalkowski." *Sports Illustrated*, June 30, 2003.

Mehta, R.D., and J.M. Pallis. "Sports Ball Aerodynamics: Effects of Velocity, Spin, and Surface Roughness." In *Materials and Science in Sports*, edited by F.H. Froes. Minerals, Metals, and Materials Society, 2001.

Meir, R.A., R.P. Weatherby, and M.I. Rolfe, "A Retrospective Analysis of Major and Significant Injuries and Their Consequences Reported by Retired Australian Baseball Players." *The Open Sports Medicine Journal* 4 (2010): 119–126.

Mishra, Dev K., Jan Friden, Mary C. Schmitz, and Richard L. Lieber. "Antiinflammatory Medication After Muscle Injury: A Treatment Resulting in Short-Term Improvement but Subsequent Loss of Muscle Function." *Journal of Bone and Joint Surgery* (Am) 77 (1995): 1510–1519.

Nathan, C.F. "Secretory Products of Macrophages." *Journal of Clinical Investigation* 79 (1987): 319–326.

Nazarian, Levon N., John M. McShane, Michael G. Ciccotti, Patrick L. O'Kane, and Marc I. Harwood. "Dynamic Ultrasound of the Anterior Band of the Ulnar Collateral Ligament of the Elbow in Asymptomatic Major League Baseball Pitchers." *Radiology* 227 (2003): 149–154.

Nosaka, Ken. "Muscle Soreness and Damage and the Repeated-Bout Effect." In *Skeletal Muscle Damage and Repair*, edited by Peter M. Tildus. Champaign, IL: Human Kinetics, 2008.

"100-mph Club." The Baseball Almanac, www.baseball-almanac.com.

Paige, Leroy (Satchel), and David Lipman. *Maybe I'll Pitch Forever*. Lincoln: University of Nebraska Press, 1993.

Pizza, Francis X., "Neutrophils and Macrophages in Muscle Damage and Repair." In *Skeletal Muscle Damage and Repair*, edited by Peter M. Tildus. Champaign, IL: Human Kinetics, 2008.

Posnanski, Joe. "Thirty-Two Fast Pitchers." *Sports Illustrated*, September 7, 2010.

Potteiger J.A., D.L. Blessing, and G.D. Wilson. "The Physiological Responses to a Single Game of Baseball Pitching."

Bibliography

Journal of Applied Sport Science Research 6, no. 1 (1992): 11–18.

Preston, J.G. "The History of the Record for Baseball's Longest Throw, a Tale That Involves John Hatfield, Honus Wagner, Sheldon Lejeune, Don Grate, Rocky Colavito and Glen Gorbous, Among Others." http://prestonjg.wordpress.com, December 4, 2009.

Rall, Jack A. "Energetic Aspects of Skeletal Muscle Contraction: Implications of Fiber Types." *Exercise and Sport Sciences Reviews* 13 (1985): 33–73.

———, and Roger C. Woledge. "Influence of Temperature on Mechanics and Energetics of Muscle Contraction." In *Thermal Dependence of Muscle Function*, Proceedings of the American Physiological Society (1990): R197–R2003.

Rasmussen, Blake B., and Stuart M. Phillips. "Contractile and Nutritional Regulation of Human Muscle Growth." *Exercise and Sport Sciences Reviews* 31, no. 3 (July 2003): 127–131.

Ribowsky, Mark. *Don't Look Back: Satchel Paige in the Shadows of Baseball*. New York: Da Capo, 1994.

Roberts, Thomas J., and Emanuel Azizi. "Flexible Mechanisms: The Diverse Roles of Biological Springs in Vertebrate Movement." *Journal of Experimental Biology* 214 (2011): 353–361.

Rosser, B.W., B.J. Norris, and P.M. Nemeth. "Metabolic Capacity of Individual Muscle Fibers from Different Anatomic Locations." *Journal of Histochemistry and Cytochemistry* 40 (1992): 819–825.

Ryan, Nolan, with Jerry Jenkins. *Miracle Man Nolan Ryan: The Autobiography*. Dallas: Word, 1992.

———, and Tom House with Jim Rosenthal. *Nolan Ryan's Pitcher's Bible: The Ultimate Guide to Power, Precision, and Long-Term Performance*. Simon and Schuster Fireside, 1991.

Sakurai, S., Y. Ikegami, A. Okamoto, K. Yabe, and S. Toyoshima. "A Three-Dimensional Cinematographic Analysis of Upper Limb Movement During Fastball and Curveball Baseball Pitches." *Journal of Applied Biomechanics* 9 (1993): 47–65.

Saltin, Bengt. "Muscle Fibre Recruitment and Metabolism in Prolonged Exhaustive Dynamic Exercise." *Ciba Foundation Symposium* 82 (1981): 41–58.

Sayers, Stephen P., and Monica J. Hubal. "Histological, Chemical, and Functional Manifestations of Muscle Damage." In *Skeletal Muscle Damage and Repair*, edited by Peter M. Tildus. Champaign, IL: Human Kinetics, 2008.

Schwartz, Jerry. "Javelin Thrower Shows Braves His Stuff." *The New York Times*, August 8, 1996.

Schwarz, Alan. "Pitchers Go Down for the Count." *Baseball America*, May 12–25, 2003.

Seene, Teet, et al. "Overtraining Injuries in Athletic Populations." In *Skeletal Muscle Damage and Repair*, edited by Peter M. Tildus. Champaign, IL: Human Kinetics, 2008.

Selin, C.W. "An Analysis of the Aerodynamics of Pitched Baseballs." Doctoral dissertation, Iowa State University, 1957.

Seymour, Harold. *Baseball: The Golden Age*. New York: Oxford University Press, 1971.

Sheehan, Joe. "Pitcher Workloads." Prospectus Today, BaseballProspectus.com, June 18, 2003.

Sherman, W.M. "Recovery from Endurance Exercise." *Medicine and Science in Sports and Exercise* suppl. 24 (1992): S336–S339.

Sickels, John. *Bob Feller: Ace of the Greatest Generation*. Washington, DC: Brassey's, 2004.

Srinivasn, R.C., M.P. Lungren, J.E. Langenderfer, and R.E. Hughes. "Fiber Type Composition and Maximum Shortening Velocity of Muscles Crossing the Human Shoulder." *Clinical Anatomy* 20 (2007): 144–149.

Bibliography

Test Operations Procedure 4-2-805. Appendix B, "Measurement Technique and Instrumentation," and Appendix F, "Translation of Instrumental Velocity to Muzzle or Striking Velocity." Aberdeen Proving Ground, MD.

Thomas, Henry W. *Walter Johnson, Baseball's Big Train.* Lincoln: University of Nebraska Press, 1995.

"Throwing Smoke." *Time Magazine*, June 2, 1975.

Treder, Steve. "Delving into the Dalkowski Depths." *The Hardball Times, www.hardballtimes.com.* May 29, 2007.

———. "Examining the Relief of Relieving." *The Hardball Times, www.hardballtimes.com.* July 4, 2006.

Tye, Larry. "Satchel Paige." Society for American Baseball Research, http://sabr.org.

Urban R.J., et al. "Testosterone Administration to Elderly Men Increases Skeletal Muscle Strength and Protein Synthesis." *American Journal of Physiology* 269 (1995): E820–826.

Vailas, A.C., et al. "Physical Activity and Hypophysectomy on the Aerobic Capacity of Ligaments and Tendons." *Journal of Applied Physiology* 44 (1978): 542–546.

Vaughn, Ross E. "Three Dimensional Kinematics of the Baseball Pitch." In *Biomechanics in Sports II*, edited by J. Terauds and J.N. Barham, 72–78. Del Mar, CA: Research Center for Sports, 1985.

Walsh, John. "In Search of the Sinker." *The Hardball Times*, www.hardballtimes.com, June 6, 2007.

Ward, S.R., G.J. Loren, S. Lundberg, and R.L. Lieber. "High Stiffness of Human Digital Flexor Tendons is Suited for Precise Finger Positional Control." *Journal of Neurophysiology* 96 (2006): 2815–2818.

Wendel, Tim. *High Heat: The Secret History of the Fastball and the Improbable Search for the Fastest Pitcher of All Time.* Cambridge, MA: Da Capo, 2010.

Werner, Sherry L., et al. "Relationships Between Ball Velocity and Throwing Mechanics in Collegiate Baseball Pitchers." *Journal of Shoulder Elbow Surgery* 17 (2008): 905–908.

———, Glenn S. Fleisig, Charles J. Dillman, and James R. Andrews. "Biomechanics of the Elbow During Baseball Pitching." *Journal of Orthopaedic and Sports Physical Therapy* 17, no. 6 (1993): 274–278.

Index

Aberdeen Proving Ground 8, 16
adenosine triphosphate (ATP) 44, 45, 46, 47, 48, 49, 101, 139, 143
aerobic capacity in fast-glycolytic fibers 141–145
agonist and antagonist muscle pairs 61; activity ratio 71
USS *Alabama* 174
Alexander, Shaun 73
Alvin, Texas 9, 10, 144
American Sports Medicine Institute 27
Anabolic Steroid Control Act 114
anabolic steroids 97, 113, 114, 115, 129, 132
anaerobic endurance 139, 140, 141, 145, 144
anaerobic energy system 44, 45, 101, 140, 141
anaerobic exercise 139, 142
Anaheim, California 22
androgenic effects of testosterone 130
angle of extension 29, 31, 54, 76
anti-inflammatory drug effects 100
arm cocking 26–27, 29–30, 55, 61–63, 65–66, 69, 71, 94, 103, 121, 134
arm speed 30, 176, 181
Atlanta Braves 37
Atlas, Charles 107, 111

ballisticians 8, 16
Barnstorming Tour 110, 135, 159, 174
Baseball Almanac 42, 69
Baseball Magazine 171
Baseball Prospectus 137
Bennett, George 93
Berra, Yogi 25
biceps activation in pitching 50; eccentric contraction 54, 104
Big Train 11, 179
biological springs 27, 28, 29, 32, 55, 60, 61, 63, 182; series and parallel 62; weak links 95

Birmingham, Alabama 27
Bloomington, Illinois 98
Bonds, Barry 130
Boston Red Sox 148, 162, 171
Bradley, Alva 36, 180
Brooklyn Dodgers 110, 178
Brown, Mordecai 162

Cain, Pat 57
California Angels 9, 12, 68
calisthenics 110, 118, 119, 123, 124, 155
Cantillon, Joe 10–11
capillaries 43, 44, 45, 143
centrifugal force 31, 54
Chapman, Aroldis 24, 78
Chattanooga White Sox 160
Chicago Cubs 162, 177
Chicago White Sox 20, 156, 160
chin-ups 8, 121, 122, 123, 128
Cincinnati Reds 24
Clemens, Roger 179
Cleveland Indians 5, 7, 36, 156, 184
Cleveland News 169
Cleveland Plain Dealer 169
Club Azules 159
co-activation 69
Cobb, Ty 11, 130
cocking movements 26, 61, 62
Colavito, Rocky 39
collagen fibrils 60, 62, 86–91
Collier's magazine 159
color of muscle by type 47
complete games (pitching) 137–139, 141, 147, 148, 150, 168
complexity of pitching coordination 52
concentric muscle contraction 93
connective tissue 87, 89
Costill, David L. 140
cultural shift in pitching 12
Cy Young Award 29, 42, 63, 76, 139, 148, 150, 168, 178, 179

Index

Dalkowski, Steve 57, 181; end of career 72; power and elasticity 65; quotations about speed 59; speed measurement 58–59; strikeout and walk stats 59
damping of elastic recoil 68, 69
Dean, Dizzy 6, 156
Delahanty, Jim 11
delayed onset muscle soreness (DOMS) 98, 99
Detroit Tigers 8, 11, 22, 24, 42, 170
Dickey, R.A. 89
differential cooling effect 104
differential fatigue 71, 91, 103, 166; effect on curveball or slider 167
DiMaggio, Joe 156
Donovan, Richard 159
drag coefficient 17–18
drag crisis 18, 83–84
drag on a baseball 18
Durocher, Leo 6

eccentric muscle contraction 93–96
Einstein, Albert 15
elastic band exercises 71, 118, 124, 155
elastic limit 88
elastic-strain energy storage and return 37, 60, 94, 133, 181; effect on pitching economy 67–68; of ulnar collateral ligament 62
elbow extension 27, 30; timing and angle 53–54
elbow joint gap 88
electromyography 49, 94
endurance 137–141
energy balance 167
Evansville Baseball Club 39

fast-fatigable muscle fiber 44, 182
fast-glycolytic muscle fiber 43, 44, 47, 50; fuel supply variability 145; susceptibility to damage 96
fast-oxidative-glycolytic muscle fiber 43, 45–47
fastball attributes 12, 182
Feller, Bob 5, 34, 36, 40, 133; complete games 138; downward trend 172; farm work 8–9; first Major League appearance 5–6; muscle-bound 110, 128; slump 169; speed measurements 16–17; strikeout record game 170; weight training 110; World Series 162
Fenway Park 179
Ferrum College 133
fibrils (myofibrils) 43
filaments (myofilaments) 43

Fleisig, Glenn 27, 28, 30, 31, 54
flexor carpi radialis 31, 47, 49, 50, 79, 81, 90, 91, 103
flexor carpi ulnaris 31, 47, 49, 91, 103, 123, 167
flexor digitorum profundus 31–32, 47, 50, 166
flexor digitorum superficialis 31, 47, 49, 50, 90, 103, 104, 166
flexor muscles weight 50
Flying Tiger Airlines 175
forcing frequency of pitching 63, 66
forward arm rotation 27, 30
Fullerton High School 10

Galileo 63
Gehrig, Lou 183
Gillick, Pat 59
glucose 44, 45, 48, 49
glycogen 44, 48; conserving 146; deficits 152, 153; diet effect on restoration 142; levels in muscle 140; reduction rate in weight lifting 127; restoration period 48, 101, 102, 153
Gorbous, Glen 39
gracilis tendon 67, 180
Grate, Don 39
Greenberg, Hank 170
Griffith Stadium 16
Grillo, Ed 13
Guinness Book of World Records 19

Hall, John 20
hand speed 62, 73, 74, 75, 76, 78, 79, 85
Hardball Times 136
Harvey, Doug 59
hierarchy of muscle activation 50, 141
hop of fastball 75, 80, 83–85, 164
hormone 97, 114, 115, 130, 131
House, Tom 38
Houston Astros 133, 138, 163, 177
Houston Post 9
Humboldt, Kansas 10
humerus 30, 90, 107, 122

inconsistency and overtraining 102, 136, 152, 174
inefficiency of fast-glycolytic muscle fibers 44, 101
inflammation 89, 91, 92, 97, 99, 100, 105, 116, 140, 153
infrared laser device 20
infraspinatus 54, 61, 65, 69, 65, 71, 94
injury incidence 94

Index

innings pitched: in career 92; per week 171
intramuscular storage of energy 101, 140, 145, 153
isometric muscle contraction 93

Jacobi's Theorem 40
javelin throw 37, 38, 40
Jefferson Medical College research on pitchers' elbows 88
Jobe, Frank 49, 87
John, Tommy 86–87
Johns Hopkins Hospital 93
Johnson, Ben 115
Johnson, Randy 178
Johnson, Walter 10; complete games 138; fastball sink 83; first Major League appearance 11; off-season strength training 110; pitching masterpiece 172; pitching mechanics 34–35; slump 170–171; speed measurement 23; strikeout ability 12, 73; twentieth anniversary observance 183; Walter Johnson High School 10
joint stability 37, 51, 87, 90, 106
Jones, Dalton 59
Judge, Joe 172

Kansas City Monarchs 159
kinetic and potential energy exchange 63, 64
kinetic chain 12, 25, 32, 34, 35, 37, 41, 51
Koufax, Sandy 14, 131, 135, 139, 178; 1965 World Series 81; strikeout records 82; throwing harder with less effort 68
Kupperman, Herbert 130

Laabs, Chet 8
lactic acid 44, 49, 120
Lasorda, Tommy 148
late acceleration 53, 74, 78, 181
launching movements of pitching 26, 52
Lederer, George 19, 20
Lejeune, Sheldon 39
Lieber, Richard L. 99, 115
lift 83–85
ligament and tendon healing 89
Lincecum, Tim 29, 168
long-throw competition 39–40
long toss 50, 117, 126, 134, 150–152, 154
longevity in pitching 138, 150, 155–156, 158
Lopez, Andy 130
Los Angeles Dodgers 87, 148

Los Angeles Times 20, 73, 81, 110
Lumiline timing device 16

Mack, Connie 11, 73–74
macrophage 97, 102, 116, 140
Maddux, Greg 139
Martinez, Pedro 146, 148–151, 156
Mathewson, Christy 141, 148, 153
max-effort pitching 13, 117, 141, 147, 170, 172, 174, 180
McAuley, Ed 169
McGwire, Mark 130
Million-Dollar Arm Contest 38
Milo of Croton 113–114
mitochondria 43, 45, 46, 49, 143, 144
moment of inertia 40
momentum 17, 27, 28, 61, 62, 94, 119
Montreal Expos 148, 178
Montreal Royals 110
motor neuron 43, 44, 45, 51, 67, 166
motor units 44, 46, 51, 55, 78, 117, 118, 119, 122, 125, 145
Moyer, Jamie 86, 87
muscle activation 55, 117
muscle biopsies 47, 101, 127
muscle contraction speed 37, 41, 42, 46, 108, 153
muscle damage from eccentric contractions 94; benign 116; effect on muscle fatigue 100, 101
muscle fatigue 101; effect on the elbow 105
muscle fiber 42–43; recruitment 55; type distributions 46
muscle repair 99, 114–116
muscle strengthening: abdominals 124; criteria 116–117; lattissimus dorsi 125; legs 124; obliques and glutes 123; triceps 125; wrist- and finger-flexors 123
myoglobin 43, 44, 45, 46, 47, 143

National Aeronautics and Space Administration (NASA) 19, 40
natural frequency of the arm 63, 66
Nebraska, Steve 5
neutrophils 97, 140
New England Journal of Medicine 132
New York Giants 148
New York Mets 9, 13, 21, 89
New York Times 177
Nolan Ryan Junior High School 10

off-season strength training 125–126
Olinda, California 10
O'Neil, Buck 73

213

Index

outliers 165, 167
overtraining 102, 103, 105, 122, 126–129, 136, 144, 174, 182

Paige, Satchel 73, 85, 156–160, 175, 184
Patel, Dinesh 38–39
Pearland, Texas 10
periodization of training 126
Philadelphia Athletics 173
Philadelphia Phillies 39, 86, 135, 150
pitch counts 151; per complete game 139
PITCH f/x pitch tracking system 19, 24, 42; calculated spin rates 79, 85; fastball hop 84 pitching movements 29, 34, 53, 74, 107, 119, 123; Strasburg speed readings 179
pitching ligament 86–87
pitching machine 41
Pittsburgh Pirates 39
plasticity 43, 91, 131, 136, 176
plyometrics 118–119
Posnanski, Joe 156
Povich, Shirley 172
power 36; amplification 41, 61, 69; transfer rate 41
Price, David 80
progressive-overload weight training 113, 115, 132
Providence Grays 97

radar 12–13, 20
Radbourn, Charles "Old Hoss" 97, 98
rechargeable arm 101
recoil velocity 60
relaxation time of muscle 69
release point error 166
relievers' workload 136
Remington Arms Company 23
resonance 63–69
Ribowsky, Mark 159
Rice, Grantland 11
Ripken, Cal, Sr. 57, 58
rising fastball 84–85
Rockwell International 20
Rusie, Amos 146–147, 150, 175, 183
Ruth, Babe 148, 170, 172
Ryan, Nolan: career records 10; complete games 138; entering the Major Leagues 9–10; final season 160–161; forearm injury 144; longevity 156, 158; pitching in high school 9; rate of velocity loss 92; recovery ability 168, 183; seventh no-hitter 164; speed measurement 20–22; weight-lifting 111

Sabathia, C.C. 63
St. Louis Browns 160, 173
St. Louis Cardinals 6
San Francisco Giants 29
sarcomere 43, 90, 95, 99, 145
satellite cells 43, 114, 130
Schwarzenegger, Arnold 38, 111
The Scout 5
Seaver, Tom 59, 76, 77
Sheehan, Joe 137
Sherry, Norm 68
Sikorsky, Igor 18
sinew 86, 92
Singh, Rinku 38–39
slow-oxidative muscle fiber 43, 45
softball pitching 93
soreness in antagonist muscles 104; *see also* delayed-onset muscle soreness
sounds of the fastball 11, 17, 57
Sports Illustrated 93, 156
Stansfield, George 130
stem cells 96, 97, 131
stimulus for muscle growth 115–117
Strasburg, Stephen 179
stride 26, 27, 28, 41
subscapularis 41, 49; activity in pitching 122; leverage 107, 108, 113; strengthening 121

Tampa Bay Rays 80
temperature effect on contraction speed 48
teres minor 54, 61, 65, 69, 71, 94
testosterone 114–115, 130–133, 135–136
Texas Rangers 89, 164
Thomas, Henry 11
Time Magazine 6, 13
timing and coordination 51; of elbow extension 53–54; improvement 55; of trunk rotation and trunk flexion 54; of wrist-and-finger flexion 53
titin 45, 95; energy storage 90
Tommy John surgery 180
Toronto Blue Jays 164
torque curve 52, 60, 64
transmission efficiency 37
Treder, Steve 136
triceps activation in pitching 50
trunk-and-shoulder rotation 26, 28, 33, 41
trunk flexion 26, 28, 29, 32, 33, 35, 41
twitch speed 37, 133, 143
Tye, Larry 158

ulnar collateral ligament 87
underhand pitching 93

214

Index

Van Meter, Iowa 6
Veeck, Bill 160
Ventura, Robin 160
Verlander, Justin 42
Vitt, Ossie 169

Wagner, Billy 29, 42, 133–135, 144–145
wake turbulence 11, 17
Walter Johnson High School 10
Washington Post 172
Washington Senators 10, 11, 16, 172, 183
Washington Star 13
Weaver, Earl 59, 177, 182
weight-lifting 113; controls 119–121; effect on glycogen 154; effect on injury potential 128; long-term investment 129
weighted baseballs 118
Weiser, Idaho 10

Wheaties 8
wildness related to elastic recoil 67
Williams, Ted 13
Wilson, Hack 156
Wood, Kerry 177
Wood, Smokey Joe 69, 148, 162
Wrigley Field 177
wrist-and-finger flexion 27, 31; angle 53, 76–77; velocity 75
wrist curls 79, 120, 123, 127, 154
wrist extension angle 53, 75–76, 78–79

Young, Cy 138, 141

Z-disks 43, 90, 95
Zelezny, Jan 37–38
Zumaya, Joel 24

www.ingramcontent.com/pod-product-compliance
Ingram Content Group UK Ltd.
Pitfield, Milton Keynes, MK11 3LW, UK
UKHW041957140426
5217IPUK00015B/852